Other Books by Robert Hargrove

Masterful Coaching, 3rd Edition

Masterful Coaching Fieldbook

Mastering the Art of Creative Collaboration

Your First 100 Days in a New Executive Job

E-Leader in a Connected Age

Your Coach in a Book

Virtuoso, Consultative Selling (ebook)

The 7 Secrets of a Strategy of Preeminence (ebook)

Colossal Bootstrapping (ebook)

Are You a Multiplier or a Diminisher? (ebook)

The CEO & the Consigliere (ebook)

YOUR FIRST (NEXT) 100 DAYS IN POLITICS

You're in the Same Business as
George Washington

ROBERT HARGROVE

Masterful
Coaching
PRESS

Copyright @ 2022 by Masterful Coaching Press

Published by Masterful Coaching Press
640 Lexington Street
Waltham, MA 02452
www.MasterfulCoaching.com

For information regarding special discounts for bulk
purchases, please contact Masterful Coaching at
617-953-6230.

Designed by Susan Youngquist
Cover painting of George Washington by Fan Huang

Library of Congress Control Number: 2021906325

ISBN 978-0-578-86798-4

The book is dedicated to...

...all those who have the courage to throw their hat into the ring (win or lose) of American politics, with the dual goal of finding the path to power, while at the same time holding the sincere and honest intention to help everyone become better off.

This book was inspired by the warm human stories I've read about our greatest presidents, members of Congress, governors, mayors, and others who used their time in office to bring about historic change, consistent with the great public values laid out in the Declaration of Independence and Constitution.

I hope these stories about our greatest presidents—George Washington, Abraham Lincoln, Franklin Roosevelt, Lyndon Johnson—and others and what they did in their first (or next) 100 days to change the face of things, will inspire, empower, and enable leaders at all levels of politics and government to do likewise.

Contents

On July 24, 1933, President Roosevelt gave a radio address in which he coined the term "first 100 days." Looking back, he began, "we all wanted the opportunity of a little quiet thought to examine and assimilate in a mental picture the crowding events of the hundred days which had been devoted to the starting of the wheels of the New Deal."

Author's Note

In My Heart I'm a Democrat, In My
Mind a Republican

I was born in Boston, the seat of the American Revolution, where the "shot heard round the world" was fired. I was taught in grade school about America's ennobling ideals and enduring values. Because my Aunt Dorothy worked at the Book Clearing House in Copley Square and supplied me with books, as a boy I read stories about the great leaders of American history—George Washington, Abraham Lincoln, Franklin Roosevelt—and I grew up wanting to be like them.

My grandparents on my mother's side were Russian Jews who chose the "US of A" solution to escape religious persecution, coming to a new land of possibilities. Approaching Ellis Island in New York Harbor, they were thrilled when they saw the torch on the Statue of Liberty, learning later that under her marble feet, she was stomping on chains, and they were grateful when the country took them in and protected them.

My grandparents on my father's side were from the south. Their ancestors came to Jamestown in the Virginia Colony in 1634.

My grandfather, nicknamed "Rebel," was a Minor League Baseball player and took me to Fenway Park in Boston to watch the Red Sox. I remember one day as we were sitting in the bleachers in center field, people started to boo Ted Williams. My grandfather turned around, faced the crowd, and said, "Shut your yaps. You couldn't even lift the bat."

My mother was a Democrat who voted the straight Democratic ticket, no matter who was running. I can remember as a boy one late Fall seeing all the neighborhood grandparents, parents, aunts, and uncles gathering outside our apartments on Iffley Road near Franklin Park Zoo. Everyone was wailing and sobbing. When I asked my mother what the heck was going on, she looked down at me and said simply, "Mayor Curley died."

It did not matter to my mother that Curley, who had served four terms as Boston Mayor, also served five months in jail for mail fraud during one of those terms. She told me that he was good to the immigrants—the Irish, the Jews, the Italians—good to the poor, giving them jobs for votes, good to just about anyone who asked him for anything.

My father was a dyed-in-the-wool Republican, who believed in Republican ideals such as individual freedom, taking personal responsibility for your life, and living within a budget rather than on credit. He loved to help people, and when we drove from our summer place in Ogunquit, Maine, he would often stop at the bus station and offer people a ride.

As for me, I have taken a different path. The pivotal moment of my life was when I heard John F. Kennedy deliver his "Ask Not…" speech during his inauguration, a speech that changed a generation. It determined that my life would be about doing something to make a difference in other people's lives, rather than just make a living and worry about the stock market and a 401k. It was then that I decided I wanted to be a leader and make a difference, not a foot soldier in the long march of history just making a living.

I went to Boston University, studying American presidential history, and often hung out in the Martin Luther King Exhibition and Reading Room that contained his donated papers and memorabilia. I marched and sang and protested about civil rights and the Vietnam War, then continued my graduate studies at Tufts University.

HOLDING TWO OPPOSING IDEAS IN YOUR HEAD AT THE SAME TIME

Genius is the ability to hold two opposing ideas in your head at the same time and still be able to function. -Albert Einstein

Now that you have given me the honor of picking up this book intended for leaders in politics and government, you might be wondering what side of the fence I sit on. The truth is that all my life I have been an iconoclast that marches to the beat of my own drum, not a conformist who follows the madding crowd.

I draw my identity from being an American, and not with any particular political party. You might say that I am neither a Democrat nor a Republican. Except that statement is not entirely true. The truth is that in my heart I am a Democrat, yet in my mind I am a Republican, and I have voted for both Democrats and Republicans all my life and will continue to do so.

When I say that in my heart I am a Democrat, I was born with a natural empathy for rising human aspirations and throbbing human needs. I believe that the leader's job is to care and that government has an important role to play in helping people caught in the tentacles of circumstances who cannot help themselves.

When I say that in my mind I am a Republican, it is because I believe that making the "American Dream" available to everyone involves a lot more than tax and spend programs and doing crazy stuff like giving everything away for free. I have been a CEO and entrepreneur my entire life, starting successful businesses from scratch. I believe everyone has a pathway to do the same regardless of the circumstances into which they were born. And I do believe government can play a role in helping.

That said, following Donald Trump and many Republicans' endorsement of the "Big Lie" that the 2020 presidential election was stolen, it became increasingly hard for me to identify with the Republican party, especially after 147 members of Congress voted to refuse to certify the legitimate election of Joe Biden. In contrast, I was very much inspired by Republican leaders like Mitt Romney and Congresswoman Liz Cheney, who not only had the courage to take a stand and tell the truth during the former president's impeachment, but they also had the courage to hold their ground, even when personally attacked.

I AM A COACH, HELPING PEOPLE FIND THEIR GREATNESS

I have written this book, not from the point of view of a professor, historian, or political scientist who is telling stories, describing, or coming up with an explanation for what is happening in American politics or government.

I have written this book from the point of view of someone who makes their way in the world as an advisor, coach, or mentor—whose job it is to make a human connection with leaders in business, politics, and government, elevate their aspirations and motivations, and do whatever is possible to cause their success. I have always looked at people who work in places like the White House, State House, or Town Hall as people whose job it is to help everyone be better off.

I wrote the landmark book *Masterful Coaching* in 1995 with the goal of creating a new category of coaching that goes beyond providing good, anecdotal, grandmotherly advice. The book is focused on developing the next generation of leaders, guiding them to find the path to power and to make their vision of hope and change a reality, something that always involves helping people grow through adversity.

One thing I have discovered in coaching many leaders on their first (or next) 100 days is that in America, we tend to focus too much on individual leadership and not enough on collective leadership, which is what is required for democracy to work. The Founders feared someone would become king and abuse their power, so they laid down a system of government based on the permanent separation of powers. Yet at the same time, they also laid down a template for making the American system of government work based on the power of shared purpose, collaboration, and compromise.

While doing one-to-one coaching, I wrote another book called *Mastering the Art of Creative Collaboration* and developed a process called the CollabLab to help leaders form fast collaborations that deal with moonshot goals, complex problems, and intractable conflicts. It has been used with great success in business, politics, and other fields, and I will refer to it in this book.

WHY THIS BOOK

I first had the idea to write this book in thinking about the then-upcoming 2020 election, where we would not only be voting for the next president of the United States but also voting to fill thirty-five seats in the Senate and every one of the 435 seats in Congress.

I thought that the election presented a strong possibility of being what political scientists call a "strategic inflection point"—a reset election where leaders could join together in their first 100 days to help get the country back on track after it seemed to have gone so far off track for a long time. I saw it as an opportunity to rally leaders to restore the American Spirit—who we are and what we stand for—at home and around the world. I thought there was a realistic possibility to turn the page and begin the next chapter in American history.

Then just as I was finishing the book, America wound up smack dab in the middle of the worst disruption to our democracy since the Civil War, with the worst pandemic in one hundred years and the worst economic meltdown since the Great Depression.

It became obvious that America needs great leaders now to fix America. Further, we not only need great leaders in the White House and Congress, but we also need great leaders everywhere. It is time to democratize the work of leadership to include leaders in State Houses and Town Halls across the nation.

As I said, in my heart I am a Democrat, but in my mind I am a Republican. I believe democracy requires that both Democrats and Republicans be strong and healthy to work. I also believe that both sides have good ideas for building a nation that will help everyone be better off. I have written this book for you, and I will be happy to serve anyone from either side who is looking for one-on-one coaching, help in building a team of rivals, or who wants to sponsor a CollabLab that addresses the pressing issues of our day.

Let the good times roll!
Robert Hargrove
Boston, Massachusetts, 2022

Introduction

Toward the Next American Century:
An Optimist's Playbook

I am an optimist by nature, in part because I have absorbed the American "spirit of optimism." I grew up in greater Boston, known as "The Hub," the place where Governor John Winthrop arrived three hundred years ago on the ship Arbella and announced to his crew that they would build a shining city on a hill that would be a beacon of light to the rest of the world.

I feel lucky to have grown up in one of the country's top destinations for history, a center of civilization filled with great universities, architecture, museums, and statuary. Growing up here not only gave me a Boston accent, but it also instilled an appreciation for leaders who have found the courage to take on the impossible and bend history in the right direction, guiding a nation through its darkest hours.

When I was a young boy, my mother with her pillbox hat, white gloves, and black high heels, would take me on the MBTA elevated rail from Dudley Station in Roxbury to Park Street, adjoining the Boston Public Garden to take a ride on the swan boats that

Robert McCloskey wrote about in his book *Make Way for Ducklings*. Walking through the park, my mother would point out the statues of the heroes of the American Revolution—George Washington and Ben Franklin—as well as abolitionist Charles Sumner, who was caned (and paralyzed) on the Senate floor for his stance on abolition.

As I came of age, the American spirit of optimism was fueled in me by leaders whose paths crossed the pivotal moments of my life—such as listening to John F. Kennedy, our hometown hero, inaugurate his first 100 days by delivering his rousing "Ask Not..." speech. When he spoke the words: "Ask not what your country can do for you, but what you can do for your country," I felt he was talking directly to me. From that point on, I wanted to be a leader, not just a follower, and to make a difference, not just a living.

My soul was stirred when President Ronald Reagan said, "It's morning in America," followed by another zinger in Berlin a few years later: "Tear down that wall Mr. Gorbachev, Mr. Gorbachev tear down that wall." My heart soared when President Jimmy Carter held the Camp David Accords between the Egyptians and Israelis, ending an armed conflict that had being going on for 5000 years.

I have almost left out the optimism that comes from being a lifelong Red Sox fan, whose grandfather took him to watch Ted Williams. We all had become accustomed to the idea that the Red Sox never seemed to have the right pitching or hitting, and at the end of the season, we'd say, "Just wait 'til next year." Then, miraculously, after not having won the World Series in eighty-five years, in 2000 the Red Sox finally won the big one, and did so four more times over the next decade.

Today, I make my way in the world as a trusted advisor to leaders in business, elected officials, political appointees, and public managers, with the goal of helping them realize an impossible future and fix America's problems, so how can I be anything but an optimist?

Of course, I am not a blindfolded optimist who believes that climate change is a hoax or that Putin did not try to interfere in the recent/past few US elections, or that cutting taxes on billionaires and corporations results in wealth trickling down to the average Joe.

I believe that the ability to maintain confidence driven by optimism in the face of adversity, is the ultimate definition of being a leader. Our greatest presidents—Washington, Lincoln, and Roosevelt—maintained a sense of optimism, even when they woke up in the wee hours of the morning in sheer terror regarding the awesome burden of their responsibilities.

George Washington remained optimistic about winning the American Revolutionary War despite fighting the mightiest nation on earth and a year of humiliating defeats and retreats. This is what allowed him to keep going despite everyone saying, "It's impossible!" "You can't win!" "Give up!" "Go home!"

Lincoln took office at the beginning of the Civil War when the nation was cut in half and 600,000 people were about to die. Lincoln reportedly said, "I am an optimist because I don't see the point in being anything else." After the Union victory at Gettysburg on July 7, 1863, he wrote a note to Major General Henry W. Halleck, "Now, if Gen. Meade can complete his work so gloriously prosecuted thus far, by the literal or substantial destruction of Lee's army, the rebellion will be over." Unfortunately, the victory was followed by a string of defeats just a few days later.

Franklin D. Roosevelt realized that for a leader, optimism is not just a state of mind but also a strategy for winning hearts and minds. He restored confidence and optimism in his inaugural speech. One of my favorite quotes from him is: "I assume unhesitatingly the leadership of this great army of people dedicated to a disciplined attack upon our common problem [the Great Depression]." He then cheerfully delivered those unforgettable words, "The only thing we have to fear is fear itself." Within a few days, the mood of the country shifted, and people were feeling more positive and upbeat.

Finally, it is my belief that for a leader, the combination of optimism and outrage is essential if you want to make a difference and leave a legacy. You need optimism to believe you can impact issues like climate change, an inclusive economy, and healthcare. You need outrage to speak, listen, and act in a way that puts these on the political and economic agenda.

President Lyndon Johnson was optimistic that he could pass a landmark civil rights bill, but he fueled his mission with a sense of outrage. "Their cause must be our cause too. Because it is not just Negroes, but really it is all of us, who must overcome the crippling legacy of bigotry and injustice. And we shall overcome."

All great leaders combine a sense of optimism about the future and outrage about the present.

AN OPTIMIST'S PLAYBOOK

I have written *Your First (Next) 100 Days in Politics* from the point of view of an optimist with a sense of outrage about many things that are happening in America today. I have written it as an optimist's guide for leaders in politics and government, as well as the "office of the citizen"—those who feel a sense of outrage about the things happening in this country and want to make a difference, have an impact, and leave a legacy. I have written it for anyone who wants to play their part in creating a better America—a land of freedom and equality, where the doors of opportunity are wide open to everyone.

I use the subtitle *You're in the Same Business as George Washington* for several reasons. Presidents Washington, Lincoln, and Roosevelt all viewed their first 100 days as not just an onboarding experience, but also as something that had the potential to be the hallmark of their entire careers. They recognized an opportunity to make a difference when it was presented to them and then took bold and uncompromising action. When you were elected or appointed to office, you stepped into that very same opportunity.

If you are tired of the whole *first 100 days* lollapalooza or the moment of opportunity has not yet presented itself, you have the power to choose your *next 100 days* to make a bold promise that will help to change the face of things so you can pull out all stops to deliver it. For example, Lincoln used his first 100 days to "preserve the Union," then arbitrarily used a period of time known as "Abraham Lincoln's 100 days" to issue the Preliminary Emancipation Proclamation, promising to abolish slavery in 100 days or less.

Likewise, many other great leaders who were well past their first 100 days have arbitrarily chosen their "next" 100 days as the defining moment of their career. President Johnson used his first 100 days to pass the Civil Rights Act of 1964. He then capitalized on the personal credibility, political capital, and momentum he had achieved to launch a plethora of bills in his "next" 100 plus days known as the "Great Society" programs.

Finally, in times like these, following a pandemic, economic meltdown, and social protest, we need leaders who not only have a sense of what is important, but also a sense of urgency about what really needs to be done—leaders who arrive ready to pick up the mantle of those who have come before them and jump into action.

JOE BIDEN'S FIRST 100 DAYS—GOLDEN NUGGETS ANYONE CAN LEARN FROM

I have spent decades coaching leaders in business, politics, and government to find their greatness. One thing I have learned is that the first or "next" 100 days is not just a check-the-box onboarding process but has the potential of being the hallmark of your career. I have witnessed firsthand how this exciting, pressure-packed period is an opportunity to make a difference, have an impact, and leave a legacy.

Still, I have always found that it is much easier to make a point by telling a warm, human story about real people, than by giving a lecture. I am not saying this to be partisan, but the story of Joe Biden's first 100 days contains many golden nuggets that could be helpful in your first or next 100 days, regardless of what side of the political fence you sit on.

* * * * *

During the campaign for the 2020 election, when Joe Biden was running for president, he turned on the TV and heard Stephen Colbert refer to him as "that nice old man." Joe Biden got on the phone the next day and called Colbert telling him. "Listen buddy, if you ever call me a nice old man again, I am going to come down there and personally kick your ass." Colbert joked, "I promise you I won't, sir. You're clearly not that nice." As it turned out, Joe Biden was a much stronger candidate than anyone expected, won the election, and started kicking ass throughout his first 100 days.

When Joe Biden became president, he had already been both a teacher and student of the first and next 100 days for a long time. He had been through many leadership transitions himself during his thirty-six years in the Senate and had been President Obama's most trusted advisor on the subject. He seemed to know not only the kind of leader America needed as a president during such tumultuous times, but also just what needed to be done to make his own leadership transition successful.

By the end of his first 100 days, President Biden received widespread job approval, with 63% of Americans approving of how he was handling his job as president; 71% approved of how he was handling the coronavirus pandemic; 62% approved of how he was handling healthcare; 57% approved of how he was handling the economy; and 54% approved of how he was handling foreign affairs. Also, 54% of Americans thought the country was going in the right direction, the highest since 2017, although it was split by party: 84% of Democrats approved of the direction, while only 20% of Republicans did.

Let's look at some of the lessons to be learned from Biden's first 100 days.

Grace Under Pressure

Joe Biden showed tremendous leadership maturity and grace under pressure in the days following the aftermath of the 2020 election, as he dealt with the Trump Administration's refusal to cooperate in the peaceful transition of power, demonstrating that emotional intelligence (EQ) is more important than IQ. It would have been tempting for most of us mere mortals to be baited into an argument with the "former guy," President Trump, who told the Big Lie that the election had been stolen.

It would have been a snap to run to the barricades with muskets pointed at the domestic terrorists who led the first armed insurrection on Capitol Hill since the war of 1812, or for that matter, the 147 members of Congress who refused to certify his election that same day. Yet Biden kept his cool, acting as a unifier versus a divider, never once saying or doing anything that could be remotely construed as polarizing. This in itself signaled to many that when it came to being the leader America needs, Joe Biden had the right stuff.

Setting the Tone

Presidential historian Doris Kearns Goodwin says, "A leader's job is to set the tone." Think Ronald Reagan and "It's morning in America," George H. W. Bush's "A kinder gentler nation," Barack Obama's "A vison of hope and change" and "Yes we can." Joe

Biden set the tone as the new president in his victory speech with just three words "American is back," immediately restoring confidence and optimism after the Trump Administration.

He wanted to tell both Americans and the people around the world that during his administration, he would affirm the American ennobling ideals and enduring values that had become lost during the years of the previous administration. Suddenly, millions of people in the United States and around the world breathed a collective sigh of relief, as if a huge weight had been lifted off their shoulders.

The country had been through the worst threat to our democracy since the Civil War, the worst pandemic in 100 years, and the worst economic collapse since the Great Depression. Still, Biden proclaimed in his speech, "I have never been more optimistic about America than I am this very day." He had reason to be optimistic. He had received more votes than any other president in history (81 million votes to Trump's 74 million), giving him a mandate.

He sent out his first tweet after his inauguration on the way back to the White House: "There is no time to waste when it comes to tackling the crises we face," Biden wrote. "That's why today, I am heading over to the Oval Office to get right to work delivering bold action and immediate relief for American families."

VISION: TOWARD THE NEXT AMERICAN CENTURY

When President Biden entered the Oval Office, there was no customary handwritten note left by his predecessor on top of the Resolute Desk. So, Biden took a few moments to practice what my friend Kevin Cashman calls "pause leadership" or stepping back and reflecting to lead forward.

His presidency could result in two possible scenarios. One would involve Americans taking the "high road" toward the *Next American Century*. Henry Luce, publisher of *Time* magazine, coined the term "The American Century" to describe a period starting after the end of WWI in 1918, when America's ennobling aspirations and enduring values combined with extraordinary leadership, resources, talent, and dynamism to make us the most powerful nation in the world, with a way of life that is still unequaled. It was during this time that America also became a world leader in global politics. Due to American influence, the world went from mostly accepting kings, potentates, and czars to an increasing aspiration for democracy.

The other scenario could involve Americans taking the "low road" toward an increasingly brittle, polarized, and divided nation on the verge of fracturing. Biden reflected on his deeply held beliefs that were contrary to this approach, as he expressed in his inaugural address: "There is nothing Americans cannot accomplish if we do it together." He also thought about Abraham Lincoln's words: "a house divided against itself cannot stand."

Biden later said in a speech that the greatest threat to our country is whether democracy will survive in the years ahead. He made note of his conversations with President Putin of Russia and President Xi of China, who told him that in a world of accelerating change, it takes too long in a democracy to reach the consensus that is needed to solve problems. Today, China has a goal of making this *The Chinese Century,* to which Biden has said, "That's not going to happen on my watch." Clearly, if we want to make this the Next American Century, we will need leaders who know how to build a shared purpose, collaborate, and compromise with people with whom they differ.

BUILD A HIGH-PERFORMANCE TEAM

Biden has a healthy enough ego to be president, yet not so healthy as to believe that one person can do it alone. Even before he was elected, Biden had been consulting with his Chief of Staff

Ron Klain, whom he had known for years, about his goals and plans, viewing Klain as a thinking partner on his choices.

He was determined to choose a Cabinet made up of people who "look like America," with women, Blacks, Latinos, Asians. He chose Kamala Harris as his vice president, the first woman to hold that position. He appointed John Kerry, a very "senior guy," as his special climate change envoy. He appointed Merrick Garland, a constitutional scholar and former Supreme Court candidate, as his Attorney General. He appointed the highly decorated and esteemed Lloyd James Austin III, a Black four-star general, as his Secretary of Defense. He chose Deb Haaland, the first Native American in a cabinet post, as Secretary of the US Department of Interior

In their first week on the job, while visiting the State Department, President Biden and Vice President Harris delivered a motivating master class. "[I]t's one of our highest priorities, to thank you," Harris said as she opened her remarks to the employees and diplomats in the audience, explaining that their work is important and that it matters. When Biden got to the stage, he sincerely thanked everyone for the sacrifices they and their families make on behalf of the US, flying all over the world to do their jobs.

His main message was that what you do matters: "You are the center of all that I intend to do in the world. You are the heart of it…the strength and success of our nation depends in no small part on you." Harris had similar thoughts: "Everything you do, every policy you advance, every partnership you forge makes a difference in the lives of everyday Americans," she said.

TREAT YOUR FIRST 100 DAYS AS IF IT IS THE HALLMARK OF YOUR CAREER

When Franklin Delano Roosevelt ("FDR") took office in 1933, he said, "there is an awfully sick patient called the United States of America." He called himself "Dr. New Deal" and said he was going to apply the cure. When Joe Biden took office, he felt very similarly and was ready to see and meet the calling to become Dr. Joe.

Biden idolized FDR and wanted his first 100 days to not just be about overcoming Trump's attempts to block the peaceful transfer of power, but also to be the hallmark of his entire career. Biden was fascinated and intrigued by the legendary first 100 days during the Great Depression where FDR restored confidence and optimism, and along with Congress guided fifteen bills to passage. Yet he was perhaps even more intrigued by FDR's "next" 100 days where he passed a torrent of transformational legislation that resulted in an Economic Bill of Rights for all Americans. Biden said he wanted to do something like that.

Like LBJ, Biden believed that the power of the Federal Government is to help people who are caught in the tentacles of circumstance, especially those less fortunate amongst us who are fighting forces too big for them to fight alone. He wanted to be a transformational leader who uses his first 100 days to fix America's problems that were caused by the nation-encumbering crisis, and his next 100 days to drive transformational change by shifting the government's social contract with its people.

A POWERFUL FIRST 100 DAY PROMISE YOU GO PUBLIC WITH

When Biden gave his State of the Union Address before a joint session of Congress on the eve of his 100th day, it was obvious that "this nice old man" had gotten off to a strong start in his first 100 days, and in fact, in his first ten minutes, when he jumped into action and began signing a number of executive orders designed with American ideals and values in mind. He had a very clearly spelled-out first (and next) 100-day plan.

First 100 Days—Fix America. While the first 100 days is a tremendous opportunity to get off to a fast start and score some early wins, it is also fraught with risks that most people in politics and business do not appreciate. A lot of people get it wrong! Think John F. Kennedy and the disastrous Bay of Pigs invasion. Think Richard Nixon's second term as president and the Watergate Scandal. Think Barack Obama getting shut down by Mitch McConnell after steam-rolling Obamacare through.

Joe Biden may not be a perfect president and he may not be a perfect human being, but he got a lot of things right about his first 100 days. He had had a vision for his presidency for a long time, and he also arrived with a strategy with which he would approach his first and next 100 days. It involved using his first 100 days to fix America, which was dealing with multiple crises, and his next 100 days to drive transformational change. With that in mind, he steered a clear course as a leader taking charge, building a team, and getting fast results, while laying the groundwork for driving transformational change later.

One of the most important things that any newly elected official, political appointee, or public manager can do to make their first 100 days successful, is to go public with a BIG PROMISE, and deliver on it. On January 20, 2021, President Biden promised to get 100 million vaccine doses delivered into arms in his first 100 days. Only 65 days later, on March 25th, he increased that number to 200 million.

By April 22nd, the United States had met Biden's goal of 200 million vaccinations, a week ahead of his goal. Biden also announced on January 20th the American Rescue Plan which was passed into law just two months into his term, securing a major win that would build momentum. It appropriated $1.9 trillion to expand unemployment benefits and make direct payments to 150 million individuals so they could pay their rent and buy groceries, while funding support for healthcare and covid vaccines.

FDR had taken care of the "forgotten man" (who had lost his job) by providing unemployment insurance to workers and providing the elderly with Social Security. LBJ provided the "forgotten man" with Medicare. Biden used the American Rescue Plan to move the children of the "forgotten man" out of poverty, and he was just beginning. He wanted to pass a bill for universal day care that would allow the parents of minorities to get 9 to 5 jobs, helping them to climb the social/ economic ladder. He also created a plan to make a two-year college education available to every American with no strings attached, which would ultimately translate into jobs.

The Next 100 Days—Drive Transformational Change. Ever since FDR, people have viewed the *first* 100 days as if it's the first and *only* 100 days for driving transformational change, after which they have to content themselves with transactional improvements. This tends to put sky-high expectations and pressures on new leaders that no human being can fulfill.

The single most important discovery I made in writing this book was that the legend of FDR's first 100 days was less a fact than a myth. Like Joe Biden, he used his first 100 days to Fix America—with the goal of putting people back to work during the Great Depression—and then used a period of time known as "FDR's second 100 days" to drive transformational change. It was during this time that he greatly expanded the powers of the presidency, changed the social contract between the US government and its people, and passed an Economic Bill of Rights for all Americans.

Biden also scored early wins in his first 100 days that allowed him to build personal credibility, political capital, and momentum. He then launched into his second 100 days with the idea of building on FDR's and LBJ's legacy of building the Great Society in an era of globalization.

He has set BHAGs (big hairy audacious goals) for tackling global climate change, in a way that would serve to totally transform the global economy. He also wanted to pass the John Lewis Voting Rights Act to affirm our democracy and prevent further gerrymandering of election districts and racist voter suppression bills aimed especially against people of color.

He wanted to build on the momentum of the American Rescue Plan by passing the American Jobs Plan (investing in infrastructure) or, as he said, "Build Back Better" after the pandemic. It not only included things like bridges, roads, and railroads, but also other elements of 21st century infrastructure, like universal internet access.

Biden took a trip to Lake Charles, Louisiana and stood in front of the Calcasieu River Bridge, built in 1952, and twenty years overdue for renovation, in a state hit thirty times in the past ten years by natural disasters that have cost up to $50 billion in damages. "I've never seen a Republican or a Democrat road. I just see roads." Biden said. He called for a once in a lifetime investment in roads, bridges, electrical grids, schools, childcare, job training, and broadband to make America competitive in the 21st century. Biden called for funding this investment by raising the corporate tax rate from 21% to 28% —still lower than the 35% it was before Trump's 2017 tax cut—and making sure corporations could no longer get out of paying their taxes.

THE BIDEN BOOM

Biden had said that the president's job is to care. It turns out that Biden's sincere and honest intentions around this, which were reflected in his climate change agenda, the American Rescue Plan and American Jobs Plan, electrified not only most American citizens, but also the economy. Trump had said that if Biden were elected, the stock market would crash, and people's 401(k)s would be emptied of their life savings. Yet the opposite was true.

By the end of his first 100 days, the stock market was soaring to a high, unmatched in the first 100 days of any president since FDR took office in 1933. Further, the economy had created over a million new jobs. The *Wall Street Journal* reported that a record share of companies were beating earnings estimates by 22.8% above expectations. In the first quarter of 2021, the economy grew at an annual rate of 6.4%. Biden said this was just the beginning.

THE POTENTIAL FOR A BIDEN BUST—OR ROOM FOR IMPROVEMENT

While there was no question Biden had a strong start with his first 100 days, there was also some room for improvement. He felt that he had to play a bit of the "king of the rock" game, issuing executive orders and laying out principles and policies that he could push through by leveraging the Democrats' majority in Congress. The rationalization was that this would be necessary in order to promptly deal with the multiple crises the country was facing.

However, whenever a leader plays the "king of the rock" game and pursues their agenda unilaterally, they run the risk of people from the other side trying to pull them off the rock and take their place. By the end of Joe Biden's first 100 days, Senate Minority Leader Mitch McConnell declared that "One-hundred percent of our focus is on stopping this new administration," rather than doing the American people's business. Republican House Leader Kevin McCarthy flew to confer with Donald Trump at Mar-a-Lago and came back with little to say about collaborating with Democrats to take on America's toughest problems and a lot to say about winning back Congress.

As I have argued already, because the Founders were afraid someone would start playing the old "king of the rock" game, they laid down the Constitution based on the permanent separation of powers. They also laid down a template with marching orders to future presidents and members of Congress that the way to move the country forward was by combining top-down power with the art of shared purpose, collaboration, and compromise.

I believe that while Biden may have needed to take executive action to affirm his vision and values, the page on shared purpose, collaboration, and compromise may have inadvertently dropped out of his "presidential playbook" without him being aware of it. He said with respect to the American Rescue Plan, to paraphrase, "I tried the bipartisan approach with Republicans, but they set a low number and would not budge."

One take away is that in order for a president, governor, or department head to collaborate with the other side to solve our toughest problems, there are several conditions that must be satisfied: 1) Leaders need to be dedicated public servants, focused on helping people be better off, rather than focused on winning elections or making the other side lose, 2) There needs to be a shared purpose big enough to inspire people on both sides to sit down at the table and negotiate, and 3) Both sides need to be honest brokers. This was (and is going forward) the area with the most room for improvement for President Biden or leaders in Congress to be able to make a difference, have an enduring impact, and leave a legacy.

America Needs Great Leaders at Every Level

Although President Biden was able to accomplish much of what he wanted to achieve in his first 100 days, as time goes by, he will most likely discover as most presidents do that his power is very limited. Political scientist Richard Neustadt wrote that the president's power is not to give orders, it is the power to persuade America to steer a course toward the *Next American Century* rather than fall off into the abyss of a continuing uncivil war. Clearly we need leaders at the top of the pyramid, but we also need leaders at every level.

The first sign of leadership is what John F. Kennedy called a "profile in courage". Congressman Jamie Raskin was a profile in courage in his soulful, heartrending impeachment case against the former president for his conduct. He said Trump's presidential conduct not only violated the law, but also violated the sanctity of the Capitol Building. It mattered because the Capitol is a physical representation of our constitutional government. Raskin was rewarded with winning praise from many in both parties and death threats to him and his family from others.

Congresswoman Liz Cheney from Wyoming was also a profile in courage when she said on the eve of Trump's impeachment trial, "The president not only incited a riot, but did not try to stop it." Declaring that it was a violation of his constitutional oath, she said, "I will vote to impeach." Her reward was that her Republican colleagues stripped her of her leadership in Congress, hoping to prevent her re-election.

Representative Liz Cheney, the number three House Republican, remarked one hundred days later at a behind-closed-door conference in Sea Island, Georgia, that her party cannot accept the "poison" of the idea that the 2020 election was stolen and should not "whitewash" the January 6th Capitol riot and Donald Trump's role in fomenting it. "We cannot embrace the notion the election is stolen. It is a poison in the bloodstream of our democracy," Cheney said, undeterred by the threat of losing her seat in Congress, adding, "We cannot whitewash what happened on January 6 or perpetuate Trump's big lie. It is a threat to democracy. What he did on January 6 is a line that cannot be crossed."

On May 10, 2021, Republican House Leader Kevin McCarthy held a speedy vote to oust Cheney from the House GOP Leadership. The closed-door, secret ballot was a "voice vote" so that no one would have to say whether they voted for or against. After the vote, Cheney went in front of the cameras to say that she would lead the fight to reclaim the party from Trump, "I will do everything I can to ensure that the former president never again goes anywhere near the Oval Office."

In being demoted by her colleagues on Capitol Hill, Cheney seemed to rise like a phoenix from the ashes to a leader of national prominence, gaining respect from Democrats and Republicans alike. Many colleagues suggested she could soon be a presidential candidate. Cheney said in an interview airing on NBC's "Today" show, "I intend to be the leader in a fight to strengthen our democracy and to help to restore our party."

Yet to steer a course to the *Next American Century* and avoid falling into the abyss of division, we not only need leaders in the White House and on Capitol Hill who lead from the top, we also need leaders in the State House to make sure our democracy survives in the face of voter suppression, and leaders in the Schoolhouse to make sure our children have the best education in the world.

> *It turns out that leadership may be the art and practice of getting out in front of the parade and shouting "this way!"*

We need leaders who are not just elected officials and political appointees, but also leaders who are CEOs and entrepreneurs, police chiefs and school superintendents, scientists and engineers, architects and artists, writers and musicians who can help spread the word.

One of my favorite quotes comes from Supreme Court Justice Louis D. Brandeis, who said, "The most important political office is that of the private citizen." I believe that this is not just words (nice rhetoric), but also something that reveals a powerful truth. As Abraham Lincoln once said, "Public sentiment is everything. With public sentiment, nothing can fail; without it nothing can succeed."

If we look at America's story through a different lens, rather than seeing only the "great man theory" of history, we will notice that most of the great changes in our country came not from the president, governor, or mayor's office (or top-down), but from the bottom up—populist movements that the people at the top followed. These changes came from people who protested and marched and who sang in order to fight for a shot at the American dream, freedom from tyranny, and equal justice under the law.

Change came from people like Harriet Tubman and the Underground Railroad and from Rosa Parks, who refused to move to the back of the bus. Most recently, it came from Darnella Frazier, a 17-year-old girl who witnessed the murder of George Floyd and had the presence of mind to pull out her phone and create a 9-minute and 20-second video so that the perpetrators could later be brought to justice.

Frazier said she wasn't looking to be a hero and is "just a 17-year-old high school student, with a boyfriend and a job at the mall, who did the right thing." She said she was not a person to take a stand or speak out. "I suffered from social anxiety, I bottle things up." George Floyd was already cuffed on the ground, a knee to the neck. "When you're already restrained it is absolutely unnecessary," she wrote. "That man was begging for his life and Derek Chauvin did not care." As the crowd shouted, "check his pulse…he actually was kneeling harder," she said. "He was shoving his knee in his neck."

During cross-examination, the defense attorney asked Frazier if she was surprised the video she recorded went viral. "Definitely," Frazier responded. "It changed your life, right?" Nelson asked. "Are you asking me?" Frazier asked. Nelson said he was. "It has," she said. In December 2020, Frazier virtually accepted the 2020 PEN/Berenson Leadership Courage Award from Oscar-winning director Spike Lee for capturing Floyd's death on video.

I wrote this book because I saw that America needs great leaders at every level. My view is that if we can acknowledge that great leadership is missing and see that as an opportunity versus a threat, we can begin to call forth the leaders that are needed and wanted.

Throughout the book, I tell stories about great leaders from American history as seen through the exclusive lens of their first or next 100 days, with the idea of raising the standard and setting the bar for both today's leaders and future leaders. This is balanced with "how to" chapters where I get down to the nitty gritty, like mobilizing people with a shared purpose, creating a strategy that matches the political situation, and creating a 100-day plan.

THE LEADERSHIP CREDO

I wrote this book with the very clear goal and intention to bring out the highest and best in you as a leader. I wrote it knowing full well that we all have a bright side and a dark side, and most of the time we go back and forth between our bright side and our dark side, without even realizing it, especially in the absence of coaching and meaningful feedback.

My goal here is to play my part in helping to win the "Battle for the Soul" of America, to encourage you (and every person who picks up this book) to lead from your bright side—what Abraham Lincoln called the "better angels of our nature." It is also to help you develop the self-awareness to recognize when your dark side is being reactivated by stress and pressure, and to reign in the negative impulses that go along with it.

I was pondering what I could do in this book to specifically support you in doing that, and then walking through the Boston Public Garden one day and seeing the statues of American Patriots, I had an "aha" moment. The idea came to me of creating a Leadership Credo that could help leaders in the White House, State House, Town Hall, and the Schoolhouse navigate the opportunities and challenges of their first 100 days.

Every newly elected official or political appointee wants to uphold America's ennobling ideals and enduring values when dealing with the greater issues of the day. Yet it is sometimes hard to keep that in view while in the face of leaders who play the old "king of the rock" game and who put the nation's interest and public interest second to party interest and personal interest.

It is also hard for leaders to maintain the right mindset in the face of 24/7 news anchors who are paid to make people angry, dumb, and foolhardy, or in a world of Tweets, Instagram, and TikTok videos.

Following is the Leadership Credo. I believe that putting your signature down on the Leadership Credo and reviewing it every day with colleagues is a powerful way to gain direct access to being a great leader as a natural self-expression.

LEADERSHIP CREDO

- I am in the same business as George Washington, Abraham Lincoln, and Franklin D. Roosevelt and have a sacred duty to "improve the general welfare."

- My job is to uphold the American Spirt—who we are and what we stand for—in interacting with people and the political climate of the times.

- I am leading when I am putting all my soul, heart, and energy into mobilizing people around a shared purpose that contributes to the betterment of society.

- I will remember:
    - *Leadership is not a job but a moral crusade and action.*
    - *You can only lead when you have empathy for the people you lead.*
    - *Both optimism and outrage are needed to make vision a reality.*
    - *No individual, political party, or department can do it alone.*
    - *It takes shared purpose, collaboration, and compromise.*
    - *Instead of just "talk," leverage the power of "do."*
    - *Go for real outcomes that make a difference in other's lives.*

I also believe that asking colleagues once a day "How am I doing?" could be a powerful way to stay focused on your own True North and to adjust your speaking, listening, or actions according to the feedback you are getting. I suggest carrying the Leadership Credo it in your back pocket and post it in your office and on your refrigerator, where you will be able to see it every day.

It would be a cool idea for elected officials and political appointees to have a leadership signing ceremony in their office where they and others respectfully sign the document. Then post it proudly to celebrate it and commemorate it, as well as to hold yourselves publicly accountable for it.

Let me close this introduction with a quote from Robert Kennedy: "Few will have the greatness to bend history; but each of us can work to change a small portion of events, and in the total of all these acts will be written the history of this generation."

Let's keep the conversation going!

Ben Franklin:
Great Compromisers Make
Great Democracies

Great heroes do not make great compromisers. Great compromisers make great democracies. -Benjamin Franklin

Our Constitution was not the work of one extraordinary leader or solo genius who laid down a vision of the United States and inspired people to execute it. Rather, it was created by an extraordinary constellation of leaders who met in Philadelphia in 1787 at the Constitutional Convention to gather individual slices of genius for the purpose of shaping a new government.

The Constitutional Convention was convened after the American Revolutionary War when there was no nation, just a collection of former British colonies and easily as much frenetic incivility, polarizing goals, and division as we have seen in recent years.

The Constitutional "Framers" bestowed upon us the American system of government based on a separation of powers between the president, the Congress, and the judiciary, as well as a path forward for avoiding the kind of "democracy in deadlock" we face now.

I believe that every leader about to start their first 100 days at the national, state, or local level should read and recount this story of the Convention. For it was there that the Framers laid down the template for moving the country forward by means of civil dialogue, shared purpose, collaboration, and compromise.

IT TAKES LEADERSHIP TO CONVENE AN EXTRAORDINARY COMBINATION OF PEOPLE

In 1787 Benjamin Franklin—one of the most important Founding Fathers, a delegate to the Constitutional Convention from Pennsylvania, and occupant of Mrs. Mary House boarding house in Philadelphia—was enjoying a hearty breakfast of a small beer, blueberry muffins, some Philly cheese, and salted fish.

As he ate, Franklin read a letter from John Adams, which included a reminder from Adams's wife Abigail who often shared her own wise political views. Franklin smiled softly as he took in her strong request that he remind the Framers of the Constitution to "remember the ladies," telling her husband that "all men would be tyrants if they could."

Ben Franklin was not just a kindly Founding Father, a bespectacled dispenser of aphoristic advice, and famous for his dangerous liaisons with women; he also played a key role in the Revolution. Once he was playing chess with his equal the Duchess of Bourbon, who made a move that inadvertently exposed her king. Ignoring the rules of the game, he promptly captured it. "Ah," said the duchess, "we do not take Kings so." Replied Franklin in a famous quip: "We do in America."

After eating his breakfast, he strolled over to the State House determined not to take himself too seriously, even though he and his colleagues were about to draft a document that was intended to "alter the course of history." It was one where government would be ruled not by accident of a king's birth or by force, but by democratic choice and reason. The story of that idea would be the story of American history.

As he approached the State House, he glanced up at the great clock over the door, referred to as The Clock of History. It was a reminder to the delegates of the Convention that the eyes of the world would be upon them, and what they did in that building would be judged by history.

It had taken real leadership to get delegates to come to the Constitutional Convention. This did not just happen on its own. James Madison knew there had to be a convener to bring the states together for such a daunting task, and that it could not be him. Madison was a diminutive man who stood 5'5", with a weak voice, who had been sickly all his life. He lacked the personal credibility needed to convince others to attend the meeting. Acknowledging his limitations, he pondered who might bring them together. The answer was obvious—George Washington.

For six months, Madison skillfully courted Washington to get him to come out of retirement and attend the convention but was met with some resistance. Given the failings of human nature, Washington had doubts whether democracy could work, believing a ruling elite might be necessary. Washington also realized that many of the delegates believed the Constitutional Convention would be a power grab by an all-powerful, quasi-Royalist government. He knew if he attended, he might be drafted to be the "president" and, as he was fiercely protective of his reputation as a dedicated public servant, he did not want to be seen as grasping for power. Finally, at the urging of friends, and for the welfare of the country, he agreed, and the states started choosing delegates to attend.

Both John Adams and Thomas Jefferson declined the invitation to attend. Jefferson called it "an assembly of demigods who were trying to reinstate George Washington as king. In truth, he was in Paris as an ambassador to France. Likewise, John Adams was in Europe serving as an ambassador to Great Britain. Patrick Henry ("Give me liberty or give me death") also turned down an invitation to attend, saying "I smell a rat in Philadelphia tending toward a monarchy."

Still, it was an extraordinary combination of people from different professions and occupations who came together to collaborate on framing the principles of the Constitution—politicians, ambassadors, doctors, lawyers, planters, investors, shipbuilders, generals, printers, postmasters, inventors, and journalists.

A CONVERSATION THAT CREATED
OUR CONSTITUTION

Preparation was important. Madison leveraged his network in the different states to gain firsthand insight into the delegates. He studied the constitutions of the thirteen states, as well as the noble efforts of other democracies, and circulated these to the delegates to study. He prepared an agenda with the different topics to be discussed, asking Washington and Peyton Randolph, the delegate from Virginia, for their reactions.

The fifty-five delegates from twelve states convened that summer in long coats and knee breeches, in sweltering heat and secrecy, with the windows of the Hall nailed shut to prevent eavesdropping. The delegates decided to facilitate a free and open exchange of ideas; however, inside the Hall, Federalists (Big Gov) and anti-Federalists would hurl veiled insults at each other, and once got into a bar room brawl at the end of one day.

Ben Franklin was a "man in full" at the convention, charming and disarming yet deeply purposeful, lighthearted, and funny. He offered to help Madison in any way he could—super host, moderator, after-hours confidant. A native of Philadelphia, he would convene small gatherings at the Mrs. Mary House for dinner and drink, where delegates from different states could establish positive human relationships, despite their divergent views. This is where the greater good would be emphasized amongst combatants, mind melds would happen, and conflicts ironed out.

Franklin was not a religious man, but sensing the potential for personal quarrels and rancorous debate, he suggested offering a daily morning prayer "imploring the assistance of Heaven" in being reminded of the greater goal "and its blessings on our deliberations," so that people would be able to successfully find a meeting of the minds.

The delegates came to the Convention ready to have a conversation about improving the Articles of Confederation of autonomous states. They switched the conversation to creating a constitution that would define a totally new country, and this would rest on establishing shared purpose and mastering the art of creative collaboration and compromise.

NAVIGATING THE CLASH OF DISSENTING VIEWS

Much of the dialogue centered on picking a topic that was a bone of contention and then scanning each state's constitution and discussing whether a particular aspect of the "Massachusetts Plan" or the "Virginia Plan" provided the best alternative. Should there be a president for life, or one president every four years? Should there be two houses of Congress or one?

The Framers were legitimately torn between having a strong presidency and federal government—which could lead to the kind of abuse of power seen with the British monarchy—or having too weak a presidency and federal government—which could lead to anarchy. There was general agreement about having two houses of Congress, but there were many squabbles, wrangles, and wars of words about representation. The larger states wanted representation in Congress based on size of the population, not including slaves. The smaller states wanted representation with an equal number of seats from each state.

Madison would speak up on the convention floor, not to air his views, but to return people to a shared purpose that was big enough to subordinate their egos to—that of drafting the Constitution of the United States, based on the idea of "One Nation, conceived in Liberty for All of Us."

He would hold up a fistful of parchment and remind people that the job was not to make fanciful speeches, floating thoughts that would disappear the moment they were spoken, like steam from a teapot. It was one of creative collaboration in drafting a joint document that everyone in the room could sign. As the summer rolled along, this would require the delegates to learn to think and work together with others who saw things differently.

Franklin would intervene when arguments got too heated or there were too many digressions, interrupting with a bit of humor: *"Gentlemen, there are two kinds of people. Those who have something to say and those who just need to say something."* This would generally produce a laugh. He would add, *"Speak not but what may benefit the noble purpose to which we have come here."* When people would step over each other's words, he would say, *"Listen first so as to show you care what others think."* When people would digress, he would say, *"Gentlemen, let's avoid trifling conversation."*

Yet even when the conversation cooled from outright clashes to superficial conviviality, there were always issues boiling below the surface. Washington worried that the power of the presidency and federal government would be too small. Madison, along with Jefferson, felt trapped in "the bigness of the Federal government." Jefferson wrote a letter to the Convention saying, "I firmly believe that Virginia is my country."

George Washington did not say much on the convention floor, always concerned about being seen as power hungry. He listened in a way that embraced the ambitions, appetites, and prejudices of the delegates, whether he agreed or disagreed. He would skillfully use his power and influence to orchestrate behind the scenes.

Hamilton, a Federalist, could generally convince Washington of his views and would speak with great passion and eloquence on the floor. He was a shrewd politician who had a transformative vision of the United States as being one of the greatest political and economic powers in the world, but he was not above entering into the transactional world of brokerage and making trade-offs.

His style was to listen to everyone intently whenever controversial issues came up in the "markup sessions"—like presidential power, a national bank, or standing army. He would write notes as if doodling on paper, searching for middle ground. He would then show others what he had written down, asking "Could this work?" He would add, for instance, "What if the national bank paid off the states' Revolutionary War debts?"

THE MIRACLE AT PHILADELPHIA

Madison would later say that the "miracle at Philadelphia," as it was later dubbed, was the result of the explosion of creative ideas that emerged from the constant wrangling of many delegates with conflicting views and opinions. This was catalyzed by the time pressure to get the Constitution down on parchment before the first session of Congress in September.

As the summer wore on with fierce argument and 24/7 toil, the delegates rolled up their sleeves and got down to business. Their collaboration was a process of shared creation that involved generating rapid iterations of rough drafts of the Constitution or part of it. They were able to find creative solutions by connecting the dots between their conflicting views.

It was to be neither a government of kings and queens, nor a government of the mob. It was to be a government based on the permanent separation of powers between the president, Congress, and Supreme Court. It was believed that the glue that would hold this new democratic system together was the same kind of debate and collaborative problem-solving they had experienced at the convention.

Even as the Constitutional Convention neared its end, there were still sticking points that most people found hard to agree with. How long would the president's term be? Would large and small states have equal representation in Congress? Who had power over the budget? Who could declare war?

One of the key issues was that of representation. Larger states favored representation by population. Smaller states favored equal representation by states. Franklin, who sensed a deadlock, decided to back off his original position of representation by population.

In his final speech at the Convention, Franklin said, "I doubt whether any other Convention we can obtain, may be able to make a better Constitution: For when you assemble a number of men to have the advantage of their joint wisdom, you inevitably assemble with those men all their prejudices, their passions, their errors of opinion, their local interests, and their selfish views. It therefore astonishes me to find this system approaching so near to perfection as it does; Thus, I consent to this Constitution because I expect no better, and because I am not sure that it is not the best. The opinions I have had of its errors, I sacrifice to the Public Good. Within these walls they were born, and here they shall die."

The last version of the Constitution contained the Connecticut Compromise which said that there would be two houses of Congress. The Senate or upper chamber would be elected on the basis of equal representation of each state. The House of Representatives would be elected by population, with each slave being counted as three fifths of a person. The president or either chamber would also originate legislation or a budget, but the House would have full financial control. Further, only Congress could declare war.

As John Quincy Adams, the sixth president of the United States, observed regarding the power of shared purpose and collaboration, "The mutual influence of these two mighty minds upon each other is a phenomenon, like the invisible and mysterious movements of the magnet in the physical world."

Washington said the Constitutional Convention went from a cacophony (which reminded people of the Tower of Babel their enemies would delight over) to a beautiful symphony. He wrote later to his friend the Marquis de Lafayette, "it appears to me, little short of a miracle, that the Delegates from so many different States [so different from each other] should unite in forming a system of national government," one that the world would be watching and waiting to see and that would last hundreds of years. Madison commented toward the end of the summer, "The happy Union of these States is a wonder, their Constitution a miracle; their example the hope of Liberty throughout the world."

By the middle of September, the delegates had drafted a proposal written on four pages of parchment. They sent that draft to the printers who set the type of its soaring preamble with a giant W, sharp as an eagle's claw.

We the People of the United States, in Order to form a more perfect Union, establish Justice, insure domestic Tranquility, provide for the common general Welfare and Secure the Blessings of Liberty to ourselves, and Posterity, do ordain and Establish this Constitution of the United States of America.

On September 17, 1787, the Constitution was read aloud and signed. The delegates went forward to lend their names to the document, and Benjamin Franklin followed and wept as he inscribed his name. As he left the convention, someone asked him what they had created. "A republic," he answered, "if you can keep it."

In the end, the Framers punted and left some things up to George Washington to decide once he became president. Washington and his Cabinet met for weeks at the beginning of his administration to sort the issues of a strong Congress and Supreme Court. Still, the Framers were able to go before Congress and get the whole thing ratified so the country could be brought into existence.

This was nothing short of miraculous since at least one third of the United States population did not identify with being American at the time and would just as likely have preferred to return to the protection of King George and the British Empire.

THE PROCESS OF HOW WE ACHIEVED THE CONSTITUTION MUST NOT BE FORGOTTEN

Today, we celebrate and commemorate who the Framers were and what they achieved in drafting the Constitution of the United States. What we have forgotten is the process of how they achieved it, which is essential to reinvigorating our Democracy today.

The Framers, including George Washington who referred to the "Miracle of Philadelphia," really did think it was a miracle that such an extraordinary combination of people with conflicting visions and values was able to produce the Constitution.

Yet, the "Miracle of Philadelphia" was also due to the fact that James Madison acted as the convener who brought people together, and Ben Franklin acted as a skilled facilitator as well as a super host, so people could make human connections.

The "Miracle of Philadelphia" was also achieved by people treating each other with civility when emotions were running strong, leveraging the power of shared purpose, collaboration, and compromise.

If you are about to start your first 100 days as a new leader with or without a big title, in a polarized political context, you can still impact the issues you and others passionately care about by following the template the Framers laid down for us.

Chapter One

A Hero's Journey:
Be the Leader America Needs

In today's turbulent times, American needs great leaders, not just in the White House, but also in the State House, Town Hall, and the Schoolhouse (everywhere). This book is for newly elected officials, political appointees, and public managers who are ready to step up to the challenge of being the leaders America needs. It will show you how to use your first 100 days not just to onboard into a new role, but also to become the hallmark of your career.

I have spent my whole life chasing one goal: inspiring, empowering, and enabling leaders in politics, government, and business to find their greatness. I guess you could say I am both an expert and a student on the subject, having spent decades searching for and sharing the best ideas I can find.

I have written "landmark books" on becoming a leader anchored in America's ennobling aspirations and enduring values, traveled the globe on countless red-eye flights to give keynote talks about the need for great leaders—not only at the top, but everywhere—and have had the privilege of coaching many people in positions of power in their first 100 days to find the courage to take on an impossible future and realize it.

Jeffrey Pfeffer of Stanford Business School and author of *Leadership BS* says that the $50 billion leadership development and training industry has failed. It teaches you about great leaders, breaks down the leadership characteristics and traits you should have, and provides 360 eye-opening feedback. Yet, for the most part, it does not give you direct access to becoming a leader who others will want to follow—nor does it make your vision of hope and change a reality in your first or next 100 days, because most of the stuff they teach is not actionable.

People are left asking themselves questions like: How do I become a leader who is as tough on Russia as Ronald Reagan, as kind and caring as Barack Obama, and as good a deal maker as John Boehner? Or how am I going to remember all the things that a great leader is supposed to do when the stakes are high, emotions are running strong, and there is no obvious path forward?

My goal in this book is not merely to teach you about being a great leader, nor is it to provide you with a first 100-day playbook that helps you onboard into your new role. Rather, it is to help you make your first 100 days the hallmark of your entire career by showing you a pathway that gives you direct access to being a great leader as a natural self-expression, with the ability to lead effectively in any situation.

I chose the words "direct access" carefully. I use direct access because it implies that there is a pathway to being the leader America needs, and that it is actionable. My intention here is to shine a light on that pathway that combines your goals, who you need to be, and what you need to do to achieve them.

To give you an idea of what I am talking about, take five to ten minutes to make three lists that you think would give you direct access to being the leader America needs. Start with a "To Be" list that represents who you need to be in the matter, then create a "To

Do" list—which includes strategic to-dos—and then make a "To Connect & Collaborate" list—how you will work with others to make things happen. (More on this later in the chapter.)

I also chose the phrase "first (next) 100 days" very carefully. It means you can use your first 100 days in office to do something to bend history in the right direction, or you can forget about the whole "first 100 day" lollapalooza and arbitrarily choose any next 100 days to do that, whenever the timing is right.

Abraham Lincoln is a classic example of a great leader. He used his first 100 days as president to seal his leadership with his team of rivals and preserve the Union at the outbreak of the Civil War and reminded people to choose the better angels of their nature stating that "We are not enemies, but friends. We must not be enemies." He then arbitrarily chose a period known as "Abraham Lincoln's 100 Days" to issue the Emancipation Proclamation. (See more on this in the Lincoln interlude).

AMERICA NEEDS GREAT LEADERS
NOW MORE THAN EVER

As Thomas L. Friedman points out in his New York Times Opinion piece "We Need Great Leaders Now–and Here's What It Looks Like," in ordinary times when our democracy is chugging along and there is peace and prosperity, great leadership matters—and leads to sustained success. Yet in extraordinary times, when America is facing a nation-encumbering crisis like the founding of the nation, the Civil War, the Great Depression, or today's rapidly approaching post-pandemic world, great leadership not only matters more—but it also matters exponentially more.

In her book *Leadership in Turbulent Times*, historian Doris Kearns Goodwin asks: "Are great leaders born or made?" The answer she gives is "both." Great leaders may have leadership in their DNA, possessing the qualities all great leaders have—ambition, empathy, responsibility, humility, self-reflectiveness. Yet it is the actual throwing one's hat into the ring, extracting vision from a nation-encumbering crisis, and weathering the storm of making it a reality—that is often the crucible by which great leaders develop.

That is why today is such a golden leadership opportunity for elected officials, political appointees, and public managers, whether this is your first (or next) 100 days.

We live in uncertain times. As Tom Peters, author of *Excellence Now, Extreme Humanism*, points out, climate change is not only coming, but is already here, and as the Texas energy blackout in subzero temperatures showed, we are not prepared for it. We have recently been through one of the most fractious elections in American history, culminating in the armed insurrection on Capitol Hill, causing many to take note that for the first time since the Civil War, our democracy has been so divided that people were ready to go to war against each other.

The Covid-19 virus took well over 500,000 American lives, and the pandemic job-wrecking machine sent millions to collect unemployment checks. The murder of George Floyd led to mass protests all over the country in the name of racial justice, income equality, voting rights, immigration, and a path to citizenship. Schools, restaurants, airlines, and hotels were locked down for over a year, making us all feel like shut-ins.

One result of so much uncertainty is that leaders at every level experience a leadership stress test. The stress is not only felt by occupants of the White House, but also by governors and mayors, CEOs and entrepreneurs, heads of schools and coaches of youth sports.

Leading during a crisis is a stress test where your leadership strengths, as well as you vulnerabilities are on full display. Do you play the old "king of the rock" game—my way or the highway—or do you mobilize people around a shared purpose, collaboration, and compromise? Do you tend to sound off with preconceived opinions and beliefs, or do you work hard at making listening to your constituents your profession, and translating that into policies and programs?

Do the decisions and judgement calls you make on a day-in, day-out basis (on both the big and little stuff) result in your being considered a national, state, or local hero, or are you considered someone who people secretly believe was the wrong choice for the job? Most importantly, are you very proactive in making your vision a reality and fixing problems, or are you more reactive?

In turbulent times like these, decisions (or lack of decisions) that cause even a slight delay in being able to pass something like a robust American Rescue Plan can result in millions of people not being able to pay their monthly rent or put food on their families' table.

In turbulent times like these, a president, mayor, or even a restaurant owner who politicizes the wearing of masks or getting a Covid-19 vaccine can suddenly become the catalyst for a super-spreader event, or the next surge in the disease.

In turbulent times like these, a CEO must be prepared to become someone who is a profile in courage. This must be a person who takes stands on issues—voter suppression, gun control, immigration—to contribute to an "enlightened democracy," while at the same time, reinventing the business model for a post-pandemic world, knowing that failure to do so will result in a long, slow decline, followed by irrelevance, followed by death.

In such turbulent times, a school superintendent's ability to collaborate with teachers in making the shift from 100% in-person learning to effective hybrid learning is often the difference between kids losing a year of school or finding ways to use virtual classrooms to accelerate their progress in math, English, history, and social responsibility.

You and I (all of us) need to realize that going to work in the morning is not just a job but an opportunity to demonstrate moral leadership. How long is it going to take for you to become the leader America needs in your organization? How long is it going to take for you to lead in impacting climate change by getting your organization to zero emissions, or to lead in protecting voting rights for all Americans in your community, or to lead in creating an inclusive economy, or to lead in immigration and a path to citizenship?

WHAT DOES GREAT LEADERSHIP LOOK LIKE?

> *Great leaders are transformational and transactional.*
> *-James MacGregor Burns*

In conducting Leadership Weekends with people all over the world, I am most often asked this handful of questions: What is great leadership? Are leaders born or made? What skills do great leaders have? What role models can I use? I prefer to answer such questions in a transformative, rather than merely informative way, and that is what I would like to take a shot at here.

WHO IS A ROLE MODEL FOR GREAT LEADERSHIP?

One of the things you discover, if you study great leaders, is that behind every great leader there is a coach or mentor who serves as a role model of some kind. George Washington's role model was Cincinnatus, the Roman general who after victory returned to the life of the plow. Abraham Lincoln's role model was Washington. When he was a lawyer on the road and stayed in people's homes, Lincoln entertained their children with stories about Washington. Teddy Roosevelt's role model was Lincoln, who he idolized to the stars. Franklin D. Roosevelt's role model was Teddy Roosevelt.

I was struck when I sat down to write this book, amidst the chaotic ordeal of the Trump administration, that there was an absence of admirable, inspiring, successful leaders in America to-day whose stories could serve as a role model to the upcoming generations of leaders. The problem was not just in the White House, but equally in the halls of Congress, where many members place serving the nation's interest and the public interest behind serving their party's interest and their personal interest.

Even House Speaker John Boehner referred to his time in office as Speaker and head of the GOP as "the Mayor of crazy town" made up of a bunch of "publicity seekers" and "knuckleheads who are against everything."

I see many signs that this backward slide is being reversed since the election of Joe Biden as president—in Jamie Raskin's eloquent impeachment arguments against Donald Trump and the Big Lie, aimed at returning the country to its moral center—and again in the passionate proactive stance of Chuck Schumer, Nancy Pelosi, and Amy Klobuchar in moving the American Rescue Plan Act of 2021 through the House and the Senate within Biden's first 100 days.

Still, as we were a bit early into the new administration when I wrote this book, I chose to go back to the gold standard as seen throughout American history. Part of my purpose in writing this book was to inspire new leaders with stories about great American leaders as seen through the exclusive lens of their first 100 days. I also wished to raise the standard and set the bar for leaders going into politics and government, as well as for the public who must ultimately hold our leaders accountable for what they say and do.

America has had three undeniably great presidents we can identify with and learn from: George Washington, Abraham Lincoln, and Franklin Roosevelt, none of whom was a perfect human being; each had many faults and flaws. What makes their stories interesting is that despite their faults and flaws, they were all anchored to America's ennobling ideas and enduring values so that they were able to rise to the occasion in applying these to the greater issues of their day.

WHAT IS A GREAT LEADER?

If I had to define it, I would say that great leadership is having the ability to employ superhuman talents, gifts, IQ and EQ to mobilize people around a transforming vision that is big enough for people to subordinate their egos to, while at the same time having the ability to enter the world of transactional politics and master the mechanics of influence to advance the cause of freedom, equal justice under the law, and prosperity for all.

When Washington became president of the nation, there was no nation. People did not identify with being citizens of the United States but with their former British colony, and many people wondered whether the dream would die. Washington was a unifier, not a divider, and labored tirelessly at mobilizing people around the shared purpose of starting a new country that would be an "Enlightened Democracy."

He used his first 100 days to establish the federal government itself, as well as to support the drafting of the Bill of Rights, ten amendments to the Constitution that were ratified soon after his first 100 days were completed. It was not long before people began to identify with being citizens of the United States, and the "Great Experiment" was underway.

All the great leaders of American history tend to be innate unifiers versus dividers, as demonstrated in a tweet by historian Michael Beschloss that showed a picture of the lining of the coat that Abraham Lincoln wore to Ford's Theatre on the night he was assassinated. The hand-embroidered lining featured an eagle carrying a banner reading "One Country, One Destiny."

ARE GREAT LEADERS BORN OR MADE?

I would have to say that while some people seem to have leadership in their DNA code, great leaders are mostly made and often in the crucible of a crisis. According to historian Doris Kearns Goodwin, Theodore Roosevelt said that if it were not for the American Revolution, George Washington would have spent his life expanding his Mount Vernon estate. If it were not for the Civil War, the name of Abraham Lincoln would not be known.

All three of our great presidents were dedicated public servants who extracted a powerful vision from a national crisis. Curiously enough, none of them played the old "king of the rock" game, despite having a majority. Rather, they realized that to drive transformational change and get big things done, they needed bipartisan support, and as a result, they became masters of the mechanics of power and influence. Over time, they came to be held in warm affection and highly regarded by people on both sides of the political fence.

Each also demonstrated during their first or "next" 100 days that they were capable of success by securing early wins that built personal credibility, political capital, and momentum. George Washington ratified the Constitution and Bill of Rights, Abraham Lincoln preserved the Union by keeping the border states from packing up and leaving, and Franklin D. Roosevelt stabilized the economy and passed the New Deal legislation.

These great leaders are each very much with us today, reminding us that rock solid character and America's ennobling ideals are the coin of the realm when we look at our dollar bills or watch an HBO special like David McCullough's *1776* or Steven Spielberg's *Lincoln*.

Following the 2020 election, President Biden evoked Washington and Lincoln in his inaugural address, making a plea for national unity and ending this "uncivil war" by summoning the "better angels of our nature" to be friends, not enemies. Many members of Congress on both sides also evoked Lincoln during the Trump impeachment hearings.

WHAT SKILLS AND CAPABILITIES DO GREAT LEADERS HAVE?

Washington, Lincoln, and FDR came from different backgrounds, yet they had a similar leadership DNA code made up of a handful of basic human qualities (the keyword being human).

AMBITION: Washington, Lincoln, and FDR were all personally ambitious, which played a huge role in their seeking the path to power, yet they found their path to greatness in connecting personal ambition to their ambitions for the nation.

EMPATHY: Washington, Lincoln, and FDR also felt a profound, innate sense of human connection and empathy for people. Lincoln as a young boy scolded a group of friends for putting hot coals on a turtle's back, brushing them off, and setting the turtle free. His empathy for millions of Black people who were enchained and enslaved led him to have a vision of guaranteeing the rights promised in the Declaration of Independence to all Americans. Nicholas Hay, Lincoln's secretary, reported that after issuing the Emancipation Proclamation, Lincoln made a trip to the army camps to visit wounded soldiers. On his way back, he passed a brigade of black soldiers who rushed forward to greet the president shouting: "Hurrah for the President. Hurrah for the Liberator." Their "spontaneous outburst" moved Lincoln to tears "and his voice was so broken by emotion that he could hardly reply."

HUMILITY: When I say humility, I do not just mean humbleness and bowing and scaping. I mean the willingness to acknowledge you don't know all the answers when starting out and to be the first one to acknowledge and own up to mistakes. When FDR became president, he was terrified because he did not really have a 100-day plan. He told his team he was going to experiment: "We will try one thing and if that fails, admit it frankly and try another. But above all, try something."

SELF-REFLECTION: Following the humiliating Bay of Pigs invasion, John F. Kennedy met with former President Dwight D. "Ike" Eisenhower at Camp David, despite their testy relationship, and asked: *Where did I go wrong?* Ike asked a crucial question: "Mr. President, before you approved this plan, did you have everybody in front of you debating the thing so you got the pros and cons yourself and then made the decision, or did you see these people one at a time?" President Kennedy admitted it was mainly a presentation made by the CIA: "I just approved a plan that had been recommended by the CIA and by the Joint Chiefs of Staff. I just took their advice." Ike told him that is where he made a mistake and, next time, he should do it the other way—encouraging diverse opinions and debating the issues. Kennedy followed Ike's advice and during the thirteen-day period of the Cuban Missile Crisis, his national security advisors (EXCOMM) held the longest executive offsite in history and, as a result, Kennedy was able to ward off the threat of WWIII and thermonuclear warfare.

SELF-AWARENESS (SELF-RESTRAINT): It is very easy to say things we later regret when the stakes are high, emotions are running strong, and disagreements suddenly seem too hot to handle rationally. President Obama so enjoyed reading Doris Kearns Goodwin's book *Team of Rivals*, that he invited her to visit him in the White House to discuss it. He said one of the things he liked most about the book was the part where Lincoln would feel anger regarding his critics and write hot letters at night, putting them in his desk unsent and unsigned. Goodwin asked him with a big smile, "Did you ever try that?" he replied, "I do that all the time." He said he discovered that leadership is not just making speeches or debating a point, it is often about what you do not say.

TREAT YOUR FIRST 100 DAYS AS A LEADERSHIP OPPORTUNITY, EVEN IF IT IS NOT

One thing I have learned in conducting leadership weekends and coaching leaders in business, politics, and government is that we all have greatness in our DNA. We all want to make a difference in other people's lives, make an impact, and leave a legacy that will be remembered after we are gone, even if it is simply to make a positive contribution to a few folks' lives.

The problem for most people is that they often lack the leadership opportunity where they can spread their wings and fly. Part of this has to do with the fact that leadership opportunities in politics and government bureaucracies are monopolized by a few very senior people at the top, such as the president, Speaker of the House, Majority Leader, or government bureaucrats. The issue is that these people often do not have knowledge of the challenges and opportunities, or the bandwidth and boots on the ground (local knowledge) to help fix all the problems that America faces.

To get around this, we need to democratize leadership so that more people, especially younger people, have more leadership opportunities. This starts with a shift in mindset from "leadership at the top" to "leaders everywhere." It also involves people in more senior roles consciously and intentionally empowering younger people to take the lead in a myriad of situations.

Yet often a lack of leadership opportunity simply comes down to being in a job where you do not have real political power to drive historic change, consistent with the great public values of a people. My advice, if you are an elected official, political appointee, or public manager in your first or next 100 days, is to look at the job as your leadership opportunity of a lifetime (even if it is not), and approach it with a one hundred percent commitment to make the most of it, rather than having it be just the next step on the ladder.

YOUR FIRST (NEXT) 100 DAYS CAN BE THE HALLMARK OF YOUR ENTIRE CAREER

The fact is that there is an underlying truth that a leader's power is often at its zenith when they first win an election (or get hired) and the face of their leadership is still new. They are basking in a halo of victory, they have a mandate to govern, and public opinion is on their side. The power of a leader to govern is even higher during a nation-encumbering crisis when someone takes charge and fixes the problems.

As such, when coaching clients in their first or next 100 days, I always ask them to approach this period not in terms of "onboarding" or "getting up to speed," but as the hallmark of their entire career. This creates a powerful shift in mindset that gears people up to not waste any time in finding their voice, instead taking a stand on the issues they passionately care about and driving transformational change.

A good example of a leader who approached both his first and next 100 days as the hallmark of his entire career is Lyndon B. Johnson, who became president at the crack of a gunshot. As vice president, Johnson had complained of being kept out of the inner circle by Robert Kennedy and being in a "wretched state of powerlessness." When the moment of leadership opportunity came, he jumped on it.

He flew back to Washington on Air Force One and, on that same day when he got home, he put on his pajamas and sat up in his bed surrounded by a few loyal friends. He told them that his most important and urgent priority was to convey to the American public that, even though one president on a trajectory to achieve greatness had died, another president was taking charge—one who would not only protect the Constitution but also build on the fallen leader's legacy. Where JFK said, "Let us begin," LBJ would say, "Let us continue."

Then standing in his vision of the Great Society (not yet a bumper sticker), Johnson proceeded to sketch out his 100-day plan. Thinking out loud to those present, he wrote down five goals: 1) Pass JFK's tax cut that had been stalled in Congress; 2) Pass a landmark civil rights act; 3) Pass a voting rights act; 4) Initiate a war on poverty: and 5) Pass a healthcare security act (which was to become Medicare). He was successful in passing every one of these bills he had set down in his 100-day plan, and he is remembered for having done so. It did not all happen in his first 100 days, but who is counting?

Once Johnson had his 100-day plan, he pursued it with commitment, passion, and zeal. He jumped into action, treating his 100-day plan as if he would passionately pursue it in the next ten minutes, or nothing at all. He called a meeting of his top advisors to introduce his major goals and priorities. When one of his advisors said he would burn all his political capital if he tried to pass a civil rights act, he delivered one of the most famous lines in American history: "Then what the hell is the Presidency for?" (More on this in the Johnson Interlude.)

ACT AS IF WHAT YOU ARE DOING IN THE NEXT TEN MINUTES IS EVERYTHING

In ordinary times, people do not care a lot about who sits in the White House, State House, or City Hall, but in extraordinary times like we face today, they care a lot. That is why in the 2020 election cycle, more people voted for the presidency and other offices at the state and local level than ever before. As mentioned, we are at an enormous strategic inflection point where there is a real opportunity for a leader at every level to take a stand that a difference can be made and to drive historic change.

In times like these, the best leaders not only approach their first or next 100 days as the hallmark of their careers, but as if what they will do in the next ten minutes is everything or nothing at all. They approach their job not in a passive way of trying to figure out "the vision thing" or "standing their watch and reacting to events." Rather they approach it with passion, commitment, zeal, and they use disciplined intensity to take a very proactive stance.

It requires full engagement on your part, empathizing with rising human aspirations and throbbing human needs, taking a stand that a difference can be made, and being very proactive. Today with the American dream fracturing, with millions being paid starvation wages, the GOP state representatives putting almost 300 voter suppression bills forward, police taking the lives of innocent Black people, and a humanitarian crisis on our border, anything else would be unconscionable.

Joe Biden served for eight years in the Obama administration and thirty-six years in the Senate, much of which was spent marked by "hail fellow, well-met" relationships, caution and compromise. There was not very much in Joe Biden's character, personality, or in his voting record to suggest that he would be anything more than a sound, vastly experienced, capable, regular president, who would if nothing else cause millions of Americans to feel a sense of relief as if a huge weight had been lifted off their shoulders.

He proclaimed that his victory was not just a victory for himself personally, but a victory in the battle for the soul of America. In just one short phrase, "America is Back," he affirmed the American spirit—who we are and what we stand for—at home and around the world. Suddenly many people at home and abroad felt that his presidency might just be that.

Biden knew he had been presented with a remarkable leadership opportunity as the president of the United States, a role he had waited a lifetime for. The fact that he arrived center stage in the middle of a nation-encumbering crisis only made the process all that much more enticing. He jumped into action less like a grandfather, and more like an experienced fire chief facing a three-alarm blaze.

From his first hours sitting behind that big desk in the White House, he acted as if his first 100 days was really the next ten minutes. He started signing executive orders at a furious pace to restore America's ennobling ideals and values after the previous administration had left them behind.

Biden said that "the president's job is to care," and he behaved as if he meant it. He worked hand-in-hand with Senate Majority Leader Chuck Schumer, "Help is coming. Help is on the way." Together with Congress, he passed the American Rescue Plan and started working on the American Jobs Plan, immigration, and gun control. He promised that before the first 100 days passed we would put 100 million Covid-19 shots in people's arms. He met that goal and upped it to 200 million shots in people's arms and then surpassed that. There is a good chance that this will be remembered as the greatest single accomplishment of any president in his first 100 days in office.

* * * *

When John Kerry woke up on the morning of Nov 2, 2020, the day of Joe Biden's election, he was a recovering Washington politician who had been a presidential candidate, Secretary of State, and served twenty-eight years in the US Senate. One might think that at the age of seventy-seven, there was not much of a future in store for him besides writing his memoirs and kissing and hugging his grandchildren. However, Kerry was convinced that while Donald Trump was in office, you did not spend your time sitting in a rocking chair. During the Trump presidency, he met with contacts from his long list of US diplomats and others around the world to apply pressure to preserve the Iran Nuclear Deal he had worked so hard to craft.

Shortly after the 2020 election, he received an unexpected call from President-elect Biden in which he was presented with a phenomenal leadership opportunity that would put him back in the saddle again. He was asked to be Joe Biden's special presidential envoy for climate, and as the man who had negotiated The Paris Agreement (climate accord), he considered the gig an opportunity of a lifetime.

The President not only announced that rejoining the Paris climate accord would be a cornerstone of American foreign policy, but he also appointed Kerry as a member of his National Security Council to emphasize it. According to Kerry, the President "gave me full authority and said, 'you report to me directly, if you need me, walk over to the White House and come in and see me'—he couldn't have been more direct about it." Biden understood that having somebody who has been in the belly of the beast, who knew the levers of government, would be critical to the outcome.

Kerry's new role put him back on the global stage and in the spotlight—a place he has always coveted. Kerry jumped into action. He got the Covid-19 vaccine and boarded a commercial red-eye flight to London, Brussels, and Paris with one aide and the unspoken mission of saving the planet. Kerry had a reputation for showing up at meetings with "obsessive zeal," "hyper prepared", and "ever optimistic" that there is a solution to the world's most intractable problem.

"I just emphasize to everybody," he said, "this is exciting... the stakes couldn't be higher." Kerry not only sought to make a Cassandra-esque plea to nations to cut emissions, but also insisted it was an opportunity for a global breakthrough—an opportunity to draw trillions in investment, create new industries and millions of new jobs, and the development of powerful new technologies.

At the Davos World Economic Forum, when asked "Can we do it?," Kerry remarked, "We actually can. But not unless we summon greater political will, not unless we harness the full energy of the marketplace, not unless we ask the private sector to help our financial institutions mobilize essential trillions in innovation and the finances that we need."

Kerry emphasized the point I am pushing in this book, "We all have to work together, this is a matter of multilateral leadership, not any one country or any one group of people… and I can't wait to be at it with everybody."

* * * *

Alexandria Ocasio-Cortez is another good example of someone who treated her first 100 days, not only as an opportunity of a lifetime, but also as the hallmark of her career. She breezed into Washington after being elected to Congress in 2018 without even enough money to rent an apartment. In less than a week, she was taking a stand on issues such as the Green New Deal, voting rights, cancelling students' college debts—and in the process, stirring up a lot of attention.

During one of the breaks at the freshman orientation for new members of Congress, she reflected on how she had previously been a bartender who got into politics as a volunteer for Bernie Sanders. She would swipe her NYC subway card and walk through the turnstile unnoticed and get on a train in Queens with hundreds of people jammed into the cars.

When she took her oath of office and began her first 100 days, it was as if she went through a life-altering experience. "Literally overnight I went from no one caring who I was unless I was swiping my MetroCard too slow, to everyone being like 'who is she, what is this?' … A couple of days after the primary, I was in my neighborhood and I turned around this corner to get on the street and this woman saw me and just started crying, she just broke down crying." Ocasio-Cortez added, "It was just a completely alien change… it felt like everything I said had so much more weight overnight."

She was determined to approach her first 100 days as the hallmark of her career and operated as if what she would do in the next ten minutes was everything, or it was nothing at all. She realized that even though she was the "new kid" on the block, this did not have to hold her back from being a passionate, relentless champion of democracy—*government of the people, by the people and for the people.*

She realized she could amass political power using her Twitter account as a bully pulpit to lead a moral crusade on the issues she passionately cared about. She ceaselessly and tirelessly sent out punchy tweets on the Green Revolution, voter suppression, dark money in politics. She soon had a 12.5 million following and as many as 500,000 "reactions" on her Tweets.

It would take her a while to win Nancy Pelosi over rather than compete with her, and to realize that one must learn the rules before going around them. However, she picked her battles, focused on friends and allies, ignored enemies and soon began to secure tangible early wins that would build rapid momentum.

One of the things that made her stand out from the crowd is that she held herself publicly accountable for the result of her first 100 days and beyond. On Dec 11, 2020, she sent out a video via Twitter where she declared the accomplishments of her first term, which were numerous. "I authored and introduced the Green New Deal Bill with Senator Ed Markey and secured 115 House and Senate co-sponsors on it. Regional versions of the New Green Deal were also adopted by ten local governments." She may not have succeeded in passing the bill, but she was successful in putting it on America's political and economic agenda. She also introduced more amendments to bills than ninety percent of her freshman class.

BECOMING A LEADER

There are two approaches to being the leader America needs: one is based on transactional learning, the other is based on transformational learning. The transactional learning approach is one where you try to learn about leading by reading a book or spending time in a classroom. This approach is based on studying great leaders, analyzing leadership characteristics and traits, and doing 360 feedback on your strengths and vulnerabilities.

Transactional learning teaches you about being a great leader but does not actually give you access to being a great leader when you show up for work Monday morning. What you get out of most books and courses are the seven steps to epiphany, a gazillion PowerPoint bullets, and a long list of things to try to remember.

The transformational learning approach, by contrast, is designed to transform you into being a great leader. My transformational approach is designed to give you direct access, a direct pathway to being the kind of leader America needs today as a natural self-expression, without having to go through the long process of the many steps in the transactional approach. As I said in the beginning of the chapter, I chose the word direct access very carefully to imply there was a straight and clear pathway for you to follow that is actionable.

One of the simplest ways to understand the transformational learning approach is to read the stories of people like Lincoln, FDR, and LBJ. Upon taking their oaths of office and becoming president, each of them reported something to the effect of a weird "transforming feeling" when they walked around the White House halls late at night and saw the portraits of great leaders from American history. Recognizing their own responsibility to contribute to the everlasting life of the nation had the impact of connecting their personal ambitions (to amass political power) to their ambitions for the nation.

THE PATHWAY TO BECOMING A LEADER

- Read and recount stories of great leaders in their first 100 days
- Find the path to power and influence
- Take a stand for something bigger than yourself
- Employ the power of shared purpose, collaboration, and compromise
- Use "action learning" to produce results and develop as a leader

Let's look at each.

1. READ AND RECOUNT STORIES OF GREAT LEADERS

I believe that the first thing you can do to gain direct access to being a great leader is to become both a student and teacher of American history. When you read and recount stories of America's great leaders, you immerse yourself in America's ennobling ideals and enduring values.

Abraham Lincoln once said that the greatest way to protect our democracy is to read, react, and recount stories of the great leaders, of the Founders, and rededicate yourself to their ideas and ideals. When Lincoln was riding the circuit, he would stay in homes of different families and would often tell mothers to read to their children bedtime stories of great leaders if they wanted them to become leaders in society.

George Washington, Abraham Lincoln, and Franklin Roosevelt recounted that as children they read stories about great leaders, which fostered a desire to become like them when they grew up. Washington wanted to be like Cincinnatus, Lincoln wanted to be like Washington, Roosevelt wanted to be like his third cousin Teddy—who he idolized.

I have super-charged and power-packed this book with stories about the great leaders of American history who lived in times as turbulent and polarized as our own to help you apply the lessons of the past to your life today, as well as a way of transporting you to them and the ennobling aspirations and enduring values they stood for. I am talking about an enlightened democracy based on freedom, equal justice under the law, and prosperity for all. You will discover that you have direct access to becoming a leader as a natural self-expression when you speak, listen, and act from these ennobling ideals and enduring values—and you are not a leader when you wander elsewhere.

I believe that while Donald Trump and his administration seemed to feel nothing but thinly disguised contempt for these values, there have been many signs of hope emerging on the political scene recently from leaders in both parties including John Boehner, Mitt Romney, Liz Cheney, Chuck Schumer, and Amy Klobuchar.

If you were looking for a senator or congressional representative to put on an 18th century gentleman's suit and play the role of Thomas Jefferson, James Madison, or Alexander Hamilton to prosecute the Donald Trump impeachment trial, Congressman Jamie Raskin would have little trouble fitting into their inner circle on the topic of Constitutional Law and Intent.

In his brilliant Senate prosecution against Trump in 2021, he wasn't merely trying to hold a president to account for being the Inciter-in-Chief, he said his goal was to provide a "moral center," to defend American history. "President Trump may not know a lot about the Framers of the Constitution," said Raskin, "but they certainly knew a lot about him" when they designed the Constitution to prevent an abuse of power that would divide our country and destroy our democracy.

He then went on to quote Republican Representative Liz Cheney: "On January 6, 2021, a violent mob attacked the United States Capitol to obstruct the process of our democracy and stop the counting of presidential electoral votes. This insurrection caused injury, death, and destruction in the most sacred space in our Republic. The President of the United States summoned this mob, assembled the mob, and lit the flame of this attack. Everything that followed was his doing... There has never been a greater betrayal by a President of the United States of his office and his oath to the Constitution. I will vote to impeach the President."

Raskin said of Cheney, "She was right; she based her vote on the facts, on the evidence, and on the Constitution." Raskin concluded, "President Trump must be convicted for the safety and security of our democracy and our people."

2. FIND THE PATH TO POWER AND INFLUENCE

Robert Caro, the iconic presidential historian and author of *The Years of Lyndon Johnson* series says that the ability to be a great leader depends less on your vision when you are starting out and more on your ability to amass political power. When someone challenged him on that in an interview he said, "Would you rather be a leader with a vision and no political power to make it happen, or a leader with no vision, but the ability to come up with one?"

Caro's question spoke volumes in terms of recognizing what seems like the obvious: one of the things that gives you direct access to being a leader is the ability to amass political power so that you can begin to make your vision of hope and change a reality. One way to do that is to throw your hat into the ring and run for office, and then climb to the next rung on the ladder. After John

F. Kennedy ran for Congress as a war hero, he then ran for the Senate, during which time he published his book *Profiles in Courage.*

Yet Kennedy soon became frustrated with the little power and influence he could wield as just one of one hundred senators and decided to climb further. He said, "I want to become president of the United States because it is the center of action." He added, "A president can get more done with a stroke of a pen in one day than a senator can in six years."

Yet, when Lyndon Johnson became president, he proved that his years as "Master of the Senate" had made him a much more effective legislator than Kennedy who passed no major bills during his time in office. Johnson had an incredible capacity to translate his natural-born empathy into strategies for amassing political power and then translating that into government action.

Caro's book about Johnson, *Master of the Senate*, is about how he amassed political power by befriending the grand old daddies of Congress (like Richard Russell), got on the right committees, and learned the arcane rules that determined the way the Senate worked, as well as about what he did with that power. Johnson not only became Master of the Senate for six years but made the Senate work better than it had since the Civil War. And then, when he became president, he used his power and influence to pass the landmark civil rights bills.

> *Political power rests in never forgetting that you are the steward of the people. -Theodore Roosevelt*

The Difference Between Being In and Out of Power. On the morning of January 6, 2020 at 7 a.m., Senator Chuck Schumer got into his car in Park Slope, Brooklyn, having slept just three hours after it was announced that Georgia had officially elected two Democrats to the US Senate, ensuring that he would be the next Senate Majority Leader. He had suffered through the previous fifteen years or so with Mitch McConnell in the Senate Majority Leader role, relegating Schumer to a wretched state of powerlessness where every proposal by Democrats was blocked.

He had dreamed of a moment such as this. "My first reaction is joy. You know, when you have set a serious goal [such as becoming Senate Majority Leader] and it takes a long time to get there, there are detours in the road and logs in the pit, when you get there, Whoa! What a feeling."

"So that was expected. But about three minutes later, I had another feeling, and I call it one of awe," he remembered. "Like, when the angel saw the face of God, they trembled in awe."

Schumer had gotten so used to not being able to realize his vision and values that he had almost forgotten what they were. Seeking to find his ground, he labeled himself alternatively a Law-and-Order Guy, Angry Centrist, and Business Democrat who dined at JP Morgan the night of the 2008 election.

Now was the opportunity to make his vision of an "Enlightened Democracy" a reality, and he decided to take a progressive stance and make an abrupt shift to the left (in part considering a primary challenge from AOC in the next election in New York). Schumer said he learned a powerful lesson from Theodore Roosevelt, and that is that the power of a president or senator lies in never forgetting that you are "the steward of the people," not the steward of Congress, or a political party.

Schumer visits every one of New York State's sixty-six counties every year and spends more time listening to people's rising aspirations and throbbing human needs than he does talking. When the pandemic struck, Schumer stood out for his empathy, promising as the economy collapsed that he and his Senate colleagues would prevent foreclosures and evictions—the biggest concern of New Yorkers. He also promised relief so people could put food on the tables.

It was Schumer who convinced President Biden to shift from a $1 trillion American Rescue Plan to an almost $2 trillion American Rescue Plan to help Americans with small businesses and families in dire need. It was Schumer who guided the bill through Congress, bringing West Virginia Senator Joe Manchin onboard. It was Schumer who, when the bill passed, went before the cameras and declared: "Help is on the way. We can get things done to make lives better. Help is on the way!"

3. Take a Stand for Something Larger Than Yourself

Taking a stand is one of the most powerful things an ordinary individual can do to gain access to the possibility of being a great "real" leader. Yet what does it mean for an individual to take a stand? If you look at Twitter, which is where many politicians express themselves, taking a stand is often thought of as giving your opinion on something, or taking a side on an issue, or making a statement about what should be.

The truth is that taking a stand is none of these things. Taking a stand is exercising your power as an ordinary individual and stepping up when faced with a situation that is inconsistent with the American spirit—who we are and what we stand for (human values). It is acting in a way that matters instead of acting as a bystander.

Think about America's Founders signing the Declaration of Independence in the face of British tyranny. Think about Abraham Lincoln, a prairie lawyer, taking a stand for the abolition of slavery in the Lincoln Douglas Debates. Think about Franklin Roosevelt declaring war on Nazi Germany in WWII.

On April 21, 2021, I was watching CNN and saw the headline "Breaking news." Derek Chauvin was convicted in the murder of George Floyd on all three counts. Like most Americans,

I breathed a sigh of relief. If 17-year-old Darnella Frazier, a witness to the murder, had not decided to take a stand, taking out her smartphone and making a nine minute and twenty second video which she then posted to Facebook, instead of just being a bystander, it is doubtful that a conviction would ever have come to pass.

You are being a leader, when you take a stand that a difference can be made and act in a way that matters, rather than being just a bystander.

Similarly, had Governor Ted Walz of Minnesota not taken a stand by calling his friend Attorney General Keith Ellison and asking him to personally investigate the Floyd case, the chances of getting a conviction through the local Hennepin County DA, a known racist, would have been equally doubtful.

And had many people (called by Supreme Court Justice Louis D. Brandeis the "office of the citizen") not gathered night after night to sing, march, and protest, the result might have been very different.

I give Governor Walz a great deal of credit for taking a stand, not only for making sure the case was prosecuted and justice achieved for George Floyd according to the principle of equal justice under the law, but for making it a landmark case that contributes toward putting an end to systemic racism in his state and in the rest of America.

Walz, in making a statement after the conviction was turned in, took a stand for a new shared vision of Minnesota. He said that Minnesota was widely considered by many to be one of the best states in the country to live in according to the Happiness Index—women in leadership, economic opportunity, education, and healthcare. Yet, he added, high marks depend on whether you were a White person or a Black person.

He threw down the gauntlet to his administration and to the Minnesota legislature (half Democrat and half Republican) to join with him in making Minnesota the best state in the country for all its citizens.

4. EMPLOY THE POWER OF SHARED PURPOSE, COLLABORATION, AND COMPROMISE

The meteoric rise in politics of Bernie Sanders is a vivid example of the fact that leadership emerges the moment an individual takes a stand that a difference can be made. Although he is seventy-nine years old and calls himself a Democratic Socialist who was born in Brooklyn, New York, he has won more than twenty state primaries in Vermont. His strength is his ability to speak with passion, authenticity, and empathy where he makes a psychic connection with plain and simple Americans for whom the American dream is fracturing. His typical tweets run along the lines of: "It's wrong that billionaires pay less taxes than a schoolteacher, police, or fireman," or "I happen to believe that getting an education should not leave you in crippling debt for decades."

Bernie, as a progressive senator, has put many issues on the political and economic agenda—the Green New Deal, Medicare for All, Cancelling Student Debt, among others. Yet he has signed his name to very few pieces of major legislation and although he has played a role in introducing amendments to main bills, his strength of "being a crusader," may also be his weakness. He is not seen by leaders in the Senate as being very effective in leveraging the power of shared purpose, collaboration, and compromise to get big things done.

In contrast, when Speaker of the House John Boehner was in power, he took few strong stands on issues but was known for his proficiency as a dealmaker. He consistently broke the Hastert Rule that said that no bill would come before Congress unless it was supported by most of the party in power. He created the "Boehner rule" which said a bill could pass with a minority of a majority. He guided many major bills to passage that would help the American people by bringing Democrats and Republicans onboard.

Boehner retired from office when he felt that "knuckleheads" in his own caucus, like Ted Cruz and Kevin McCarthy, were less interested in leading and legislating than they were in fundraising and drawing attention to themselves by taking outrageous positions on issues.

> *You are being a leader if, when you are trying to reach a goal and a stalemate arises, you reach across the aisle and get people to sit down together and negotiate.*

Chuck Schumer, on the Democratic side, may be a good example of Jefferson's idea of a leader: "Great leaders are neither dictators or dreamers, but masters of the mechanics of influence." Schumer's political power may have a lot to do with his ability to make human connections with colleagues, whether they agree or disagree with him. He loves the famous Ben Stein quote "Personal relationships are the fertile soil from which all advancement, all success, all achievement in real life grows."

Schumer gets things done by staying in communication, targeting bipartisan issues, and marching toward common ground. He calls most of his forty-nine Democratic colleagues daily, and some even more often, reminding them they can do whatever they need to do in support of their state's politics, if they stick with him on the big votes. "Even if Schumer is up to his ass in alligators, he answers the phone and he'll say, 'Tammy, I'm talking to the president, can I call you back?'" said Senator Tammy Duckworth of Illinois. Other senators also feel they have a special relationship to Schumer since he calls them so often.

Dealing with Democratic conservative Manchin is another story, one that is friendly but contentious. For years, Schumer and Manchin made an unlikely pair. They were comfortable being very direct with each other, which could occasionally lead to intense arguments, but it also paved paths for cooperation. Still, when people in West Virginia asked Manchin about his best friend in the Senate, he would point to Schumer.

With the American Rescue Plan Act, which at first seemed easy to drive through the Senate with a majority of one, Manchin jammed the Senate into a surprise halt by flirting with a Republican provision to just extend unemployment insurance instead of the Democratic plan, which was more expansive.

For twelve hours, Schumer and other middle-of-the road Democrats in the Senate worked on the West Virginian, trying to build a shared purpose and collaboratively problem solve and find compromise policy that would work for Manchin, the rest of the Democratic caucus, and the more liberal House Democrats, all of whom would have to vote "yes" on the bill.

Schumer acted as the project manager with Biden and White House chief of staff Ron Klain all day. Schumer said of his relationship with Klain, "We can almost finish each other's sentences." He got Manchin on board only after paring back the plan and making the case that if he sided with Republicans, he risked tanking the entire package.

5. Use Action Learning to Produce Results and Develop as a Leader

There are two approaches for learning to lead. As mentioned before, the first approach is learning from a book or classroom, which is pretty theoretical. Your typical leadership weekend can spark your motivations and aspirations, as well as provide you with descriptions and explanations of leadership. You walk out the door with a list of things to remember but without a way to access being a leader when you show up for work Monday morning.

The other approach to learning to lead is what I wrote about in my book Masterful Coaching and is one that gives you direct access to being a leader as a natural self-expression. It is not based on theoretical learning but rather on "action learning." This involves learning to lead in the process of making your vision of hope and change a reality. You start with your vision of hope and change and then think backward to a live project, goal, or outcome that can be tracked. You learn to lead in mobilizing people around a shared purpose and overcoming adversity as you strive to achieve it. This is an approach that gives you direct access to being a leader.

One way to get your arms around the "action learning" approach to being a leader is to make three lists: 1) a To Be List, 2) a To Do List, and 3) a Connect and Collaborate List.

CREATE A "TO BE" LIST

How do you want to play it? Today America has been through a nation-encumbering crisis of epochal proportions. People's lives have been disrupted by the pandemic, lost jobs, and civil unrest. Whether you work in Washington, the State House or City Hall, think about your main objective during the coming period and ask yourself: Who do I need to be in the matter? Then when you show up in the morning, you may soon discover that you actually feel that way. Here is a sample "To Be" list to get you started.

- Be positive
- Be ambitious
- Be passionate
- Be compassionate
- Be goal-oriented
- Be collaborative
- Be self-reflective

CREATE A "TO DO" LIST

Let's say that you are about to start your first or next 100 days and you want to make it the hallmark of your career. What would be an opportunity to both make your vision of hope and change a reality and to transform yourself into a real leader in the process? Here is a sample "To Do" list using the action learning approach:

- Formulate a vision of hope and change
- Mobilize your team to make the vision reality
- Ask: What is a key objective I want to achieve?
- Designate specific key results that are measurable
- Focus on actions you need to take in the next 24 hours
- Expect that each step you take will create support and opposition
- Grow through adversity: Pain + Reflection + Determination = Progress

CREATE A "CONNECT AND COLLABORATE" LIST

It's a great idea to be a visionary leader and to want to get big things done, but the reality is you can't do it alone. Nor can you do it with people only on your side of the political fence. One of the most powerful tools you can use is to form fast collaborations and hold Camp-David-like meetings to deal with a looming crisis, big goals, or complex problems.

The key is to bring unlikely collaborators together to light creative sparks through a dialogue where diverse views and perspectives are seen as a strength in coming up with win/win solutions. It is important in any collaboration to not just talk, but also be outcome oriented.

Here is a sample "Connect and Collaborate" list:

- Follow George Washington's rules of civility
- Never waste a lunch with supporters and opposers
- Look for existing areas primed for bipartisan action

- Set a shared goal people can subordinate their egos to
- Form "fast collaborations" to solve big problems
- Get all stakeholders in the room and explore diverse perspectives
- Come up with exciting win/win solutions

Put your lists in a place where they are easy to access and review. They become a powerful reminder that who you "be" is as important as what you "do," and to get big things done, you can't do it all on your own. Learn to collaborate!

George Washington: Character is Destiny

The Greeks believed that one's destiny or fate is not determined by external forces, but by one's inner character and force of personality. "Character is destiny" is a universal principle that you as an elected official or political appointee must keep utmost in your mind as you begin your first 100 days in office, for it will largely determine your success or failure and good or bad reputation.

I would like to illustrate this interlude with some stories about George Washington, who was by far the most important Founding Father and probably our greatest president. He is an iconic leader whose life blended public principles with private virtue.

George Washington was not a brilliant original thinker like Thomas Jefferson, who wrote the Declaration of Independence and brought a new country into existence with the stroke of a pen. He was not a brilliant orator like John Adams, who could speak in a way that elevated people above their everyday selves and rouse a revolutionary fervor. Yet George Washington was indeed a leader who could get people to follow him, even though he lived at a time that tried men's souls.

He had rock solid character. He was impossibly heroic, undaunted by difficulty, and absolutely incorruptible. His character was forged by the inextricable link between personal and national ambition, his promise of integrity—doing the right thing—over mere expediency, and firm adherence to universal principles in making wise decisions and judgement calls at all the defining moments in his life.

He was the unanimous choice to be Commander-in-Chief of the Continental Army, the unanimous choice as chairman of the Constitutional Convention, and the only person in history to be unanimously chosen to be president of the United States.

It is not that George Washington was a perfect human being, and neither are you, nor is anyone who assumes a job in government. Like most of us, he wore a mask of confidence in public that often belied his inner struggles, self-doubts, and flaws.

Like many great leaders, George Washington was highly self-reflective. His letters to friends showed his desire to strengthen his character and personality, improve his competency in politics, and not allow pride to keep him from honestly acknowledging mistakes.

By telling stories that reflect how George Washington became "George Washington" through the voice of his times, stories that show his strengths and vulnerabilities and how he grew through adversity and self-reflection, we don't aim to take him off his pedestal or revere him any less. Rather, the intention is that you will be able to identify with him, put yourselves in his place, and learn from him as you begin your term of office.

NO WAXEN FIGURE WITH POWDERED WIG AND CROOKED SMILE

In 1796, Gilbert Stuart boarded a ship in London and went to the United States for the specific purpose of painting a portrait of George Washington. Unfortunately, in his attempt to show reverence for the great man, he portrayed a waxen figure with noble bearing, boringly wise, and solemn to the point of being unapproachable and ultimately unknowable. This false portrait was itself perhaps reinforced by Washington's putting on a façade in public that masked that he was a real human being in every sense of the word. George Washington was only about forty-three years old when he took over as Commander-in-Chief of the Continental Army.

He did not wear a white powdered wig in his youth, nor did he have a distorted smile due to his wooden false teeth. His hair was in fact reddish brown, and he had a perfect toothy smile and sense of humor. He stood a head taller than most Virginians from Fairfax County and is often referred to by biographers as a "magnificent physical specimen."

In his younger days, he was an extraordinary horseman, always at the front of the fox hunt, jumping fences in hot pursuit, sometimes for almost eight hours. He flirted with the ladies at parties and was known to be charming and disarming. He was proud of his plantation at Mount Vernon and loved architecture and interior decorating.

Washington had an ambition to rise to the top of Virginia society. He had read Heraclitus, who said "character is destiny" and realized that his task was not to conquer external foes, but to completely conquer himself. He started as a young boy when he copied out of a book from France one hundred rules of civility, most of which involved showing respect for others.

Some of his favorite rules of civility were: "Every action done in company, ought to be with some sign of respect, to those that are present" and "Do not open the mouth and bedew no man's face with your spittle by approaching too near him when you speak."

Washington may not have had a lot of formal education, but he was always reading about the great leaders of history and other topics. Washington, who was to later play a real role on the stage of the revolutionary backdrop, loved going to the theatre. He learned a lot about leadership from plays like Julius Caesar, Hamlet, Richard the Third, Robinson Crusoe, and Don Juan. Imagine Washington laughing heartily while seeing a musical called The Romp, or A Cure for the Spleen.

He read books about the great leaders of history and went to the theater in part with the goal of finding role models, but also to test principles that he could use to achieve complete mastery over himself, as well as to use as a compass to navigate decisions, judgement calls, and a course of action. Some of these principles were: stewardship—putting service over self-interest; integrity—bringing men together around a higher moral purpose; a willingness to sacrifice for the cause, "the glorious cause"; self-reflection and self-control; and showing respect to everyone.

Nothing won Washington more respect than when, at the end of the Revolutionary War, he relinquished power as Commander-in-Chief. At that point in his life, he could have been anything he wanted—King, Emperor, Potentate. Yet, at the very moment that he could have had all the power in the world, he gave it up. He followed the example of the Roman General Cincinnatus, whom he had read about in his youth; the conquering hero who leaves the sword behind to work the plow on his farm. His resignation—letting go of power when he could so easily have seized it—saved the Republic from becoming another monarchy.

There is a story reported about King George of England who asked the painter Benjamin West, "Now that George Washington and the Americans have won the war, what is he going to do next?" West replied that he was going to relinquish power and go back to being a gentleman farmer in Virginia. "Well," said King George, "if he does that, he will be the greatest man in the world."

Truth be told, Washington played the role of the great man in public yet masked a canvas of inner struggles with self-doubts, rages, rants, and flaws. He often fought strong emotions, even tears. There is a great story about him that illustrates this after he resigned his post with the military.

A farewell toast was arranged at Francis Tavern in New York City with his generals and key officers. Fighting back emotions, Washington broke the silence in the room as he saw his comrades in arms. He raised his wineglass, "With a heart full of love and gratitude, I now take leave of you…I cannot come to each of you, but I shall feel obliged if each of you will come and take me by the hand." As the men stepped forward, the tears flowed from his eyes as he kissed and hugged them.

A lifelong public servant who never accepted a penny in remuneration, Washington was then drafted by the other Founding Fathers to preside over the American Constitutional Convention. Though this role was largely ceremonial in nature, he was never a neutral figure. Like the Japanese Kagemusha, or shadow warrior, Washington worked behind the scenes amidst all the squabbling to lobby for national unity against divisiveness and a strong Federal government as a bulwark to shore up the half-starved, weak, and tottering states.

Washington, Hamilton, and Madison, who believed in a strong Federal government, stood their ground in verbal battles with Jefferson, Adams, and Patrick Henry, who were concerned that the British Empire came from the concentration of power in the hands of a few and thereby advocated for states' rights. In so doing, Washington set the stage to, when he became president, transform a loose confederation of English colonies into a country based on democratic principles.

TAKING CHARGE

On the morning of April 30th, 1786, George Washington prepared to take the oath of office to become the president of the United States. He dressed that day in a suit of brown broadcloth spun in Hartford, with gold buttons showing an eagle with wings spread. To make his outfit stand out, he wore white hosiery, black shoes with silver buckles, and yellow gloves.

A little after noon, following a morning filled with the deep ringing of brass church bells and prayers, a detachment of troops on white horses, followed by black carriages loaded with legislators, stopped at the Franklin House on No. 3 Cherry Street where Washington was staying. Escorted by David Humphreys, who had accompanied him from Mt. Vernon, Virginia, the president-elect stepped into his appointed carriage, which was trailed by foreign dignitaries and throngs of joyous citizens.

The president-elect was escorted to Federal Hall in New York City. At the top façade of the building was carved the Great Seal adorned with the American Eagle. It made him strongly aware, at a subliminal and gut level, that he was not only about to take up an important role in history, but that he would be judged by history as well. He bowed many times to the crowd as a consummate sign of respect and passed through the House of Representatives and entered the Senate Chamber before the two Houses of Congress.

Robert Livingston, a Founding Father and a New York lawyer known as "The Chancellor," administered the oath of office from a balcony overlooking Wall and Broad Streets, with Samuel Otis holding out the Bible to Washington, who put his hand on it. Washington, with a solemn expression, then lifted the Bible and kissed it.

Livingston had to lift his voice over the cheering from the crowd inside and out and said, "It is done." He then declared, "Long live George Washington, President of the United States." The spectators responded with hurrahs and chants of "God bless our Washington!" As Washington looked out at the crowd, his bearing was that of a powerful new head of state, yet profoundly humble. It was obvious he was deeply moved. He put his hand over his heart and slowly bowed multiple times.

A spontaneous cheer surged from the crowd, whose members were packed cheek-by-jowl on Wall Street and Broad Street and on every roof in sight. His ceremonious outside appearance before them would be a confirming act of his authority over the nation and the cheering citizens teeming below.

In the opening remarks of his inaugural address, Washington showed genuine concern about his fitness for the job as president. He said he had grown melancholy over his prospects for success in the job and he spoke with candor about "inferior endowments from nature in political matters, and governmental affairs." His spirits rebounded, however, when he considered that the "Almighty Being" had overseen America's birth. "No people can be bound to acknowledge and adore the invisible hand which conducts the affairs of men more than the people of the United States."

One of Washington's most admirable character and personality traits was that he was a great unifier—and this at a time in American history when the nation was rife with divisive forces, very much like today's world. As historian David McCullough points out, Washington had to create a new country based on a Republican form of government, at a time when only a small fraction of the population saw this as desirable and the rest thought the country would be better off under the king.

He also emphasized in his inaugural address that "the preservation of the sacred fire of liberty and the destiny of the democratic model of government" were fated by "the eternal rules of order and right which Heaven itself has ordained" and staked, finally, deeply, "on the experiment entrusted to the hands of the American people." He set a template for future presidential inaugural speeches by banging the drum on his big ideas, without going into the details of policy matters.

He said that every new policy deriving from his government "would bear the name 'American'" and aim at creating the good society. He pledged to national unity, no "party animosities," and "no local prejudices or attachments" that might divide the country or even tear it apart.

He emphasized that national policy should always be grounded in private morality, embedded with "eternal principles of order and right," ordained by heaven itself. As he wished to emphasize freedom of religion in America, he did not publicly affiliate himself with any religion.

Washington's presidency was firmly established with the audience by the time he completed his speech. The Count de Moustier, the French minister who was a member of the crowd that day, wrote that there was full trust between Washington and the citizens who stood packed below him looking up toward him with jubilant faces.

De Moustier reported to the French government that rarely had a "sovereign reigned more completely in the hearts of his subjects than did Washington in those of his fellow citizens...he has the soul, look, and figure of a hero united in him." One young lady in the crowd echoed this when she remarked, "I never saw a human being that looked so great and noble as he does."

THE FIRST 100 DAYS—SETTING A NEW POLICY DIRECTION

George Washington's first 100 days stretched from April 30th to August 7th, 1789. By this measure, no president has ever achieved more at the start of their administration than Washington. Perhaps Washington's greatest achievement of his first 100 days was that he established the Office of the President itself, as the man in charge of the government.

Washington was basically given the going-in mandate of making the vision of "a new Republican form of government based on democratic principles" into a reality. His job was to transform the general outline of principles in the United States Constitution into a real government, with a policy direction and the structures and systems that would give stability to the nation, at a time when the nation was starved, tottering on crutches, and limping to the point of collapse.

Washington not only created the first Cabinet executive departments, like the State Department, Defense Department, Commerce Department, but also helped to design the nation's court system, build the Federal banking system, establish the principle of national taxation, and commence diplomatic relationships with Britain, France, Spain, and other countries.

In the year following the Constitutional Convention, Washington was personally and directly involved in ratifying the United States Constitution, emphasizing the importance of a Federal government that he felt would be needed for unity and order. He favored the adoption of a bill of rights to appease those who were wary of a strong Federal government and, once in office, Washington supported congressional lawmakers in drafting amendments to the Constitution. In October 1789, shortly after his first 100 days, Washington sent to the states copies of twelve amendments adopted by Congress. By December 15, 1791, three-fourths of the states ratified ten of these, and the Bill of Rights was born—a document that would make America a beacon of hope, as well as a role model to the rest of the world.

As you may know, Washington would establish an important precedent by not seeking a third term of office on the principle that America would be one of the world's first countries not to be run by a monarch or military dictator, but by a duly elected government under the Constitution—a government "of the people, by the people and for the people."

Washington understood that his every decision and action was without precedent. He wrote a letter to a friend where he said, "Few who are not philosophical spectators can realize the difficult and delicate part which a man in my situation had to act...

I walk on untrodden ground. There is scarcely any action I take whose motives may not be subject to double interpretation. There is scarcely any part of my conduct which may not hereafter, be drawn into precedent." I believe any new leader in a powerful job must have the same concerns.

CREATING A GREAT GROUP

Everybody knows that George Washington was a great leader and was the one person everyone in the country could trust. What is not as well-known is how committed he was to the collective leadership of his Cabinet. He was determined to build a group of extraordinarily talented people—including Alexander Hamilton, who he chose to be Secretary of the Treasury, Thomas Jefferson, who he chose to be Secretary of State, James Madison, an advisor, and others.

Washington was a Virginia plantation owner of tens of thousands of acres and many slaves, and he had been the Com-mander-in-Chief of the Army for eight years against the might-iest nation on earth. As such, he was accustomed to being "Lord of the Realm" and master of his domain, despite his democratic values. He treated his Cabinet members not as ministers on a peer level, but more like his assistants who were there to help him. It was clear to Hamilton, Madison, and Jefferson that he was the boss.

At the same time, though very bright, Washington never suf-fered from the "smartest man in the room" syndrome. He had seen firsthand that the writing and signing of the Declaration of Independence, winning the Revolutionary War, and the convening of the Constitutional Convention represented the triumph of col-lective leadership and intelligence.

Washington set up weekly Cabinet meetings with the shared purpose of establishing a government that was based on democratic principles. This was to be a forum for conversations de-signed to capture the collective intelligence in discussing the greater issues of the day. There, he tolerated dissent over his own strong Federalist views, which were grounded in a bone-deep belief that the country required unity over division. At the same time, he realized that the truth often comes from a clash of dissenting opinions.

He created lots of space in the Cabinet meetings for the free interplay of ideas between brilliant men like Hamilton, Madison, Jefferson, Henry Knox, and others, seeking to sift through it all and capture the power of multiple minds. Washington and his group met on a wide range of hot and controversial topics, such as: Shall America have a strong central government or weak one? Would it be better to have a strong central bank to grant loans?

As Chernow points out in his book *Washington, a Life,* "If Washington was not as brilliant intellectually as Hamilton, Jeffer-son, Madison, Franklin, and Adams, he was gifted with superb judgment. When presented with options, he almost invariably chose the right one." The judgment of the president was never hastily formed, but once made up, it was seldom to be shaken.

It would be a mistake to assume that Washington and his Cabinet were the perfect team of tremendously talented players focused on one goal, whose egos never got in the way of thinking and working together, not prone to minor insults, slights, or inju-ry. The truth is that Washington and his entire team were subject to individual flare-ups and team dysfunctionalities that needed to be addressed. As mentioned, Washington's whole life was about seeking to serve public values by mastering his own private emo-tions. Yet, as he was only human like the rest of us, he did not always succeed.

Once during a Cabinet meeting, he was shown a picture of a French newspaper with his head in a guillotine. He started ranting and raving with so much anger he was almost convulsive. Yet, he soon regained his composure and then acted as if nothing had happened.

He sought to keep the group squarely focused on the virtues of collective purpose, collaboration, and compromise. He warned his staff about allowing rancor and divisiveness to tear things apart, while he also gave lots of room for Jefferson and Hamilton to express their differing opinions.

Although he believed along with Hamilton in a strong presidency and a strong Federal Government as a basis for creating a new country, he tried to prevent arguments between Hamilton and Jefferson from turning into feuds. He would remind Hamilton or Jefferson privately of the other's sincere and honest intentions. However, he grew despondent when Secretary of State Jefferson, sensing that he was losing the battle, disparaged him in Congress, and then later resigned from his post.

Washington was a hard-driven perfectionist who held himself and his closest team members to a high standard. He would sometimes take out his bad moods on Hamilton. On one occasion he told Hamilton angrily, "You have kept me waiting for ten minutes. You disrespect me Sir." Hamilton, who for all his brilliance and ambition was the personification of the saying that "no man is a hero to his valet," said, "I was not conscious of it Sir, but since you have thought it necessary to tell me so, we part." In less than an hour they agreed to act as if nothing had happened.

This may make it appear that Washington's grumpiness sounded habitual rather than a momentary lapse. Like many of us, at one time or another, Washington, the father of our country, could be less than an inspiring and empowering boss. However, Washington's self-reflective quality and desire to improve his leadership often resulted in his going back and affectionately clearing the air of grievances with his subordinates through a heartfelt apology.

George Washington would always seek wise counsel about his leadership strengths and failings as seen through his many letters.

He would often engage in late night conversation with one of his most trusted advisors, Henry Knox, an officer in the Revolutionary War who later became his first Secretary of War. Washington valued Knox's advice and wrote in 1798, "There is no man in the United States with whom I have been in the habits of greater intimacy, no one who I have loved more sincerely, no one for whom I have greater friendship."

SECURING EARLY WINS

One of the most important things for any new leader in their first 100 days in office, stretching on to their first year, is to secure early wins that build credibility, political capital, and momentum. There are two varieties of early wins. The first has to do with transactional leadership, where a leader brings an incremental change or improvement by entering the domain of realpolitik and making tradeoffs or grabbing low hanging fruit and accomplishing small things that potentially could be the spearhead for a larger breakthrough. The second variety of early wins are those that we associate with transformational leadership that brings about historic change.

To be sure, Washington's greatest act of transformational leadership, based on an empowering vision and values which were a quick win, was the ratification of the Constitution along with the passage of the Bill of Rights. He offered to help James Madison with the Bill of Rights when it was facing skepticism in Congress, where many believed in majority rule and feared a Bill of Rights would go too far in protecting the minority rights of the individual. Washington wrote a letter to Madison, which he shared in Congress, stating that the amendments had his wishes for a favorable reception in both houses.

Washington was also successful using transactional deal-making in securing a succession of smaller early wins, such as the Senate approval of Hamilton as Secretary of the Treasury and Henry Knox as Secretary of War. These small wins became the spearhead for a breakthrough which led to the establishment of a national bank that would in turn grant loans, set interest rates, and send an expedition from New England to develop the Northwest Territory, all setting the stage for economic growth.

In the words of T.S. Eliot, "We shall not cease from exploration, and the end of all our exploring will be to arrive where we started and know the place for the first time." As I said at the beginning of this interlude, the Greeks believed "character is destiny." It is fascinating and intriguing to consider that George Washington spent a lifetime developing rock solid character by living in accordance with universal principles. His reputation for honesty, integrity and ethics afforded him so much natural authority, political capital, and momentum, that by the time he reached the presidency and had to deal with Congress, his word was law.

Let a word to the wise be sufficient.

Chapter Two

Onboarding is Not Enough: Focus on Mastering Your Job Assignment

When the class of 2018 roared into Washington for the three-day freshman orientation for Congress, Republicans and Democrats alike were so excited they could not believe it was really happening. Some were so pumped up they were giving each other high fives, others were singing the Star-Spangled Banner, one or two were even doing backflips. Each believed that the orientation would not only help them start their new job as a member of Congress but also help them do The People's business and make a difference.

One of the first things that occurs in this three-day onboarding event is that everyone gets a swag bag that says *Welcome to Congress* with a bunch of goodies inside. They then rush to stand in line to sign up for a lottery which will determine whether they get an office in the Capitol Building (where they wouldn't have to walk far to go vote) or they are placed in a distant government building.

"Onboarding" is the term Human Resource organizations—whether in the government or business organizations—use for the way they help newly elected (or hired) leaders make a smooth and orderly transition into a new role. Every time I hear the word "onboarding," I think about the captain and crew welcoming people onboard an airplane or ship, and that's often all that it amounts to. It usually happens in the first week of the job, and there is very little attention paid to the first 100 days, which is where the rubber meets the road.

In an article in the Harvard Business Review, Michael Watkins, author of *The First 90 Days,* points out that most organizations think they are doing a good job of onboarding leaders, when in fact, they are not. They may do a good job with the administrative aspects of onboarding—getting your badge, filling in forms, finding an office.

Yet onboarding programs do little to help new leaders master the mechanics of their new role, establish positive relationships with the right people, or help them become grounded in the vagaries of the political chessboard and culture.

For example, today every leader who is elected to Congress is supposed to put "doing the American people's business" first and "party" second, but onboarding programs often do the opposite. When Congresswoman Tulsi Gabbard participated in her freshman onboarding program, she was astounded when the entire freshman class was told upon entering the room, "Democrats go this way, Republicans go that way." This was followed by being told you are not here to pass legislation; you are here to help your party win.

ONBOARDING REIMAGINED

I believe that onboarding programs have an important role to play in orienting people into a new job. Yet I think current onboarding programs need to be reimagined to help us develop the kinds of leaders that America needs. I am talking about leaders who personify the American Spirit—who we are and what we stand for. I am talking about leaders who know how to collaborate with people with whom they have conflicting visions and values in a way that moves the country forward.

Why not use onboarding programs as a way to raise the standard and set the bar for the people we elect or hire? If the standard were higher, I do not think Donald Trump would ever have been able to pull off the first armed insurrection on Capitol Hill since the War of 1812 with the help of 150 members of Congress who gave credence to the lies he was spreading. Nor would there ever have to be a vote by the whole Congress on whether to remove Marjorie Taylor Green from committees for saying 911 was a hoax, the Parkland shooting was staged by actors, and California wildfires were the result of Jews using lasers from outer space, none of which is true.

If it were up to me, I would have the freshman onboarding process in Congress and elsewhere led by great historians, the ones who are national treasures. David McCullough, Doris Kearns Goodwin, and Robert Caro walking into the room would elevate the whole atmosphere of your typical onboarding session. Imagine them telling stories about the first 100 days of Presidents Washington, Lincoln, or Roosevelt, leaving people with something they could identify with and learn from. Now imagine another round of stories about our greatest legislators—Daniel Webster, Henry Clay, John C. Calhoun—who each knew how to advance the greater goals of the American people through compromise without walking away from principle.

Then I would seek out some of the most powerful members of Congress—House Speaker Nancy Pelosi and Senate Leaders Chuck Schumer and Mitch McConnell—to deliver the message that our job is to do the American people's business, which requires thinking and working together, rather than against each other. As Speaker Pelosi said, "We will strive for bipartisanship with fairness on all sides. We have a responsibility to find our common ground where we can, and stand our ground where we can't, but we must try."

I would then ask these congressional leaders to lead a 90-minute Q and A session designed to help newly elected officials and public managers learn to navigate the political chessboard and, at the same time, integrate into the culture and become a positive force for changing it.

A good way to approach this would be to tell stories and then help new leaders tease out of those stories what Ray Dalio of Bridgewater Associates calls "stress-tested principles" that apply to a wide variety of situations they may encounter, and that are "sticky" enough to remember.

For example, some principles might be:
- Character is destiny—find the road to character.
- Anchor everything you do and say in America's ennobling aspirations and enduring values.
- Stand your ground on issues you feel passionate about while seeking areas of bipartisan cooperation.
- It is not okay to question people's motivations; it is okay to question their ideas.
- Treat everyone as a friend and colleague; just because someone is your adversary on an issue, doesn't make them your enemy.

ONBOARDING IS ONLY THE FIRST PHASE OF A SUCCESSFUL LEADERSHIP TRANSITION

Lyndon Johnson became president at the crack of a gunshot. He literally began his leadership transition when he boarded Air

Force One and took his oath of office with Jackie Kennedy standing beside him still wearing her blood-splattered suit. The first 100 days of his leadership transition was spent re-entering the world of transactional politics, now as president, and securing an early win of passing the Civil Rights Act of 1964. His next 100 days, which occurred about a year later, was spent laying down the foundation of his Great Society programs.

I am telling you this story to highlight the idea that onboarding is only the first phase in making a successful leadership transition and involves helping the new person get oriented to the job assignment and make a smooth and orderly transition to power.

The second phase is for the person to take charge of the new job assignment, build a team, and use the rest of the first 100 days to enter the world of transactional politics and secure some early wins that help build personal credibility and momentum.

The final phase in making a successful leadership transition is one that most people never achieve. It is for the newly elected or appointed person to master the new job assignment so that they are able to make vision a reality, bring about transformational change, and skillfully navigate the political chessboard, culture, and rules.

As Michael Watkins points out, leaders need help in making a leadership transition and are often vulnerable to making unwitting mistakes that can cause them to fall into a deep hole that they cannot climb out of for the rest of their term. Unfortunately, after the initial onboarding period, most people are left to sink or swim with little help being offered. And even worse, many people sink who don't need to.

In general, people need a language and a mental framework to be able to think about their first 100 days. They also need a leadership transition roadmap that gives them an overview and is broken down into chunks. Further, they need a set of critical success strategies and key tasks. This chapter will provide you all of these.

SUCCESSFUL LEADERSHIP TRANSITIONS
PROVIDE IMPORTANT CLUES

Dwight D. Eisenhower had already had a long and distinguished military career including as Supreme Allied Commander of the D-Day invasion, where he got to call all the shots. When elected US president, he had reached the pinnacle, yet he had scant experience as a politician and soon realized that his power to call the shots as president would be limited in a divided government. It is reported that he walked into the Oval Office for the first time with his wife Mamie and said, "Well I'm here now, what am I supposed to do?" He then wrote down a list of questions about how to make his presidential transition.

At the Harvard Business School, I stumbled across a study that did a great job of answering questions about leadership transitions. It showed how successful leadership transitions follow a pattern. This pattern provides important clues that you can use to demystify and accelerate your leadership transition.

The first clue is that the more leadership transitions you have been through in your career, the better. Leaders who have been through multiple leadership transitions are like the master who intuitively knows how to take charge, build a team, and get results. Further, insiders tend to be more successful than outsiders. If you have fewer transitions under your belt, or are an outsider trying to get your nose in the tent, find a coach or mentor who can help you find answers to all of your questions.

The second clue is that not all leadership transitions are the same. Leaders who make successful transitions have sought to match their style and skills to create value in the role. The first step for you to take is to go to school on the specific job assignment, breaking down the roles, responsibilities, and tasks. Next, figure out "who you need to be" and "what you need to do" to perform in the job. If you are in a chief executive role, you will need to take charge, drive change, manage a budget, and so on. If you are a member of a team, you will need to manage the boss.

The third is that leaders who are successful in transitions are often very proactive. The best leaders are not those who, after taking the oath of office, relish sitting on the presidential, gubernatorial, or department head chair, enjoying their new position. Rather, they realize that the people who elected or hired them expect them to be the remedy to the problem, not just the repetition of what their predecessor did, and as such, they jump into action.

FOUR CRITICAL SUCCESS FACTORS

As a new leader about to start your first (or your next) 100 days in politics or government, you should already have a simple and straightforward set of goals for your leadership transition, knowing that you'll never get a second chance to make a first impression. For example, your goals might be taking charge and making a smooth and orderly transition to power, building a high-performance team you can count on, and getting off to a fast start and achieving some early wins.

I have discovered that there are four Critical Success Factors that will help you reach those goals. Critical Success Factors represent the fewest and most necessary boxes to check in order to have everything turn out the way you want. They include big ideas or a conceptual framework that, if taken on, will allow you to think about your leadership transition.

CRITICAL SUCCESS FACTOR 1.
FIND A MASTERFUL COACH OR MENTOR

The simplest and most powerful thing that can make your leadership transition successful is the one that is most often overlooked, and that is finding a masterful coach or mentor who can offer you advice that is based on your real goals and is situation specific—never theoretical or abstract.

When Harry Truman was in the White House, he went upstairs for dinner every night and talked with his wife Bess, who he called "The Boss," about whatever was really on his mind. Another example is President Kennedy. Chances are you have seen that famous photo of him talking to his brother Robert with his hand grasping his chin pensively as they walked from the West Wing of the White House to the main building.

Yet the kind of masterful coach I am talking about is a bit different than a family member or friend, or even someone you hire a chief of staff. I am talking about someone who knows something about leadership transitions and understands how to help you amass political power and influence.

Lyndon B. Johnson is an example of someone who wasted no time in finding a mentor. When only twenty-four years old, he first went to Washington as the legislative secretary to Congressman Richard Kleberg of Texas. Once there, LBJ used his family connections to wangle a meeting with another fellow Texan, House Speaker Sam Rayburn. He then invested lots of time in creating a relationship with Rayburn, inviting him to his apartment on weekends where Lady Bird would cook up Rayburn's favorite Texas specialties, after which they would sit and talk politics. Rayburn offered LBJ political pointers, things like "Don't try to go too fast" or "Don't go for a short-term victory by embarrassing someone that will lead to burning bridges long term."

After a few years in the role of legislative secretary, LBJ asked "Mr. Sam" for a favor: to intercede on his behalf with the FDR administration to get him appointed as the Texas State Director of the National Youth Administration. At first, the White House appointed another candidate and formally swore him in. Upon hearing the news, Rayburn went to the White House. It is not known what happened at the meeting, but the White House announced that a mistake had been made, and LBJ was appointed to the job—one that soon became a springboard for his political career.

Joe Biden, the Most Experienced President Since LBJ in His First 100 Days

Not since Lyndon Johnson has a U.S. president arrived at their first 100 days with as much legislative experience as Joe Biden. By the time Joe Biden opened for business at the White House, he reminded me of the storied Captain Joseph Warren Holmes from the clipper ship days who sailed around Cape Horn eighty-four times facing stormy seas and multiple crises. Biden took the wheel of the ship and started furiously issuing executive orders to put the nation back on course to its ennobling ideals and enduring values before turning the wheel over to his staff to work out the details.

Biden's success in his first 100 days was in part due to the many leadership transitions under his belt. Unlike Obama, who was a Washington outsider, and who despite sincere and honest intentions, alienated Mitch McConnell and his Republican colleagues, Biden is a Washington insider with forty-two years under his belt who knows how to get things done.

If you are a newly elected official, political appointee, or public manager who lacks confidence due to your lack of experience, take heart in this president's example from when he first arrived at the Senate. Joe Biden went from being a nobody upon his arrival to a somebody, in the same way Johnson did: by eagerly seeking coaching, mentoring, and sponsors from the "Grand Old Daddies" of Congress.

Biden placed Senator Edward Kennedy high on his list of mentors. Biden said of Kennedy, "He was my tutor, introducing me, a young Irish Catholic kid from Scranton, to a world I had never seen. When I arrived in the Senate, he would stop by my office, would take me to the Senate gym to meet the other senators, and helped me get on important committees."

Kennedy also taught him to spend most of his first year not trying to single-handedly lead the revolution, but rather to observe how the Senate worked and to listen to what was going on. Kennedy took the time to teach Biden who the power brokers and key influencers were in the Senate on both sides of the aisle. He also taught him a lot about how to master the machine, the forces and factors that determine how the Senate works.

This included the Senate's arcane rules for things like "cloture" and the "filibuster," the unwritten rules that shape the culture of the institution, as well as acknowledging that every person in the Senate had been elected by the American people and deserved to be treated with honor and respect.

Biden's views as a liberal Democrat (the moderate side) seeking bipartisan solutions were shaped by his relationship with Kennedy. Biden said that they sat in the same aisle when the Senate was debating the most important issues of the day, from Vietnam to Iraq, from the Civil Rights Act and the Voting Rights Act to the Violence Against Women Act, and they ate together at caucus lunches, mapping legislative and grass-roots strategy. Both agreed that healthcare should be a right, not a privilege.

BIDEN'S UNLIKELY MENTOR

Biden also found a very unlikely mentor in Washington, a "Senator's Senator," a man who he could look up to for his civility, brilliance, and gravitas, even though he disagreed with all his political views. It was Senator John C. Stennis from Mississippi who had served in the Senate since 1947, a segregationist who had voted against every civil rights bill that had come to the floor. Still, when Biden joined the Senate in 1973, almost a decade after

Stennis' votes against the landmark civil rights legislation of 1964, Stennis' views were in the process of transforming.

Shortly after being elected, Biden lost his wife and one-year-old daughter in a car accident. Less than a month later, Biden was sworn into office, and Stennis went out of his way to befriend him. Biden recalled in his book that Stennis asked him why he had run for office. "Civil rights, sir," Biden told him. Stennis responded, "Civil rights? Good," he said. "Good. Good. Glad to have you here."

Biden could not help but notice that Stennis, regardless of his views, seemed to possess tremendous natural authority, and this was something he wanted to develop. He once said that Stennis reminded him of Stonewall Jackson, who when he spoke, "it was like a thundering avalanche from an unexpected quarter" that shook up people's thinking and moved things forward.

Biden said in a speech he gave at Stennis' birthday party: "Mr. Chairman when you enter the Senate Floor, point your finger and raise your voice, it is like a thunderbolt from a clear sky. Everybody listens to what you have to say."

Stennis was the chairman of the powerful Senate Armed Services Committee, and he made sure that Joe Biden became a member. Biden was not just struck by Stennis' gentlemanly southern manner, but also by his ability to think on his feet and to frame national security issues.

Biden later wrote vividly of a conversation with the older senator in 1989 when Stennis retired, and Biden moved into his old office. Biden recounts the occasion in detail, including Stennis' very personal take on civil rights.

"'You see this table, Joe? This table was the flagship of the Confederacy from 1954 to 1968. We sat here, most of us from the Deep South, the old Confederacy, and we planned the demise of the civil rights movement,'" Biden wrote that Stennis had said. "'And we lost. And, Joe, now it's time that this table go from the possession of a man who was against civil rights to a man who was for civil rights.'"

"'The civil rights movement did more to free the white man than the Black man,' Stennis said," according to Biden. "He could see me looking at him, confused, and he pounded on his chest. 'It freed my soul,' he said. 'It freed my soul.'"

COACHING IS MISSION CRITICAL FOR UNDERSTANDING THE POLITICAL CHESSBOARD AND CULTURE

It was during the 2018 freshman orientation that someone snapped a picture of a quartet of new members of Congress: Alexandria Ocasio-Cortez of New York, Ayanna S. Pressley of Massachusetts, Ilhan Omar of Minnesota, and Rashida Talib of Michigan. Alexandria Ocasio-Cortez (better known as AOC) posted the picture on Instagram with a single phrase, "the Squad." It was a name that would stick.

Before long, AOC and the rest of the Squad, despite their sincere and honest intentions to take stands on issues that they passionately cared about—like the Green New Deal, campaign finance reform, voter suppression and gerrymandering—started criticizing colleagues in the media and in social media, speaking out about a geriatric dysfunctional Congress, and in the process, alienating people on both sides of the aisle and prompting President Trump to say: "they should go back to where they came from."

Nancy Pelosi found herself in a battle with AOC and the Squad in her bid to be confirmed as Speaker of the House. She wasted few words seeking to put AOC in her place, saying a "glass of water with a 'D' next to it would win" in Ocasio-Cortez's district. Pelosi also spoke about AOC's Green New Deal as "The green dream or whatever they call it."

Speaker Pelosi added that the Squad had their Twitter world but no following, or "currency of the realm"—the power to turn their activism into a coalition that could pass any legislation: "They are four people and that's how many votes they got."

However, Pelosi then did a turnabout and met for thirty minutes with AOC at Ms. Ocasio-Cortez's request. Pelosi told AOC, "In a family, you have your differences on issues that come up, but you're still family." She acknowledged that despite some personality issues, the two made their peace.

In 2020, after two years in office, AOC reflected on her first 100 days and onboarding process. "I think I have more of a context of what it takes to do this job and survive on a day-to-day basis in a culture that is inherently hostile to people like me," Ms. Ocasio-Cortez said in an interview, "I realized that if I kept up my revolutionary approach, it would make people whose help I needed mad." She joked, "They could have put me on the dog walking committee."

Imagine if the Squad had a coach or mentor when first starting out who could help them to reflect on their actions in the context of what they wanted to accomplish.

CRITICAL SUCCESS FACTOR 2.
WISELY LEVERAGE THE "COUNTDOWN
PERIOD" BEFORE YOU START

When you start a job as a chief executive, legislator, or department head, it is critically important that you spend time doing some serious work before you start. During the countdown period—sometimes called 'the 100 days before you start your job"—you need to spend some time preparing yourself for Day One.

Countdown periods differ according to whether you are a chief executive who has the power to call the shots, a legislator whose job is to collectively decide what legislation to pass, or a department head who must run an organization effectively and efficiently.

As PayPal CEO Dan Shulman told James Citrin, author of *You're in Charge, Now What?,* "Day One on the job better not be day one where you're putting your action plan in place. It should be well underway by the time you get there." You need to have a good idea of your personal agenda and be ready to take charge long before you first set foot in your office. This requires a good understanding of the opportunities and challenges you will be facing.

When Barack Obama was elected, the United States was facing a global financial crisis, two wars in two different countries, both of which America was losing, and many other hot issues. He stepped up and "took charge" unofficially before inauguration day, meeting with his Cabinet picks, and informally negotiating with members of Congress about the global financial crisis and bailout. As a result, he was able to avert another global depression that was shaping up like a perfect storm.

By contrast, many of the leaders I have coached in their first 100 days stubbornly adopt the attitude of "there is not much I can do until the buzzer starts" and later realize they have completely missed out on the opportunity the first 100 days could have presented them in getting off to a fast start.

When I ask, "What do you think you will spend your first 100 days on?" they tend to say, "Getting to know my team, setting goals and priorities, and getting some early wins." In actuality, most end up spending this period as the expression goes, "drinking from a firehose," having back-to-back meetings, and finding themselves in a state of overwhelm.

As noted previously, not all leadership transitions are the same. The president of the United States, a governor, mayor, or anyone in an executive role who can call the shots goes through a different kind of leadership transition than someone who has just been elected as one of the 500 members of Congress, the state legislature, or city council. It is important to adopt a beginner's mind and take time to understand your leadership role, responsibilities, and tasks. It is also important to do some Google research on leaders who have been successful in that role before and see what they did that worked and did not work.

THE COUNTDOWN: LEARNING + AHA MOMENTS + ACTION = PROGRESS

Immersion and Learning. For the first 100 days to be effective, immersion-based learning is essential. According to the Encyclopedia Britannica, immersion-based learning is where you place yourself directly in the environment, without any distractions, and with a singularity of purpose to accelerate your learning so that you can perform well in that environment. For example, going to China to learn the language, going to Army Ranger School to learn to become a warfighter, or a PGA golf school to learn golf.

For many people, the first 100 days of a new job is a period of immersion-based learning. The problem is that the combination of high expectations, stress, and pressure often results in people winding up trying to "get up to speed" on their new role, at the same time they are trying to perform. This can result in people resorting to "fake it until you make it" and making mistakes. The best way to avoid this is to use the countdown period before you start the job to begin the process of immersion-based learning.

Imagine that for the next few days (or weeks) you are going to go down the kitchen stairs and lock yourself in the basement—your Man Cave or Woman Cave—with your smartphone, Zoom video account, and access to Google with the idea of doing a deep dive on some questions you really need to have some answers to in order to make your first 100 days successful.

The "Aha" Moment. It is important to keep in mind that during the countdown period and first 100 days to follow, you will be drinking from a firehouse, talking to opinion shapers and movers, holding back-to-back meetings with colleagues, and trying to sort through various personal agendas, views, and perspectives. It is natural during this time to wind up in what I call the "Confusion Room" where as soon as you find the answers, the questions have changed.

When I think of the immersion process and confusion room, I think of Abraham Lincoln traveling by railroad from Springfield, Illinois to Union Station in Washington, D.C. and trying to figure out whether he should focus on preserving the Union or on abolishing slavery when he gets to Washington.

I think of FDR talking to his son James and trying to figure out whether to assume the same "dictatorial" powers that a president has in wartime, bypassing Congress to pass his New Deal and bring the country out of the Great Depression, or whether to uphold our democratic traditions and our Constitutional system of government.

The point is that if you stay in the immersion-based learning process, in your man cave or woman cave, there comes a point where you move beyond the easy and obvious answers to the questions you have been asking and come to the moment of true insight. That is the time when you see the light coming in from the mouth of the cave, and you are ready to emerge and jump into action.

Action. In the end, Lincoln, who took office with the Civil War breaking out and 600,000 people about to die, decided to focus on preserving the Union, knowing that if he abolished slavery, all the border states would secede. FDR wrote an inaugural speech where he declared that he must assume the same war powers a president has in wartime to lead the country out of the Great Depression, and then at the last minute put it aside, realizing his job was just as much about preserving democracy, as it was about stabilizing the economy and putting people back to work.

THINGS TO DO IN THE COUNTDOWN PERIOD AND PITFALLS TO AVOID

A good place to start is with yourself. Start with recalling who you are, your family background, where you came from on the map, all of which will have a big impact on your vision and values. Harry S. Truman said in his book *Plain Speaking* that who he was as a president was more than anything else shaped by the time he spent reading books about the great leaders of history and by the American values he learned growing up in Independence, Missouri where people spoke plainly and knew the difference between right and wrong.

Karl Rove, Republican campaign strategist for George W. Bush, said in a Masterclass on Politics with David Axelrod, campaign strategist and chief of staff to Barack Obama, "It's important now that the election is over and you have won, to think about why you ran for office in the first place." This is something that is very easy to forget when you are campaigning on the front lines and trying to be all things to all people.

David Axelrod advises to find one opportunity or issue you are really passionate about and use that as a basis for formulating a personal agenda, staying on message, and driving it like a monomaniac with a mission. This was the key to FDR passing his New Deal to lead Americans out of the Great Depression, LBJ passing the Civil Rights Act of 1964, and Barack Obama passing the Patient Protection and Affordable Care Act—all of which happened in their first 100 days.

CREATE A LEARNING AGENDA BASED ON THIS LIST OF POWERFUL QUESTIONS

Take out a piece of paper and write down a list of basic questions about your role, key responsibilities, and tasks. Here are some sample questions:

- What do I need to do for a smooth and orderly transition to power? Who do I want to hire for my team?
- What is my personal agenda for my first and next 100 days?
- Where can I get my hands on an organization chart, so I can understand the different departments?
- What is one singular initiative I would like to drive in my first 100 days?

On the backside of the paper write a list of questions that you want to immerse yourself in to help you gain insight into the goals.

- What is the greater issue of the day that I feel most passionate about? (For example: climate change, a more inclusive economy, immigration, a path to citizenship.)
- If there were one singular initiative I would like to drive, what would it be?
- What would be my biggest political obstacle in deciding to move this forward?
- What dilemmas, puzzles, riddles am I confused about?

DO YOUR DUE DILIGENCE—GATHERING RESOURCES

There are basically three different kinds of resources that will help you to accelerate your learning: 1) stuff to read, 2) stuff to watch, and 3) people to talk to. Once you take the oath of office, your job is to protect and preserve the Constitution.

When Harry Truman became president, he took that to heart and kept a copy of both the Declaration of Independence and Constitution in his back pocket, and he would often take them out to read when he was pondering the greater issues of the day. In time, he discovered that the vision and values in those ancient documents began to have a transforming effect on him.

Truman was born in the post-Civil War America in Missouri, a border state, and was subject to the racial hatred and bigotry of his era. He once said that every American ought to have an equal opportunity except "niggers and Chinamen." Yet as a result of reading the Declaration of Independence and Constitution while in office, Truman went from being a civil rights denier to a civil rights activist, desegregating the military by executive order during his time in office. (More on this in the Truman interlude.)

Also spend time reading news commentators and columnists respected by both sides. Chris Wallace of Fox News, Thomas Friedman of the New York Times, and David Brooks of the PBS News Hour are examples of opinion shapers and movers who not only have a commitment to the truth rather than conspiratorial lies, but also are very good at explaining the megatrends, the forces and factors behind the news events themselves. It is okay if you disagree with what they say, you can still learn from them. They are a much more reliable source of information for you than reflexively jumping on social media where the information available is often based on fake news or extreme bias.

I have found that you can learn how to do anything in an hour on YouTube that years ago would have taken hours to find out about in a library. Just type in the words "How to ...." and fill in the blank. How to make a great Day One speech? How to find rock stars of talent for your team? How to take a stand on an issue, and at the same time put your finger on a bipartisan approach?

Conduct Due Diligence Interviews

In coaching leaders, one of the things I often advise is that when conducting due diligence interviews with your team, colleagues, the general public, and opinion shapers and movers, it is important to retain the fresh perspective of an outsider, while learning from the insights of insiders who have a good grasp of the goals, problems, dilemmas you will need to deal with. I suggest that after you create your learning agenda, you create a list of ten good questions you will want to ask people, by thinking about: What do I know about this topic? What do I need to learn? Who can help me to learn it?

The time between the interviews is a good time to practice "pause leadership"—stepping back and reflecting in order to lead forward. This starts with creating a list of "ponderables" that represent the dilemmas you face. It could include basic questions about who is going to be on your Team of Rivals, or what are going to be your principles and policies on issues, or how you can come up with an approach to winning over people on the other side of the political fence. Find someone who can be your coach or sounding board to bounce your thoughts and questions off. The idea is to engage in the inquiry long enough that you go beyond the easy and obvious answers and come to moments of true insight.

The next step is to begin to write a White Paper describing the current situation, which is a prelude to sketching out your first 100-day action plan.

CRITICAL SUCCESS FACTOR 3.
THE FIRST 100 DAYS ROADMAP

I have devised the First 100 Days Roadmap with the idea of creating something like the Rosetta Stone: light of verbiage but loaded with wisdom that explains a lot. I consciously and intentionally put the Great Seal of the United States at the top of the First 100 Days Roadmap to remind everyone who takes the oath of office that you are in the same business as George Washington, Abraham Lincoln, and Franklin D. Roosevelt. Your job is to create a more perfect union and improve "the general welfare," as it says in the Constitution.

Your First 100 Days Roadmap

E Pluribus Unum
From the Many, One

Take Charge

Set the tone with the power of your words, hold out a vision, face and embrace reality

Stand for Something You Passionately Care About

Take a stand for a greater goal, big enough for everyone to subordinate their egos to

Build Your Team of Rivals

Choose the smartest and strongest people who can play as a team

Be the Leader America Needs
Make the Great Society Your True North

Build Bipartisan Coalitions March to Common Ground

Leverage shared purpose, collaboration, and compromise

Create a 100-Day Action Plan

Set your most important 100-day goals and a strategy for how to reach them

Secure Early Wins to Build Momentum

Get going right now, immediately, and produce some results

The entire roadmap centers around the notion of becoming the leader that America needs, and having your "True North" derived from your commitment to making a "Great Society." A wonderful example is Janet Yellen, former head of The Fed and now Joe Biden's Treasury Secretary, who grew up in working-class

Brooklyn. She pledged to run "an institution that wakes up in the morning thinking about people's jobs, paychecks, hopes, struggles, and dignity."

"E PLURIBUS UNUM"—*The motto of the Great Seal is "E Pluribus Unum"*—*from the many, one.* It is a reminder that your job entails being a unifier, not a divider. Your job is not about winning for your political party; it is about building a shared purpose and collaboratively solving problems that will help everyone be better off.

TAKING CHARGE. On the left side of the First 100 Days Roadmap, it states that the leader sets the tone. On inauguration day, as Joe Biden stood on the Capitol Hill steps preparing to take his oath of office as the next President of the United States, he set the tone in his inaugural address with just three words: "America is back," silently signaling to the world that he would re-establish America's ennobling ideals and values. The First 100 Days Roadmap asks you to hold out a vision of your shining city on a hill and, at the same time, face and embrace reality and be prepared to jump into action to deal with it.

BUILD A TEAM OF RIVALS. When Lincoln became president, he had no executive experience in government and decided to build a "Team of Rivals" made up of the smartest, strongest people he could find. The key thing in building your own "Team of Rivals" is to not just hire people because they are one of "the good guys" you have known for years. Instead, think in terms of the "matching talent to the job" value. Start with specifying the character traits, competencies, and superhuman qualities that are necessary for someone to perform in the role. Then search for someone with these traits who you can trust to fill the job. Bill Campbell, the CEO Whisperer of Silicon Valley who coached

Steve Jobs, Jeff Bezos, and Larry Page, says that it's important to hire "aberrant geniuses" who can play as a team.

CREATE A FIRST 100-DAY ACTION PLAN. Michael Porter of Harvard Business School points out that good leaders need a positive agenda based on what they want to accomplish, not just an agenda for dealing with a crisis. Start by working with your team to create a First 100-Day Action Plan, coming up with the most important goals and priorities you want to accomplish before your first 100 days is up, and a strategy for how to accomplish them given the vagaries of the political chessboard and culture. President Biden set three goals that he wanted to accomplish in his first 100 days: 1) Reestablishing American leadership in the world, 2) Get Covid-19 vaccines into the arms of 100 million Americans, 3) Pass the American Rescue Plan (stimulus plan).

STAND FOR SOMETHING YOU PASSIONATELY CARE ABOUT. On the eve of his election victory, President Barack Obama pondered what would be the one initiative he passionately cared about that he wanted to drive over the course of his first 100 days. The answer was something he had never seriously considered before. It was passing a national healthcare bill. The president-elect took a stand for this, even though he knew that each step taken to realize it would create both support and opposition. This led him to drive what became known as Obamacare to success in his first year.

BUILD BIPARTISAN COLATIONS, MARCH TO COMMON GROUND. Let's face it, it is almost human nature to play "king of the rock" and just tell people that "elections have consequences" and that we have the political power to press forward on the issues we passionately care about—a New Green Deal, immigration reform, an economic rescue plan. However, there comes a point where we realize that if we want to advance our agenda, we have no alternative but to stand our ground and at the same time seek bipartisan support. This is where chanting the mantra of this book—the power of shared purpose, collaboration, and compromise—becomes essential. Start with looking for an opening for bipartisan action. Create a shared purpose that is big enough to subordinate your egos to and then debate the issues to find where there is common ground and a path forward.

SECURE EARLY WINS TO BUILD MOMENTUM. Securing early wins is a great way for a new leader to build political capital, credibility, and rapid momentum. The key to securing an early win is to break bigger goals into small bites by identifying bothersome issues and problems that can be solved in a relatively short period of time with existing readiness, available resources, and standing support. It helps if there is a good idea, a fresh approach, an innovative solution ready at hand.

CRITICAL SUCCESS FACTOR 4.
USE A FIRST 100-DAY CHECKLIST

My very good friend Hans Peter Hartman, a legendary Swissair pilot, invited me to go for a private flight in a small twin-engine Cessna over the Alps after a leadership weekend I conducted in Zurich, Switzerland. HP, as I called him, besides being brilliant and wise, was a bon vivant full of good humor, and he loved kidding around with me.

Yet when we got to the private aircraft side of the Zurich airport and got out of the car and approached the plane, he suddenly became all business. He opened the door and pulled out a pilot's checklist that was as long as your forearm and started going through each and every item.

While I appreciated his due diligence, I have to admit it seemed almost excessive to me. HP said, "You're probably wondering why I'm doing this for just a short flight. I am doing it because going through the checklist is the best way of ensuring we are going to have a successful flight over the majestic Mount Rigi or Mount Titlis in the Bernese Alps. By going over this checklist and looking over every part of the flight-plan and plane, I can almost guarantee that nothing will go wrong."

Years later, I came across a book called *The Checklist Manifesto* written by Atul Gawande that said successful surgeons also used this approach with complex, nuanced operations. Gawande discovered that without the checklist approach, it was just too darned easy for the doctor under stress and pressure to assume that his team knew what he was thinking about for the next step in a procedure without him actually saying it—or to skip some minor detail of standard operating procedures which could result in a costly life-threatening mistake.

Says Gawande, "Good checklists do not try to spell out everything—a checklist cannot fly a plane. Instead, they provide reminders of only the most critical and important steps in a process—the ones that even the highly skilled professional using them could miss. Good checklists are above all practical."

In coaching many leaders on their first 100 days, I noticed after a while that it was not enough to provide people with a book that included a first 100-day roadmap, critical success strategies, and tasks because it was too easy for people to read it and just say, "that's interesting" and not take action.

The First 100-Day Checklist that I have developed through professional experience lists the key tasks or jobs to be done. If people were to go through the whole drill and checked all the boxes, they would not only be able to successfully navigate their first 100 days, but also avoid stepping on the obvious landmines.

The following checklist needs to be looked at not just as a gentle reminder, but rather as a discipline that needs to be religiously followed or at least worked on during the transition.

COUNTDOWN PERIOD: PREPARING FOR THE JOB ASSIGNMENT

- Enlist your family's backing, given the job demands
- Find a place to live if necessary, not far away from work
- Dedicate at least one hour a day to spiritual, mental, or physical resilience
- Find a back pocket copy of the Constitution and read it
- Write a letter to yourself that describes why you ran for office in the first place: *What issue do you passionately care about?*
- Write down the name of your specific job assignment and the key roles, responsibilities, and tasks that go with it
- Conduct a professional 360 leadership assessment of your bright side and your dark side
- Search for a master mentor and invest time and attention in making it a win/win relationship

ONBOARDING PERIOD—ACCELERATE YOUR LEARNING

- Take advantage of any official onboarding program
- Create a learning agenda with 5 to 10 good questions
- Gather public resources to read, and turn every page
- Start to conduct due diligence interviews about the organization's goals, problems, dilemmas
- Don't stop until you come to the "aha" moment
- Create a White Paper that addresses the current situation
- Create a list of your most important goals and priorities
- Start reaching out to key influencers and potential leaders

First 100-Day Checklist

- Get crystal clear on your going-in mandate
- Have a story ready for Day One—remember, the leader sets the tone
- Declare your shining city on a hill and most urgent goals and priorities
- Seal your leadership with three symbolic actions
- Create a 100-day action plan
- Build your team of rivals—match talent to job assignment and values
- Define a singular initiative that, if achieved, would make a difference
- Leverage the power of shared purpose, collaboration, and compromise
- Look for an existing opening for bipartisan action on something that matters
- Secure early wins that build personal credibility, political capital, and momentum

Abraham Lincoln:
A Leadership Transition

Chief executive onboarding may well have begun at the Great Western Railroad depot in Springfield, Illinois when newly elected President Abraham Lincoln boarded the train that would take him to Washington, D.C. Lincoln had personally tied the ropes on the trunks and labeled them: *A. LINCOLN, WHITE HOUSE, WASHINGTON, DC.*

A special train had been chartered for the trip, the shining L.M. Wiley with a strong Hinkley engine, today emitting a giant cloud of steam. Lincoln climbed the steps to his private saloon car. He paused for a moment at the rear of the car to say farewell to his friends. A bystander said, "his breast heaved with emotion, so much so he could scarcely command his feelings to commence."

Over the next twelve days, the presidential train traveled almost 2000 miles over eighteen different railroad lines. Lincoln, at the request of state and local officials, graciously made frequent whistle-stop speeches to cheering crowds. He charmed the crowds with bows and repeatedly expressed admiration for "the good-looking ladies."

These whistle-stop speeches were carefully listened to by newspapermen like Horace Greeley of the New York Post, for clues about how Lincoln came across to Americans and the new policy direction Lincoln might set. Lincoln was somewhat unusual looking at 6 feet 4 inches (this at a time when the average American was only 5 feet 6 or 7 inches tall). He added to his height with a tall stovepipe hat, which he always insisted on wearing. He was rather homely, wearing clothes that were never pressed, through which protruded long, gangly arms and legs.

Lincoln said in his first political campaign speeches when he was only twenty-three years old, "Every man is said to have his peculiar ambition… [mine is] being truly esteemed by my fellow men." When he spoke, it roused people in such a way that when they heard that Abe was coming to town, farmers would leave their fields and walk miles to hear him speak. On the rear platform of the whistle-stop train ride, he remarked that we began this nation with the idea that all men are created equal and now it only applies to people of a certain complexion. He added, "A house divided against itself cannot stand."

Yet, he would also add a touch of down-to-earth mirth. As a Midwesterner, he did not want to come across as highfalutin, and so he used funny stories, often the self-deprecating kind, to lessen tension over his political positions and to humanize himself with the crowd.

He told one story on the train trip three times, which goes like this. One day a woman on horseback came across me as I was chopping wood. She stopped and looked at me and said, "My lands, you are the ugliest creature I have ever seen." I said, "Well ma'am, there isn't a lot I can do about it." She said, "Well, you could have stayed home." With that, Lincoln slapped his side in front of the crowd and laughed louder than anyone in earshot.

PREPARE FOR THE JOURNEY
BEFORE YOU START

The long train journey gave Lincoln the time and mental space to step back and reflect. He thought about how his aspirations had grown. As his law partner once said, "His ambition was a little engine that knew no rest." It had carried him from a penniless, bookless, friendless field hand to becoming an American folk hero, lawyer, congressman, and president.

Does the man make the times or do the times make the man? He was not sure, but as Ralph Waldo Emerson, who later eulogized him in a church in Concord, Massachusetts said, "Rarely was a man so fitted to the event" (addressing the great question of slavery and the Civil War). Lincoln had a long-term vision concerning emancipation, but first he had to deal with the immediate issue that, on the day he was elected, seven states seceded from the Union.

Lincoln settled back in his leather chair in his rail car, kicking his feet up on the desk and thought about his leadership transition and the immediate job of setting a new policy direction and, at the same time, stabilizing the current situation. He also needed to write his inaugural speech, pick a Cabinet team, and decide on his order of priorities. The Inaugural Address was the first item on his agenda. He would deliver it in less than a month, and he believed this was an opportunity to bend history in the right direction.

He had sketched out a speech the night before they left Springfield and put it in his satchel, which he then gave to his son Robert. When they arrived at the Old Bates House in Indianapolis for the evening, the president-elect's son set the bag down with the other luggage, which was then removed to another room. The bag was lost, and with it the only copy of the inaugural address. Young Lincoln sputtered that he had intentionally left it with the other luggage. The bag was soon found, and rather than take the speech himself for safekeeping, Lincoln handed it back to Robert, "see if you can't take better care of it." Robert said that he barely let it leave his grip for the long journey to Washington.

The whistle blew and the train puffed along on the journey to Washington, D.C., while Lincoln looked out the window pondering what to say and looking over his inaugural address. As he watched the passing landscape vista of the hills and valleys go by, he saw two visions of America. The first was that of the United States on a trajectory to become the greatest nation in the world, a political beacon of light and an economic juggernaut. The second was that of two countries, once united, on a trajectory which was a fall from grace, forever divided and squabbling. He thought to himself with a wry smile, "Those cotton republics will never amount to a hill of beans."

He believed his presidential mandate under the Constitution was to affirm the first of these visions and prevent the second from happening. At the same time, he believed in a higher power with a divine plan and saw his job as making sure the country would wind up on the right side of history by nudging things along in the right direction. Unlike presidential candidates today, he felt no obligation to lay down in his inaugural speech a clear vision with bumper-sticker-like slogans or offer a 100-day action plan with crisp timelines.

Lincoln, an actively engaged president, had an essentially passive human nature and was reluctant to take bold moves even on topics he passionately cared about. Like a lawyer preparing to go before a judge, he would debate with himself all the sides of a complex question until he could build a clear-cut winning case.

Lincoln's style in his speeches was a sharp contrast to the grand eloquent orators of his day who would speak with big words for hours. He was down-to-earth, simple, and short in what he had to say. He was met by many reporters on these whistle-stops and would graciously deflect questions designed to force him to give an easy or obvious answer to complex questions by telling funny stories, jokes, or quips. Lincoln was known to say that it was "better to remain silent and be thought a fool than to speak and to remove all doubt."

Lincoln continued to ponder his inaugural speech where he would deal with one of the greatest questions ever presented to the president of the United States. Washington, Jefferson, and Madison all struggled with the question of slavery until the last days of their lives. This speech would force Lincoln to confront the question of whether or not to take a stand and extend the gifts given by the Founders, the Constitution, and the Bill of Rights to all citizens of the United States at the risk of further provoking the South and lighting a spark of fiery rebellion that would tear the country apart.

To ease his mind on the long journey, Lincoln would get out of his car when the train stopped at night. In Findlay, Ohio, rather than don his stovepipe hat when he went out, he wore a soft felt hat. Borrowing a long cloak from a soldier, he draped it over his shoulders to disguise his height and cover his long arms and legs, walking through town unrecognized. He bought newspapers in which the headlines blared, radical Republicans from his own party (including Charles Sumner, Horace Greeley, and Frederick Douglass) imploring Lincoln to take a stand and bold action to put an end to slavery.

Lincoln was in a psychological and political pressure cooker. Although he was loyal to his party, Lincoln knew that to keep the United States from blowing apart, he would need the support of radical Democrats who did not believe in the South's right to secede, and he did not want to provoke them by campaigning for the end of slavery. Choosing patriotism over partisanship, he did not go the Republican way nor the Democratic way. He chose the third way—a hybrid from both sides.

Getting back on the train, he grabbed an apple from a barrel that had been left there for guests and started paring it with his pocketknife. He would like nothing more than to be the president who fulfills his Constitutional duty to strive "to create a more perfect union" by extending the gift of the Founders—that of freedom—to all. Yet he had an innate mastery of political timing that led him to grasp that this was not the time. Perhaps his moment would come.

As he sat on the train, he told his young private secretaries, John Nicolay and John Hay (bright young men whose company was agreeable to him), about his cares: "Any newly elected statesman must look at the whole picture and put their highest priorities in order." He stared into the coal stove in front of him in his private car, musing that he needed to put the greater goal of preserving the United States of America on the front burner and put the exceedingly good goal of Emancipation on the back burner for now.

Lincoln knew that words matter, and he was very careful as to what words he chose as he took pen to paper to write his speech. He wanted to echo the Founders' ennobling words so as to elevate people, while making sure he did not unwittingly say something radical that would touch off a maelstrom that would cause the border states to secede: "If I could save the Union without freeing any slaves, I would do it; and if I could save it by freeing all the slaves, I would do that." He would scratch down a few phrases, then roll the paper up into a ball and start again.

Lincoln had had many experiences of leadership long before he became president, but truth be told, he arrived on the job with less experience in government administration than just about any other president in United States history. The job of forming the new Cabinet also began during the train trip. He wanted to hire the best and the brightest and decided to build a "team of rivals." Some of these were men who had competed with him for the presidency, either in the Republican or Democratic Party, and who thought themselves better qualified than he was. He drew up a shortlist for starters: William Seward, Salmon T. Chase, Edwin Stanton.

At a train stop, he telegraphed William Seward, asking him to accept his nomination for Secretary of State. Lincoln, the "dark horse candidate," had delivered a stinging defeat to Seward at the Chicago Nominating Convention. A man who had assumed he was the presumptive candidate, Seward said at the time, "I have been rudely robbed by a country rube from Illinois."

Seward was the former governor of New York, a senator, and one of the wiliest politicians around. Seward accepted on the basis that he thought Lincoln, who went out of his way to woo him with flattery, would make him the power behind the throne. Seward fancied himself like Cardinal Richelieu, the éminence grise of France, who was the most trusted advisor to King Louis XIII. Louis was the absolute monarch in the public limelight, but the Cardinal made most policy decisions behind the scenes.

As the train moved eastwards, Lincoln was informed that the Pinkerton Security Agency, having uncovered an assassination plot, recommended canceling the stop in Baltimore, a city that was very sympathetic to the South. Under cover of night, while everyone in his party slept, a disguised Lincoln boarded a different train, with only his bodyguard and a Pinkerton man, to make his way to Washington.

THE WILLARD HOTEL: MEETING, GREETING, AND LEARNING

The carriage carrying Mr. Lincoln and his party from the train station stopped in front of the Willard Hotel in Washington, D.C., which was in a tired state of repair. The grand lobby inside had high ceilings with peeling paint and smelled nasty like coal smoke.

Huge dark wingback chairs with leather cushions cracked with age were arranged hither and yon around the room, each with a shining silver spittoon.

The Pinkerton man caught the attention of the extremely white-faced desk clerk and slammed his fist on the countertop. The manager jumped to attention and the Pinkerton whispered something in his ear. The manager hurried from the desk and said, "Welcome to the Willard Hotel, Mr. President." The only problem was he said it to the man accompanying Lincoln that night, Elihu Washburne, an old political crony from Illinois. Lincoln smiled widely as Washburne said, "That is the President." Lincoln added humbly, "President-elect."

The next ten days prior to the inauguration were some of the busiest in Lincoln's life. The Willard would serve as a temporary White House, even in its tired condition. Lincoln knew that the art of politics was a social activity, whether the game was winning the election itself, onboarding into a new role, picking a cabinet, or matching a new policy direction to public opinion. He would spend the lead-up to the inauguration meeting, greeting, and learning from a very large number and diverse assemblage of people.

As Lincoln stepped through the lobby and entered the restaurant the next morning, William Seward was already sitting at the breakfast table biting into the end of a big Cuban cigar, which he habitually smoked. Seward smiled and said, "I understand you had some trouble in Baltimore." Lincoln joked, "Well to be honest, the journey was so long that by the end I might have considered it a gift to be shot."

Lincoln had breakfast with Seward, the self-appointed premier, seeking his first attempt to grasp power and influence over Lincoln. Seward asked for a copy of Lincoln's inauguration speech, volunteering to help and only to make minor edits. Lincoln pulled it out of his inside jacket pocket and handed it to Seward, who spent most of the day toning down the language so as to not provoke the South, making numerous suggested changes. Lincoln, not wishing to offend him, went along with the idea and did incorporate many of the changes.

The rest of the day was spent in meetings with all manner of notables, from President Buchanan and his cabinet, to Supreme Court justices, to members of Congress of various degrees of influence. General Winfield Scott, the aging military commander from the Mexican War, arrived in full uniform with his epaulettes and medals. He bore a stark contrast to Lincoln, who greeted him in his black suit with wrinkled trousers worn from travel.

According to Lincoln's personal secretary and assistant secretary, Nicolay and Hay, who were his only authorized biographers, Lincoln was a man who had well-formed opinions on most topics concerning his new administration, but he also liked subjecting those opinions to public scrutiny and was willing to be influenced. His labor during this time was consulting with notable members of the Republican or Democratic Party who had sage words of advice to offer about the Cabinet choices, the new president's policies, or how to deal with the South's military rebellion. He also met with many everyday people who filled the Willard wishing to meet the president and have a word with him.

For ten days, every moment of the day and long hours into the evening were occupied with making human connections and interactions. Lincoln's doors, as was his custom, were forever and freely open, and he nurtured the habit of listening more than he talked to the wise counsel from people of every sector, party, and race. He had a way of talking to everyday people, "Hello, I'm Abe Lincoln" that made them feel that he not only liked them but was really listening to them, and they liked him, too.

Hay pointed out "it is safe to say that probably no president before or since has approached his task better informed of the temper of his followers and decided more deliberately upon his general course of conduct." Lincoln rarely spent much time during or after these conversations in advocacy of his views but continued in inquiry. He would keep an open mind on the issue until the very last moment, never committing himself irrevocably until the moment of execution.

He was sometimes accused by his Cabinet, party friends, or foes of vacillating on issues. One of his visitors said to him, "Mr. Lincoln, I believe you are two faced." Rather than take offense, Mr. Lincoln smiled and said, "Honestly, if I were two faced, would I be showing you this one?" At other times, when a visitor would offer his advice on the new administration or its policies a bit too strongly or ask a question that Lincoln wasn't ready to answer, he would stand up, clap the visitor on the back and say, "Mr. Smith, how wonderful it is of you to come and see me," and usher the visitor out the door with the most gentlemanly manners, and the visitor left wondering what had happened.

When Lincoln was asked later by Seward how he managed to tolerate such a drain on his time and attention, Lincoln replied that it had not been a drain at all. In fact, he said that his soul has been invigorated and spirit rejuvenated by all the meetings. Lincoln believed that the week spent meeting, greeting, and learning had helped him gain not only a much better-grounded understanding of the situation he would be facing as president, but also the stratagem and tactics to deal with them. He met many office seekers, complainers, and favor seekers.

Although Lincoln's secretaries John Hay and John Nicolay had already been allowed to move into the White House ahead of inauguration day to get things ready, it was during this week of meetings that Lincoln and his wife, Mary Todd, took a break and at the Buchanans' invitation, visited the White House for the first time. Edward, the butler, led them up the stairs, and the Lincolns exchanged looks at what they saw.

Mrs. Lincoln would be disappointed that the grand life she had envisioned in Washington would have to take place in an executive mansion that looked like the inside of a third-rate hotel. The first impression was that of shabby furniture, torn drapes, frayed carpets, and a rat-infested basement. This was at a time when Washington, D.C. was still largely a swamp (literally), and the White House windows were without screens, allowing many mosquitos and other pests to freely come and go.

The Lincolns entered the White House that morning, with some fear and doubt, and began to explore the executive mansion. They were taken aback by the size of their new house, with thirty-one rooms, a library, conservatory, and stables. The West Sitting Hall was as big as their whole house in Illinois. Mr. Lincoln did not blink an eye at the shabby décor nor express an ill word, but Mrs. Lincoln was aghast. She set about the task of looking at what it would take to refurbish the place and came up with an estimate for repairing everything which came to over $20,000—a lot of money in those days!

When Mrs. Lincoln showed her husband the estimates, he was furious, saying that it was furnished okay just as it was, and it was a better house than they had ever lived in. He confided to Hay, "I swear I will never approve the bills for flub dubs for that damned old house when the poor freezing soldiers could not have blankets." He told her to cut the price by two-thirds and he would pay for it out of his own pocket. Mrs. Lincoln nodded in agreement but found a wealthy local sponsor to pay for the extensive refurbishment and redecoration she undertook.

THE INAUGURATION

On the day of Abraham Lincoln's inauguration, few people in the country realized the caliber of the person the country was getting. Even in a work of fiction, it would be a huge undertaking to create a leader with such a complex, nuanced character and enigmatic personality to draw on in helping steer us through secession and the bloodiest days of the coming Civil War. He was in the words of writer Tom Wolfe in his book The Bonfire of The Vanities, "a man in full"—confident yet humble, personally ambitious yet publicly purposeful, empathetic yet coldly resolved, persistent yet patient.

As Doris Kearns Goodwin has noted, over the coming months and years, the new president would turn his "team of rivals" into ardent admirers, defuse high tension situations with funny stories, mediate among warring tribes, and sustain people's spirits in the darkest hour. Further, he would translate the story of the great conflict with all that was at stake into words of "matchless force, clarity, power and beauty."

As Lincoln rode through the capital in a carriage with Buchanan, there was the expected almost regal parade—the spit and polish uniformed military men, marching companies, horse-drawn floats with over thirty beautiful ladies, and carriages filled with joyous Republican politicians and Democrats with goodwill. Yet, tighter security was in evidence for those with their eyes wide open, more than in any prior inauguration in the history of the United States. Soldiers on horseback adorned the street and there were cannons surrounding the Capitol. Snipers with rifles were posted in various Capitol windows.

The president-elect climbed the stairs of the Capitol—with the Great Dome only half built—and finally stood on the inaugural platform. The Chief Justice gave Lincoln the oath of office, his hand on the Bible, with the dignitaries from Congress all in attendance. Mr. Lincoln removed his stovepipe hat with one hand and took his inaugural address out of his coat pocket with the other. There was an awkward moment, as Mr. Lincoln who was holding his hat, needed two hands to hold and turn the pages of his speech.

Mr. Steven A. Douglas, the Democratic candidate who was bested by Mr. Lincoln in the 1860 election, stepped forward and said, "Please allow me to hold your hat." Mr. Lincoln handed it to him with a broad smile and endearing glance and Douglas sat there holding it for the entire time of the speech. This event grabbed more headlines and generated more talk in Washington than almost anything else that happened that day.

Lincoln's speech echoed the themes of the speech written in Springfield that had been edited on the train ride. He asserted that as he had just taken an oath to preserve, protect, and defend the United States Constitution, this oath enjoined him to see that "In your hands, my fellow-countrymen, and not in mine, is the momentous issue of the fate of the United States and the Civil War," he reminded secessionists. "The Government will not assail you. You can have no conflict without being yourselves the aggressors."

Lincoln's final words where he reaches out to the South are the ones most remembered. "I am loath to close. We are not enemies, but friends. We must not be enemies. Though passion may have strained, it must not break our bonds of affection. The mystic chords of memory, stretching from every battlefield and patriot grave to every living heart and hearthstone all over this broad land, will yet swell the chorus of the Union, when again touched, as surely, they will be, by the better angels of our nature."

TAKING CHARGE, BUILDING A TEAM, DEALING WITH ARMED REBELLION

As he rode in the black hansom carriage that day to the White House, Lincoln would have been taken aback by all that would be written and said about him in the future. Lincoln would be cast as the rail splitter, prairie president, and great emancipator in the years to come. Speakers and writers would explore the impact of his father renting him out like an indentured servant to escape poverty, his many friends but lack of close ones, his wartime presidency in crisis, his stand on the question of slavery, and even his sexual orientation.

My aim here is to tell a story about the process of Abraham Lincoln taking charge of his new job, building a team of rivals, and dealing with the armed rebellion that threatened to become a full-blown civil war—all in his first 100 days. Lincoln had many sleepless nights, pacing the halls of the White House, and spent many days on the edge of his seat, coming up to speed on a job that no president had ever faced, which was totally new to him, and was in his own words "totally overwhelming."

Imagine how Lincoln, a man with no executive administrative experience, had to go back to the White House after his inauguration and figure out how to stabilize a government and run a country. Imagine how he managed to build a great group to help him, one that was made up of rivals who were plotting to push him aside. Imagine trying to preserve the Union and avoid a civil war without the support of Congress and without a trained army.

On the first day that Lincoln took office, he received a letter from Colonel Anderson at Fort Sumter, the last remaining Union fort which was surrounded by the Confederate militia, led by General Beauregard and an army of 10,000 men. Sumter was fast running out of supplies. The President had to make a decision and put a question before his Cabinet in simple terms: "Should we resupply Fort Sumter, and if we do, is it worth it?" (More on this later.)

That was what Abraham Lincoln's first 100 days as president essentially looked like. From his first full day in office on March 5, 1861 to his 100th day in the middle of June, Lincoln barely had time to handle the things presidents normally handle, never mind deal with the greatest crisis in 100 years—or find time for relaxation and reflection.

BUILDING A TEAM

Today we tend to view the men in Lincoln's Cabinet based on 19th-century portraits and photos that portray them as men with long beards, sober countenances, and crusty temperaments. In truth, most of these men were in their early 50's, and very much in the prime of life. At the same time, they were men who were not only smart, but also had a great deal of executive experience, the kind Lincoln lacked and needed. Further, each of them was chosen in part because of being a powerful person of influence in either the Democratic or Republican Party, or in their geographic region.

One great question before Lincoln was how he was going to transform his team of rivals, men who ran against him as president and who thought themselves superior in every respect, to embrace him as a leader and accept his authority. Another question before him was how he was going to take a group of individual superstars and transform them into a group that could collaborate with each other. Not only did his Cabinet members see themselves as Lincoln's betters, they also did not like each other very much. In truth, by some stroke of genius, he was able to transform them into a great group. How did he do it?

Lincoln had the rock-solid character, a nuanced personality, and the humanity that we associate with almost all great leaders. Like Washington, he matched his great personal ambitions with public purpose and a long list of personal virtues. He was a natural-born leader, recognized by his classmates in school as superior in intelligence, physical athleticism, and sensitivity to others. He also had natural-born empathy. One day as a boy he came upon friends in the woods, and seeing they were placing hot coals on a turtle's back, he scolded them harshly and carefully removed the coals.

He had, in today's language, not just high IQ—intelligence quotient—but also high EQ—emotional intelligence quotient. He treated everyone with dignity and respect and was almost always magnanimous and forgiving. His private secretaries said that he never acted like a dictator with the Cabinet or made arbitrary decisions. He was generous with praise and hesitant to offer harsh criticism.

When something went right, he rapidly gave others the credit. When something went wrong, he took the blame. If he made a mistake, he immediately faced up to it. He was personally self-sacrificing, taking time to visit wounded soldiers in army field hospitals, and had a good sense of humor in times of trouble. Still, it took a while for Lincoln to take charge and build a team.

His greatest test in getting his Cabinet to embrace him as a leader and accept his authority was presented by William Seward. While Lincoln was still in Springfield wooing Seward to be his Secretary of State, Seward was already cultivating a special relationship with him. Seward, who was bitterly disappointed over not being nominated as president, viewed himself as the presumptive premier who would act as a trusted advisor and make decisions on Lincoln's behalf from behind the scenes. Seward, however, began to fall from grace when he began to use this as a device to wrest power from both Lincoln and the other Cabinet members.

When Lincoln nominated Salmon P. Chase, former senator and governor of Ohio as Secretary of the Treasury, Seward saw him as a threat and wrote a letter saying he was declining his nomination for Secretary of State. Lincoln, who saw through Seward's power play, told his private secretary John Nicolay, "I must not let Seward win the first trick." Lincoln, who was forever gracious and had an innate sense of tact, pocketed Seward's letter without a word.

Lincoln was not just a master of political timing, but also a master psychologist. He concluded when he arrived in Washington that Seward, for all his brilliance, was insecure. Seward seemed to possess a dual nature, often subordinating himself to authority, along with occasional eruptions of rebelliousness. Said one Seward crony, "Mr. Seward is like ivy that needs a strong oak to lean against and grow on to reach the sky." Seward had two powerful mentors early in his life who were both very strong and domineering. He would set off with his goals and plans, then jump and fall back in line when either of his mentors rebuked him. Yet occasionally, he would push back like a rebellious teenager with a sharp tongue, only to fall back in line again.

Lincoln soon had his own experience of Seward's rebellious streak when on April 1, 1861, he received a memorandum from his Secretary of State, playing upon Lincoln's inexperience. "Some thoughts for the President's consideration," it said. In the memorandum, Seward claimed that after nearly a month in office, the new administration lacked a clear policy, either foreign or domestic. The president needed help in making it clear that the issue before the country was the preservation of the United States, not slavery. It also said the president was spending too much time with minor political appointments and patronage.

The letter might have been a cause for Lincoln to dismiss Seward, but he did not want to blow up his Cabinet. Rather than chastise Seward, Lincoln wanted to create a situation where Seward and the rest of the Cabinet would accept his authority. Also, he recognized that while the letter was impertinent, there was considerable truth in it.

Lincoln decided to write one of his famous "hot letters" to Seward stating he did have a policy on all these matters, as stated in the inaugural address. As to Seward's suggestion to the president that he or someone else should execute the government's policy, Lincoln replied flatly that "if it must be done, I must do it." The interesting thing is that like many hot letters Lincoln wrote, it is believed that he placed it in his desk, unsigned, and unsent. Instead,

Lincoln arranged to talk to Seward in a more convivial situation, over a glass of bourbon, late at night at the Willard.

One of the other issues Lincoln had to deal with in creating a great group was that his key Cabinet members—Seward, Stanton, and Chase—seemed to always press for making decisions with him in his office behind closed doors. Lincoln had chosen these men not only for their individual brilliance but also for the possibility that he would capture the collective intelligence of the group in discussing any issue of importance, whether that happened in one Secretary's office or the other.

He made the decision to have weekly Cabinet meetings that would allow him to gain insights from the different views and perspectives around the table concerning questions about the greater issues of the day. He created a powerful forum for the free flow of ideas and tended to view disagreement as a resource instead of a threat. He understood that the truth came in the clash of different opinions and could lead to original ideas and pragmatic solutions no one had thought of yet.

FORT SUMTER

On March 5th, the day after the inauguration, the first agenda item on his desk was a letter from a man he had never heard of, a Major Robert Anderson, the commander of Fort Sumter. Fort Sumter had been surrounded by Confederate ships and troops since South Carolina seceded in December of 1860. Now Lincoln learned that Anderson believed the situation at Fort Sumter was desperate. They would run out of provisions in six weeks, and would need to either be resupplied or surrender.

Lincoln's Commander-in-Chief General Winfield Scott estimated that reinforcing the fort was going to take 25,000 men— 9,000 more than the entire army—and might trigger a civil war. He recommended surrendering. On his first full day in office, Lincoln was facing the possibility of having to break three of his inaugural promises: preserving the United States of America by not recognizing the Confederacy, holding onto government property, and waiting for the Confederates to move first.

Lincoln held a Cabinet meeting to discuss Fort Sumter. In this meeting, he told them about Major Anderson's letter and General Scott's recommendation. Much to Lincoln's frustration, the majority of his Cabinet agreed with General Scott. Finding no support from his Cabinet or General Scott, Lincoln went looking for optimists and learned that not all military experts were as pessimistic as General Scott.

Lincoln stalled for time, looking for more information. The Cabinet met again to discuss what to do and a vote was taken. Half the Cabinet voted to evacuate the fort and the other half voted to provision it. Lincoln said, "You see, gentlemen, the division among you is pretty much like the one inside of my own head." With that, Lincoln made the decision that a ship would set sail from New York Harbor with the means to provision the Fort, and perhaps more. When those who wanted to evacuate pushed back, Lincoln said, "Many things can happen between now and the time the fleet reaches Charleston. It is better for us to have a range of choices than none at all."

Two weeks later, Lincoln received shocking news from General Scott, who recommended to surrender not only Fort Sumter, but Fort Pickens on the Florida coast as well, even though that fort was securely in Union hands and could be reinforced at will. He once again called a Cabinet meeting, as he needed a decision on whether attempts should be made to relieve both Fort Sumter and Fort Pickens. He put forward the plan that Sumter would be resupplied in the dead of night. The Cabinet voted and decided to go ahead.

However, before the fort could be resupplied, on April 12th, 1860, little more than a month after Lincoln's inauguration, Brigadier General Pierre G.T. Beauregard of the provisional Confederate forces demanded the surrender of Fort Sumter. The rebel forces numbered 10,000 well-equipped men, while the defenders had only sixty-eight soldiers with inferior armaments and few supplies. But Major Anderson refused to concede and, while the Union fleet lay helpless offshore, the fort was subjected to a fiery bombardment that lasted thirty-four hours.

Realizing that the resistance was futile, Anderson was forced to surrender. Although the attack resulted in the death of two Union soldiers, with no casualties on the other side, this incident marked the beginning of the exceptionally bloody Civil War.

This was the first of many political and military setbacks Lincoln and his Cabinet would experience, but he, like the rest of them, grew through adversity. Lincoln's extraordinary leadership, his vision, values, and willingness to put himself in harm's way by taking weekend rides privately on horseback to visit soldiers in the field began to rub off on these men and helped them to become the kind of leaders the country needed.

By the time of the attack on Fort Sumter, Seward, Chase, Stanton, and others concluded alone and among themselves that Lincoln was learning his job, and his forgiveness and magnanimity were "almost super-human." They were impressed when Lincoln, upon discovering one of his Cabinet members was doing something to sabotage him, would overlook it and make it clear he loved them and forgave them.

By the time the first 100 days were up, Seward and the others had done an about-face. Executive skill and vigor are rare qualities Seward told his wife, remarking, "The President is the best of us." Gideon Welles, the Secretary of the Navy, became a devoted and trusted advisor to Lincoln. He foretold that Lincoln's ability to lead would be "better appreciated in the future than now." When Lincoln was shot, Stanton, who by that time not only loved him but was totally devoted to him, said, "Now he belongs to the ages."

There is a story that a guest at a White House dinner with all Cabinet members in attendance asked how the President and his Cabinet were faring and whether service to the "Great Man," and the "Great Purpose" superseded self-interest. Seward stood up and raised his glass, "We are Lincoln men." The rest of the group rose together, raised their glasses and said, "Here, here."

THE SECOND 100 DAYS

Lincoln, like many great leaders, could not squeeze his greatest accomplishments into the first 100 days in part because the timing was not right. His second 100 days would alter the course of history and put things on a new track.

He explained to his Cabinet on September 10, 1862 that he intended to issue a preliminary Emancipation Proclamation, in which he would promise to end slavery in the South in 100 days. Explaining his reasoning for this to his advisors, who were taken aback by his pronouncement, he said, "with my president's hat I had previously felt duty bound by the Constitution to uphold the legal rights of slaveholders." Yet, he continued, he was thinking with a shift in mind and heart. If African Americans were liberated so they could fight for their country rather than work as slaves for the Confederate war machine in the fields, hauling armaments and building fortifications, he reasoned, then the North would prevail. He added that the moment he declared the emancipation, the South would struggle for a while with the idea, then realize they had no reason to go on fighting.

Then there was also the personal side of it. Lincoln, who his friend William Herndon called "The most shut mouth man [he had] ever met," had campaigned by keeping his strong feelings and policies on slavery to himself. He told the group, "I am naturally anti-slavery. If slavery is not wrong, nothing is wrong. I cannot remember when I did not so think and feel." There was much discussion in the Cabinet for and against, but Lincoln in the end did not change his mind.

On September 22, 1862, Lincoln took his pen and signed a sacred document called the Preliminary Emancipation Proclamation, declaring that exactly 100 days later, on New Year's Day 1863, he would free every slave in bondage in every state in the Confederacy. This was truly an act of transformational leadership that altered the very fabric of society, North and South.

There were many friends and advisors of Lincoln who, as soon as they heard about his promise to emancipate the slaves, said he should take it back—it was too radical and would only prolong the war. There were also many like-minded abolitionists—Horace Greeley, Charles Sumner, and Frederick Douglass—who were perplexed Lincoln had not acted boldly and done this upon becoming president. Also, 100 days was an interminable time to wait.

Frederick Douglass said that should the emancipation actually happen, it would be the most remarkable day in the "American experiment." Yet he then asked, "But will that deed be done? Oh! That is the question."

The news spread like wildfire, and hundreds came at midnight to serenade Mr. Lincoln at the White House. Lincoln broke into tears. Some were from Washington, D.C.'s population of 36,000 slaves who had already been freed. Elsewhere, the reaction was a mixed bag. The Preliminary Emancipation Proclamation, the New York Times editorialized, was as important as the Constitution and Bill of Rights. On the opposite side, the Richmond Examiner said it meant "the inauguration of a reign of hell upon earth!"

The word got out to thousands of slaves in the South. A slave called Isaac Lane picked up the newspaper from his master's front stoop and read it to every Black man, woman, and child he could find. In Norfolk, Virginia, seventeen slaves who were caught with a copy of the paper that carried the story about the proclamation were accused of armed rebellion and hung.

As autumn leaves fell and winter arrived, pressure developed for the president to abandon his pledge. They did not want it to appear that Lincoln and the North were so desperate that they would emancipate the slaves and arm them just to win the war.

Lincoln wanted to wait for a military victory to dissuade them of that idea, and luckily it came. The Battle of Antietam (also known as Sharpsburg) provided the necessary Union victory to issue the Emancipation Proclamation. Over 3650 men were killed in the relentless fiery and explosive clash. Of the more than 17,000 who survived, many would never have arms to hold their children or legs to walk their fields again.

Lincoln himself had his doubts, but in the end he said, "Fellow citizens, we cannot escape history." Lincoln preached to Congress in December, "We shall nobly save or meanly lose the last, best, hope of earth."

Charles Sumner paid a visit to Lincoln in the White House on Christmas Eve. He was worried the President might recant his promise. Lincoln told him to relax, "He would not stop the Proclamation if he could, and he could not, if he would."

In the days leading up to New Year's Eve, Lincoln went over the draft of the Emancipation Proclamation with his Cabinet. They suggested an amendment "those emancipated, to forbear from tumult," which Lincoln did not add. However, Chase suggested a new ending, which Lincoln weaved in: "I invoke the considerate judgment of mankind and the gracious favor of almighty God."

Frederick Douglass, the Black abolitionist said on day ninety-six, "The cause of human freedom and the cause of our common country, are now one and inseparable." The countdown continued, and day ninety-seven passed into day ninety-eight, ninety-nine, and then New Year's Eve, 1862, "watch night," rolled around. It came to be called the "Day of Days."

In the capital, crowds of jubilant Blacks and whites filled the streets. Thousands of slaves in Richmond, Virginia, who would not even be freed by the Emancipation Proclamation, took to the streets. Crowds of people at churches in New York, Boston, and Philadelphia—home of the American Revolution—held candles as midnight approached. At precisely 11:55 pm, churches across the country fell mysteriously silent. At midnight, the choir broke into "Blow Ye Trumpets Blow, the Year of Jubilee Has Come."

Day one hundred, January 1, 1863, sometime after two o'clock in the afternoon, Lincoln held the Emancipation Proclamation in his hand and picked up his pen. "I never, in my life, felt more certain that I was doing right than I do in signing this paper."

In his book about Lincoln, historian John Hope Franklin wrote in a chapter called The Hundred Days, the Preliminary Proclamation, that Lincoln transformed the war into a crusade against slavery. Lincoln was so proud of what he did and so desirous of spreading the word that he remarked, "Do not let the dying die until they have heard the sound of freedom."

Chapter Three

The Leader Sets the Tone: Speak Like JFK, Communicate Like Ronald Reagan

Of all the talents bestowed upon men, none is so precious as the gift of oratory. He who enjoys it wields power more durable than that of a king.
-Winston Churchill, The Scaffolding of Rhetoric, November 1897

SPEAK LIKE JOHN F. KENNEDY

On Friday, January 20th, 1961, John F. Kennedy and other Catholics were given a reprieve from the proscription of not eating meat on Friday by the special dispensation of His Holiness Pope John XXIII in honor of the first Roman Catholic to be inaugurated as President of the United States. Kennedy, despite having a dangerously high cholesterol problem, took advantage of the papal dispensation by having a wonderful breakfast—a rasher of bacon and eggs. As the grandson of Boston Mayor "Honey Fitz" and son of Joe Kennedy, the ambassador to the Court of Saint James, he was accustomed to the special treatment of the smart, the beautiful, and the well-positioned.

Unfortunately, Mother Nature did not bless the morning of the inauguration with good weather on that January day. The temperature was a frigid twenty-eight degrees, and the eight inches of freshly fallen snow on the ground shut the city down. Kennedy emerged on the steps of the Capitol Hill building at 11 a.m. and took his seat on the inaugural platform next to the other dignitaries, standing out from the crowd with his natural charisma, boyish good looks, and Florida tan. His chestnut hair, broad smile, and pearly white teeth could make both men and women swoon.

He had removed his top hat and topcoat on leaving his limousine and wore only a suit, vest, and tie that accentuated his vim and vigor. It tickled him that no one on the platform knew that underneath his suit jacket and white oxford shirt, he was wearing long underwear from LL Bean.

His carefully choreographed and costumed youthful appearance stood out in sharp contrast to the other dignitaries on the platform, the old guard—Chief Justice Earl Warren, President Dwight D. Eisenhower, and President Harry Truman—who were all bundled up and had a decidedly gray pallor. Ike was a bit hard of hearing by this point and would often bend his ear.

Chief Justice Earl Warren began to administer the oath of office, with Kennedy's hand on the Fitzgerald family Bible. During the oath, Kennedy's hand slipped off the Bible for a moment, which caused some Protestants to later claim that because of this, JFK was never officially sworn in as president.

As historians relish pointing out, there was an almost laughable tangle of hostility and small-mindedness uniting the dignitaries gathered on the platform to listen to Kennedy's inaugural speech. Eisenhower's nickname for Kennedy was "little boy blue." Kennedy referred to Eisenhower as "the old fart." Truman loathed Kennedy, because he loathed Kennedy's father Joe, whom he had once threatened to throw out a hotel window. Eleanor Roosevelt, another enemy of Joe's, had campaigned to stop Kennedy from winning the nomination and would have to sit on the platform with the other dignitaries. Jackie called Lyndon and Lady Bird Johnson "Colonel Cornpone and his little porkchop." Johnson called Bobby Kennedy "that little shitass," and Bobby spoke about Vice President Johnson as "an animal in many ways." Adlai Stevenson resented the Kennedys for naming him as Ambassador to the United Nations instead of Secretary of State, the job he thought he was owed.

Kennedy's intent was to use his inaugural address to set the tone for his new administration with the goal of helping Americans become a better version of themselves. The speech the new president delivered that day would elevate all sitting on that platform above their everyday selves, as it would millions of Americans who heard it.

Kennedy stepped to the lectern and set the tone of his new administration by being a unifier versus a divider. "We observe today not a victory of party, but a celebration of freedom—symbolizing an end as well as a beginning—signifying renewal as well as change."

Striking a note that brought out the noble ideals and enduring values of the Founding Fathers, he said, "We dare not forget today that we are heirs of that first revolution." He then added, "Let the word go forth from this time and place, to friend and foe alike, that the torch has been passed to a new generation of Americans— born in this century, tempered by war, disciplined by a hard and bitter peace."

This line had a huge amount of resonance with all those watching on TV, given that the Eisenhowers, Trumans, and Roosevelts were sitting on the stage with him, and it made millions of young Americans, who like myself were born after WWII, feel he was passing the torch directly to us.

Kennedy was both an idealist and a realist, saying that the revolutionary ideals of the Founders were very much at stake around the world that day, as they had been in the past, with a Cold War brewing with the Soviets. "Let every nation know, whether it wishes us well or ill, that we shall pay any price, bear any burden… to assure the survival and the success of liberty."

Kennedy knew that Americans needed a new sense of shared purpose, similar to the one the Greatest Generation had in World War II. He came to that now famous line, "and so my fellow Americans, ask not what your country can do for you. Ask what you can do for your country."

The speech, which became known as the 'Ask Not…' speech, is sometimes called the speech that changed America. As a young man growing up at the time, I felt that when Kennedy spoke, he spoke for all Americans, and even more importantly, I felt as if he were speaking directly to me. It was a defining moment for me, after which I wanted my life to be about making a difference, not just making a living.

Historian David McCullough heard the speech and decided to quit his job at Sports Illustrated and drove to Washington, D.C. the next day to get a job working for the US Information Agency, whose mission was to spread the word about American ideals and values all around the world.

Donna Shalala, Congresswoman and Secretary of Health and Human Services under Bill Clinton, said that hearing the speech was like a splash of cold water. She was a student at Western Reserve University, where she was considering getting a law degree. As soon as she heard that Kennedy had created the Peace Corps, she abandoned those plans and volunteered. She wound up spending the next several years in villages in the southern part of Iran, later reporting it had been an amazing life-changing experience.

Gonzalo Barrientos was a freshman at the University of Texas when he heard the speech. The son of farmers and cotton pickers in central Texas, Barrientos wanted to study hotel or restaurant management as a way to escape. "I didn't want to stay in the cotton fields forever," he said. Barrientos wanted more—not a lot more, but an opportunity to "go out and be a part of a place that had air-conditioning and carpet." Barrientos figured that a business degree was the best way to do that. Kennedy's speech made him reconsider.

Barrientos acted on his inspiration and switched his majors, focusing on sociology, economics, and government. He went on to train newcomers to the Volunteers in Service to America (VISTA) and became one of the first Mexican-Americans elected to the Texas State Legislature. He served ten years in the House and twenty-one more years in the Texas Senate. His goal: "to help the community, to help poor people, the downtrodden to empower those people to the American Dream. All of which, I think, came from John Kennedy."

COMMUNICATE LIKE RONALD REAGAN

Ronald Reagan was already referred to as "the great communicator" after he gave a speech at the Republican National Convention to nominate Barry Goldwater in 1964, a speech that launched his political career like a rocket. By the time of Mr. Reagan's Presidential Inauguration in 1981, the title had developed capital letters and acquired almost an official standing.

In the 1980s, at a presidential campaign stop in New Hampshire, the editor of the Nashua Telegraph told the sound man to turn off Reagan's microphone so he could make an announcement. Reagan, the "Gipper," stood up like he was going to whoop someone, and said, "I am paying for this microphone, Mr. Green." The crowd responded with enthusiastic cheers and hollers.

That same year, during the presidential debates with Jimmy Carter, Reagan drove home the need for change, simply by asking millions of Americans, "Are you better off now than you were four years ago?" And during the 1984 presidential debates for his second term, when Walter Mondale asked whether Reagan, then seventy-three, was getting too old to be president (a question on many people's minds), Reagan smiled broadly and put the issue to rest with one graceful good-humored quip, "I am not going to exploit, for political purposes, my opponent's youth and inexperience." (Even Mondale laughed). And who can forget Reagan's words at the Brandenburg Gate in West Berlin, "Tear down that wall Mr. Gorbachev"?

During his farewell address as president, referring to his nickname as "The Great Communicator," Reagan went on to add, "I wasn't a great communicator, but I communicated great things, and they didn't spring full bloom from my brow, they came from the heart of a great nation—from our experience, our wisdom, and our belief in the principles that have guided us for two centuries."

Reagan was, in fact, a superb orator—one of the most inspiring in American history, equally comfortable with a State of the Union address to Congress, a speech to the British Parliament, a "fireside chat" with the American citizens from the Oval Office, or a direct challenge to a foreign adversary. He could switch gears, shifting from one speech to another on short notice, based on how events were emerging.

On January 28, 1986, Reagan was preparing to give his State of the Union Address that evening. However, the speech was postponed, and everything changed that morning when the Challenger space shuttle, meant to carry schoolteacher Christa McAuliffe into orbit, was reduced to a serpentine tunnel of smoke in the sky near Cape Canaveral with millions of schoolchildren watching from their classrooms.

Reagan, just as shocked as everyone else by the tragedy, would have the unenviable job of making a speech that would help Americans make meaning out of what had happened. Reagan knew that in speaking to the children of the nation who had viewed the horrific event, that he had to "make it plain to them that life does go on and you don't back up and quit some worthwhile endeavor because of tragedy." But can such terrible things be made plain—even by a president lauded for his public speaking?

When an emotional speech was needed, Chief of Staff Donald Regan sometimes said, "get that girl...you know, have that girl do that." That girl was at that time a fairly unknown speechwriter, Peggy Noonan, who had a reputation for showing up late to the office after reading the papers, but also for writing great speeches. According to Noonan, "The president is going to have to do a speech that is aimed at those who are eight years old, and those who are eighteen, and those who are eighty without patronizing anybody."

For a former movie actor and street performer known for his way with crowds, the Challenger speech is rivaled only by Reagan's prescient "Tear down this wall!" address delivered in Berlin just two years before the Berlin Wall came down.

"Ladies and gentlemen... today is a day for mourning and remembering," he began. "We've grown used to wonders in this century," he said, "It's hard to dazzle us. But for twenty-five years, the United States space program has been doing just that. We've grown used to the idea of space, and perhaps we forget that we have only just begun. We are still pioneers. They, the members of the Challenger crew, were pioneers."

"And I want to say something to the schoolchildren of America who were watching the live coverage of the shuttle's takeoff. I know it is hard to understand, but sometimes painful things like this happen. It is all part of the process of exploration and discovery."

"It's all part of taking a chance and expanding man's horizons. The future doesn't belong to the fainthearted; it belongs to the brave. The Challenger crew was pulling us into the future, and we'll continue to follow them."

"We don't hide our space program. We don't keep secrets and cover things up. We do it all upfront and in public. That's the way freedom is, and we wouldn't change it for a minute."

Then came Reagan's—that is, Noonan's—powerful closer:

"The crew of the space shuttle Challenger honored us by the manner in which they lived their lives. We will never forget them, nor the last time we saw them, this morning, as they prepared for their journey and waved goodbye and 'slipped the surly bonds of earth' to 'touch the face of God.'"

In "Speaking My Mind," a collection of his speeches, Reagan readily acknowledged he had honed his speaking ability while in Hollywood as an actor and later as host of the television program "GE Theater." He was aware that his political success was due, in part, to his ability to give a good speech based on two things: "to be honest" in what you are saying, and "to be in touch with [your] audience." He stated that you needed to "talk to your audience, not over their heads or through them. Don't try to talk in a special language of broadcasting or even of politics, just use normal everyday words."

Reagan believed that a speech should be brief, concise. He told Peggy Noonan that twenty minutes was the maximum time that an audience should be expected to sit patiently through a speech. The president emphasized that his speeches contained ennobling ideals and enduring values that the average American instinctively identified with. He liked to use quotes from likely sources like the Revolutionary American pamphleteer Thomas Paine, who wrote, "We have it in our power to begin the world over again."

Reagan did not just write his speeches; he would often stand in his office and practice them over and over until he was satisfied with their delivery.

TIPS FOR MAKING A GREAT SPEECH

The best speakers are remembered not for what they said, but
for how they make us feel. -Maya Angelou

1. YOU ARE THE MESSAGE

What does that mean exactly? It means that when you give a speech or communicate with someone, it is not just the eloquence of your words or delivery that are the message. It is the signals you send about what kind of character, competence, and gravitas you have as a person, delivered through your facial expression, eye contact, body movement, your vocal pitch, tone, volume, and intensity, as well as your commitment to your message.

For example, George Washington was not a great orator, a great writer, or a great military strategist. Yet, he carried himself with the bearing of a king and was known for his rock-solid character and capability. People were not only willing to follow him across the Delaware, but also trusted in anything he said. He was the only president who, without giving a single campaign speech that implored people to "elect me," was elected unanimously.

Abraham Lincoln, the greatest presidential speechwriter of all time, knew that you lead with the power of your words. Yet he had to overcome the fact that he spoke in a high-pitched, squeaky voice. He opened his speeches with funny stories, built principle-based, logical arguments that made sense to plain and simple people, and he made human connections with his empathy. At the same time, Lincoln realized that leadership is often about what you do not say. "Better to remain silent and not be thought a fool, than to speak and erase all doubt."

Theodore (Teddy) Roosevelt once said of himself, "I came into life like a giant ball, as if launched by a catapult." While Teddy

Roosevelt could win people over to his speeches and policies with his enthusiasm, it would sometimes, however, lead to him going on like a windbag. A man who visited him at the White House was asked, "What did you say to the president?" The visitor replied, "My name" (and never got in another word). Roosevelt learned about how he was perceived by people from his chief of staff and decided to compensate for it by coming up with short, sticky phrases that would grab the newspaper headlines, such as "Speak softly and carry a big stick."

Moral of the story? The best thing you can do to be a good public speaker is to become a better version of yourself. Accentuate your strengths through style and substance and come up with a compensating strategy for your weaknesses.

2. Seize the Opportunity to Set the Tone

A new leader's job is to set the tone, whether it is an inaugural speech, state of the union address, talking about a natural disaster, or speaking at a funeral. When Franklin D. Roosevelt became president in the middle of the Great Depression, he set the tone in his inaugural address by delivering those profound words: "We have nothing to fear but fear itself."

When President John F. Kennedy was assassinated with the crack of a gunshot, the nation, which had been soaring based on his vision of hope and change, went into a state of hopelessness and shock. President Lyndon Johnson, not a great public speaker, set the tone by giving a great speech before a joint session of Congress called "We shall overcome." He emphasized the theme of "We shall continue to move forward with the legacy of JFK's principles." The speech was well received, and Johnson used the momentum to pass three civil rights bills in his first year in office.

As a new leader, it is important to consider that every time you have an opportunity to speak, you have an opportunity to set the tone, whether it is by giving a speech to introduce a bill before your state legislature, making a motion at a city council session, or holding a neighborhood meeting on how to create better schools.

3. What Job Am I Hiring the Speech to Do?

The first thing to keep in mind when writing a speech is that communication is a function of intention. If you are going to speak as the president, governor, or city council member, ask yourself, before you begin writing your speech, what the intention is in giving it—what do you want it to accomplish?

To put it another way, think in terms of hiring a speech to do a job for you. Ask yourself, "What is the job I am hiring the speech to do?" For example, you might say to yourself: "Many Americans have been given the gift of a 21st century education (economic opportunity, equal justice, and so on.). I want to say something that will provide these gifts, not just to people who look like me, but to all Americans."

Churchill mobilized the English language and sent it into battle. -John F. Kennedy

4. Deliver a Power Opening

The opening of a speech or informal talk is important because that is the time when everyone is the most interested in taking the measure of the man or woman, and in hearing what you have to say. I would like to suggest three strategies for a power opening:

The Power Pause. Elizabeth Cady Stanton, one of the leaders of the Woman's Rights movement in the United States, had to give a speech before a group of senators and congressmen who had never seen a woman at a lectern. She used a tactic, previously used by Napoleon, called the "power pause." After being introduced, she stood on the stage for a solid minute, during which time the audience began to have a growing sense of the gravitas of the woman before them, as well as the justness of her cause. During the time she stood there, she rehearsed in her mind the opening line of her speech. Her level of leadership gravitas and the level of audience attention, curiosity, and interest seemed to grow with each passing second.

Skip the pleasantries and get to the point with a hammer blow. Booker T. Washington was a Black American educator, orator, and adviser to multiple presidents on the issue of civil rights after the Civil War. He had an opportunity to address a group of prominent southern politicians about helping fourteen million formerly enslaved African American people create a new future. Instead of spending time thanking the host and the group, he adopted the power pause. His first words were an attention grabber. "One-third of the population of the South are Negroes." Later in the speech, he went on to describe the opportunity for his audience to help Black people be better off: "If you want to lift yourself up as human beings, lift up someone else."

Command your audience with "compression." Winston Churchill was not a natural-born public speaker. Most people do not know that even in his 20s and 30s, he struggled with stuttering and spoke in a monotonous voice. However, he realized that oratory could give an ordinary person the political power of a king and he set out to master it. Prime Minister Boris Johnson said that one of Churchill's secrets was "the power of compression"—being able to get to the essence of a topic in a single sentence.

An example was when Prime Minister Churchill gave a stirring speech to commemorate the Battle of Brittany in honor of the British RAF pilots who fought off the Nazi Blitz. He condensed everything he had to say into one Anglo Saxon sentence: "Never in the field of human conflict (war) has so much been owed by so many to so few."

5. Adhere to Ennobling Ideals, Enduring Values, and Logical Argument

Woodrow Wilson, the only president with a Ph.D., had to make a speech the first weekend in April 1917 to the joint session of Congress that called for a declaration of war against Germany. He was not sure how to start and had gone for a walk in the park to "get my mind around my conflicting thoughts." After all, he had run for president on the campaign slogan: "He kept us out of war."

Yet he was stunned by the fact that Kaiser Wilhelm and his authoritarian government had condoned the German U-boat's sinking of the American passenger ship, the Lusitania, off the coast of Ireland on its maiden voyage with 1500 passengers aboard. For hundreds of years, a ship's captain in wartime had at least the ability to surrender without being sunk by a skulking submarine.

After his walk, Wilson returned to the White House soaking wet, ordered the staff quiet, entered the second-floor study, and began to write a speech, overcome by the ignoble behavior of the Kaiser and Germany's inhumanity. Later that day, President Wilson gave his speech, asking Congress to declare war against Germany, with a simple sentence that both evoked American ideals and provided a persuasive logical argument: "The world must be made safe for democracy."

Four days later, Congress (which had pledged American neutrality in WWI) voted overwhelmingly in favor of a war declaration. The New York Times reported that the "United States virtually made its entrance into the war" with Wilson's speech. "Before an audience that cheered him as he has never been cheered in the

Capitol in his life, the president cast in the lot of America with the Allies and declared for a war that must not end until the issue between autocracy and democracy has been fought out."

6. BUILD AN ARSENAL OF ANECDOTES

Ronald Reagan is almost universally admired and respected by both Democrats and Republicans, and one of the things that made him a great public speaker is his arsenal of anecdotes.

When historian Douglas Brinkley visited the Reagan Presidential Library, he found in an out-of-the-way place, a shoebox with the words written on it "RR's Desk." It contained over one thousand file cards containing a series of Reagan's jokes, stories, and anecdotes he had used in his political speeches. (Brinkley lovingly organized the box into categories.)

Yet Reagan did not just rely on canned material. He often made up jokes as he went along. When Reagan was struck by an assassin's bullet and was rushed to the hospital, he told surgeons in the emergency room, "I hope you all are Republicans."

When he appeared before a joint session of Congress a week or so later, he read a letter from Peter Sweeney, a second-grader in Wisconsin. "Mr. President. I hope you get well soon. Otherwise, you may have to make a speech in your pajamas."

On another occasion, Reagan began his speech at the White House Correspondent's Dinner in Washington, by saying, "Mike Deaver said I had a short attention span." Then he paused as if he forgot what he was going to say and added, "Oh what the hell, let us move on to something else."

7. MAKE USE OF PROVOCATIVE STATEMENTS OR QUESTIONS

A provocative statement or question is one that is strongly worded to get a reaction, often with the purpose of getting people to think differently about something. You can use a provocative statement or question to defeat a rival, to take a stand on a controversial issue, or even to show you are not afraid to get into a fight. You can use a provocative question to force people to think differently about an issue.

Franklin Roosevelt made use of a provocative statement in a campaign speech for his second term in office at the Madison Square Garden in 1936. He spoke of the plight of the forgotten man or woman to whom politicians and big business alike were so indifferent. He said, "Never before in all our history have these forces been so united against one candidate as they stand today. They are unanimous in their hate for me…" He then raised his head and said, "I welcome their hatred." The strength of this one provocative statement, which showed he was ready to do battle on behalf of millions of Americans in the Great Depression, helped lead to his nomination.

Ronald Reagan idolized Franklin Roosevelt, and his speeches often contained provocative statements and questions designed to introduce policies to stimulate the spirit of enterprise and to counter overreliance on government. In his stump speeches, he would often say, "My fellow Americans, government is not the solution, government is the problem." He said it enough times that his message began to sink into the collective consciousness, and as a result, he was able to rescue the Republican Party from the dead.

During the 2020 presidential campaign, ex-president Barack Obama used barbed provocative statements to bolster Joe Biden's chances to defeat Donald Trump, who he said did not have the character or competence to be president: "Donald Trump hasn't grown into the job because he can't."

As a candidate or new leader in office, you can seed your speeches with provocative questions to get people to question what they have taken for granted or have not even considered: "Are you better off today than you were four years ago?"

Thomas Jefferson once said, "a good question is like a mete-or shooting across the sky." A good question can get you to see something in a new way, and act in a new way. It can also be used to (re-) frame issues. Jon Meacham, Pulitzer Prize-winning historian and author of a book on Jefferson, said in his four-minute speech at the 2020 Democratic convention (taking a rare stance as a historian against an incumbent president), "Will we continue to be prisoners of the darkness of American forces, or will we free ourselves to write a brighter, better, nobler story?"

8. END WITH A CALL TO ACTION: LET US MARCH!

The Greek scholar, Demosthenes, was once asked what the secret of great oratory was. His response was "a call to action." There is a famous story about Titus, a Roman general who compared the speeches of Cicero to Julius Caesar. He said, "When Cicero gives a speech, people say, 'How well he speaks.'" By contrast, he added, "When Caesar gives a speech, people say, 'let us march.'"

Winston Churchill is a good example of a leader whose speeches were successful due to action language. If you look at the famous quote from Churchill's "Finest Hour" speech, the keyword is 'fight.' "We shall defend our Island, whatever the cost may be, we shall fight on the beaches, we shall fight on the landing grounds, we shall fight in the fields and in the streets, we shall fight in the hills; we shall never surrender…"

In conclusion, as a newly elected official, it is important to remember that communication does not happen in your speaking, but in your audience's listening. It is not what you say, but how they hear it. The challenge is to speak to people's listening by framing your message in a way that addresses their needs, fears, hopes, and aspirations.

Franklin D. Roosevelt:
The Happy Warrior

There are some people who have the quality of joy and richness
in them and they communicate it to everything and everyone they touch.
It is first of all a physical quality; then a quality of the spirit.
-Tom Wolfe

THE ASCENT

Franklin D. Roosevelt was born into a life that was as close to the British aristocracy as an American could get. His devoted parents, James and Sara, raised him like a country squire at Springwood, their 9000-acre estate in upstate New York, overlooking low rolling hills and the Hudson River.

There was never even the slightest conflict between his parents, who spent huge amounts of time with him on his schooling, sports, and studies. They also reinforced the idea that if he applied himself, the world was his oyster. Once his father took him on a trip to Washington, D.C., where he got to shake hands with President Grover Cleveland at the White House. "My little man, I'm making a strange wish for you," the president said, placing his hand on the boy's head, "May you never grow up to be president of the United States."

On the way back from Washington on the train, James Roosevelt seemed to contradict the president, reminding his son that he had lived a life of privilege and that he should never forget that, for those for whom much is given, much is required.

* * * * *

Franklin D. Roosevelt was sometimes teased for being an overprotected mama's boy and for his father being his only best friend. He thus enjoyed telling stories later in life about "going off the reservation" at Springwood and sowing his wild oats. Later in life, he liked to tell the story about how he had been denied admission to the Museum of Natural History in London. He pulled out his Museum of Natural History card from New York and convinced the guard that he was a visiting scientist. Even if the story got exaggerated over the years, it does reflect his self-assurance and pride in improvising to get his way.

He attended Groton, an exclusive boarding school in Massachusetts, where he did not excel in academics or sports. He then went to Harvard University, rented an apartment for $400 per year and there, despite his friendly attitude, was made fun of for speaking with an English accent. His next stop was Columbia Law School and a job at a Wall Street law firm working on wills and trusts, which he found awfully boring.

One day at the office he told a group of friends, who had come to admire him as a person but were unimpressed with his performance as a law clerk, that he had his career well planned out: "first a seat in the state assembly, then assistant secretary of the navy, then governor of New York—and then the presidency."

It was the same path his cousin Theodore "Teddy" Roosevelt, who he idolized, had taken. Teddy Roosevelt had made it, disdaining the values of his genteel upbringing, which was hostile to rough-and-tumble egalitarian politics. Why then should another Roosevelt, no less endowed, no less willing to battle and bargain, not succeed in the same worthy enterprise?

For FDR things were going exactly according to plan until one day in 1921, when this robust, athletic man, age 39, went for a swim at the family estate at Campobello Island off the coast of Maine. He returned dog-tired with chills up and down his back and told his wife Eleanor he was going to take a nap. When he woke up and got out of bed, he fell to the floor and could not get up. He shouted to Eleanor to come as he was paralyzed from the waist down. He was diagnosed with polio, known then as infantile paralysis, and would never walk again.

In the process of "becoming", great leaders often have defining moments that alter what is possible and achievable for them, and these result in powerful and permanent shifts in the areas of life that matter most. This was to be the defining moment of FDR's political career and presidency.

His battle with polio become a leadership crucible that would transform him from a son of wealth and privilege (who never had to deal with any adversity except perhaps being blackballed from the elite Porcellian Club at Harvard) to a man of the people. FDR from that day forward heard the call to leadership in his empathy for the human suffering he now identified with in others.

He treated everyone he met with tremendous warmth and acted like he was on a personal mission to lift their spirits and change their circumstances, whether they were fellow polio sufferers at the recuperation center he built at Warm Springs, Georgia or the millions of Americans trapped in the jaws of the Great Depression.

His rising star as a New York State politician may have come to an abrupt end after his bout with polio, were it not for Louis Howe, his totally devoted best friend, coach, and mentor. One day when FDR remarked that given his disability, he had to be at best "cautiously optimistic" about his ability to make the ascent to power, Howe replied that he could lay on his back as a country squire at Hyde Park or he could get up and become the president of the United States.

In 1924, Governor Al Smith of New York asked FDR to nominate him as a candidate for president at the Democratic Convention at Madison Square Garden. Roosevelt rose to the challenge with glee, immediately calculating the number of steps he would have to walk on crutches wearing braces, to move from the platform entrance to the podium.

By then, Roosevelt had progressed from crawling on the library floor to develop his muscles to measuring the distance he would have to cover and trying to walk that far. Eleanor Roosevelt wrote that her husband spent hundreds of hours on crutches crossing the library in their New York City house "toward the imaginary podium."

The interesting thing is that people in the Democratic circles knew that he could not walk on his own. The press was part of it, too. However, they never took a picture of him in his wheelchair. If a young photographer did not understand the code of honor (and tried to take a picture), other members of the press would knock the camera out of his hands.

When the day of the convention came, he moved from his wheelchair to the dais, being almost carried by his two sons, who held him under his arms as he braced himself on his crutches with both hands. As he got within ten steps, his leg braces locked, and it seemed he might fall. Instead of allowing his sons to prop him up, he shrugged off their grip and lunged forward to the podium in an ungainly writhing motion.

The crowd was so excited at watching FDR full of will and determination grasp the podium itself and raise his head in a triumphant smile, that even those who did not like him, started cheering and hugging each other. Says Doris Kearns Goodwin: "Twelve thousand voices exploded with admiration, even before his speech had begun." Roosevelt delivered the famous "happy warrior" speech nominating Governor Al Smith of New York. The combination of his flashing smile, resonant voice which soared above the crowd, and well-crafted words was absolutely electrifying. Radio news commentator Walter Winchell reported that thousands in the crowd were ready to nominate Roosevelt himself as president on the spot.

THE 1932 PRESIDENTIAL ELECTION

In 1932, Franklin D. Roosevelt was nominated by the Democratic National Convention for president of the United States. FDR, who liked traveling by train and ship, broke precedent and decided to fly with his entire crew to Chicago to give the acceptance speech. He had a desk brought onto the plane so that he could work on his speech. Ray Moley, his advisor and speech writer, had written a draft that was then worked on by another advisor, Samuel Rosenman.

FDR was not thrilled with the finished product and tried to draft a version himself, which did not go over that well with the boys. He was disappointed and ripped it up. When the speech was finally read over the phone to Louis Howe before going to the mimeographers for the press, Howe—who was jealous of the time FDR spent with Rosenman and Moley—exploded, "Mein Gawd, do I have to do everything myself?" He derided the draft as "chicken feed." Staying up all night, he wrote a new draft, which he handed to FDR upon arrival in Chicago.

"It's much better than the speech you've got now—and you can read it while you're driving down to the convention." FDR snapped, "Damn it Louie, I am the candidate." Still, in deference to his most ardent friend and supporter, he read Howe's draft as the car moved along, while tipping his hat, nodding, and smiling to the crowd of well-wishers along the way.

FDR liked something at the beginning of Howe's draft about "breaking foolish traditions." Yet he also liked the ending that Rosenman had put in there about "a new deal" and a "new order of competence and courage" that would rescue the economy and the forgotten men and women from poverty.

On his way to the podium, he smiled and made a slap-dash improvisational decision that would mark his presidency. He took the first page of Louis Howe's draft and placed it on top of the draft that Ray Moley and Sam Rosenman had written. Howe was content with the beginning: "Let it be from now on the task of our party to break foolish traditions..." And Moley and Rosenman content with the now famous ending: "I pledge you, I pledge myself, to a new deal for the American people. Let us all here assembled constitute ourselves prophets of a new order of competence and courage...Give me your help, not to win votes alone, but to win in this crusade to restore America to its own people."

The next day, a cartoon in *The New York World Telegram* showed Roosevelt's airplane flying over a destitute farmer looking up at the sky. Splashed across the wings were the words "New Deal." The phrase stuck, and soon took on a trajectory that changed the course of history.

THE WAR OF TWO WORLD VIEWS

America's election contest between the unpopular Republican incumbent Herbert Hoover and the popular and rising Democratic star Franklin D. Roosevelt would largely determine whether the democratic government in the United States would survive. The election of 1932 in the middle of the Great Depression was not just a clash of two candidates who had won the nomination of their parties but also a clash between two world views about the American government's social contract with its own people.

Herbert Hoover, an engineer by training, was a good man and a charitable man in his personal life. In his professional life, he believed that the president had a role to play in protecting and defending the freedoms guaranteed in the Constitution and in "promoting the general welfare" through sound economic monetary policies. Yet, he also believed that the government did not have a social contract to provide anyone a job or relief to the poor.

He made speeches about what a good job he was doing in restoring the economy through tax incentives to the rich and cutting back on government spending. His talks were loaded with mathematical formulas which showed that the number of people suffering from poverty was exaggerated by the news. Millions of Republican fliers openly jeered at the poor, accusing FDR of providing a free lunch for hoboes, transients, and relief clients who would not work.

In 1932, FDR campaigned on the promise of ending the Great Depression—and with a promise of a new deal that would restore "basic sanity" to the American system of government. While avoiding specifics, Roosevelt made it clear that his program for economic recovery would depend on the vast power of the federal government. He did, however, give clues of what might come. He spoke about the shaping of an economic bill of rights, the need for more purchasing power, and every man's right to life—and "this means he has the right to make a comfortable living."

Besides their policy differences, Hoover and Roosevelt's personal demeanors were in stark contrast. While Hoover remained grim and dour, Roosevelt was genial and exuded confidence. "Hoover was the status quo, FDR the symbol of hope." Even his campaign appearances were accompanied by the song "Happy Days Are Here Again."

The outcome of the election was an affirmation of an observation I have made many times. The great leaders of American history, the ones we celebrate and commemorate, who have a generosity of spirit, an open heart, and an outstretched hand—versus those who have no generosity of spirit, a cold heart, and a closed fist—win the presidential elections by a landslide.

FDR did exactly the opposite of what the 2020 incumbent in the White House did to win re-election. Instead of acting as a divider who split up the country into two armed camps and inciting his base of core supporters by demonizing the other side, FDR acted as a uniter who won the election by stressing the basic human goodness of all Americans, building bridges any place he could.

In what came to be called the "New Deal coalition," disparate groups such as Catholics, Jews, African Americans, Southern whites, labor union members, and small farmers united to comfortably elect Roosevelt to four terms in the White House.

During his first presidential race in 1932 with the Great Depression at its height, he defeated Herbert Hoover by an electoral vote tally of 472 to 59. He then vanquished Kansas Governor Alf Landon in 1936 (523 electoral votes to eight), businessman Wendell Willkie in 1940 (449 electoral votes to 82) and New York Governor Thomas Dewey in 1944 (432 electoral votes to 99), winning at least 53.4 percent of the popular vote each time.

FDR'S INAUGURATION

It was on a night nearly a century ago that President-elect Franklin Delano Roosevelt took an elevator from the Presidential Suite at the top of the Waldorf Astoria Hotel in New York City to a secret underground train platform—Track 61. With his family, friends, and aides, FDR boarded his private car, called "The Inauguration Special." As the train left the station for Washington,

D.C., FDR, who conveyed an outward image of supreme self-confidence, confided that he was indeed thrilled to have the job, yet he was accepting it with humility, not knowing if he was physically and emotionally strong enough to stand up to the challenge.

By the time the train pulled into Union Station in Washington, D.C., he had put those thoughts aside and was ready to plunge into the tumultuous first 100 days of his new administration. A visitor at the Mayflower Hotel had asked him the night before the inauguration if he felt that the task of bringing the American people out of the Great Depression was just too damned difficult. FDR answered, "Absolutely not!" He added jokingly, "if you spent two years in bed trying to wiggle your big toe, anything would seem easy."

March 4, 1933 was perhaps the Great Depression's darkest hour. The stock market had dropped like a rock eighty-five percent from its high in 1929, and nearly one-fourth of the workforce was unemployed. In the cities, jobless men were lining up at soup kitchens and bread lines. In rural areas, farmers whose land was being foreclosed on, were talking openly of revolution. The crowd that gathered in front of the Capitol that day to watch FDR's inauguration had all but given up on America. They were, a reporter observed, "as silent as a group of mourners around a grave."

Roosevelt's inaugural address was written with his admiration for Woodrow Wilson in mind. He remembered Wilson had said that the nation requires leaders who, recalling the nation's ideals, could speak and listen in a way that lifted people out of their everyday selves.

The speech struck the perfect pitch combination of idealism "this great nation with high ideals shall endure as it has endured, will revive, and will prosper", optimism "the only thing we have to fear is fear itself", consolation "the nation's problems thank God are only material things", and resolve "this nation calls for action, action, action now".

He won rave reviews. Even the hardheaded Republican Chicago Tribune lauded its "dominant note of courageous confidence." FDR had elevated the minds and hearts of the American people, and close to 500,000 of them wrote to him at the White House in the following week to express their gratitude.

Hours after the Inauguration, Roosevelt broke precedent in a more behind-the-curtains manner. He invited his Cabinet to join him in his White House office and asked Justice Benjamin Cardozo to have them take the oath of office as a team, which is the first time this had ever happened. FDR laughed and joked that he was doing it so they could "receive an extra day's pay." Yet the truth of the matter was that he wanted his team to get to work immediately.

A LEGENDARY SUCCESSFUL FIRST 100 DAYS: A RICHLY COLLABORATIVE ENDEAVOR

FDR spent his first night in the White House in sheer terror because he had promised to lead the American people out of the Great Depression, and he did not really have a 100-day plan. He said his strategy would be to experiment, to try one thing, and if that did not work, try something else. He told his son James that he had to find a way out of the Great Depression but feared perhaps he wasn't physically or mentally strong enough to do so.

Oliver Wendell Holmes, who had met FDR earlier in his career, said of him, "First rate temperament, second rate intellect." FDR may not have been a genius in the academic sense, but he proved to be a genius at tapping the best and brightest minds of his generation to come up with ideas that would help him reach his goals.

He had already assembled a "Brain Trust" to advise him during the campaign for the presidency. This group consisted of Rexford Tugwell, Raymond Moley, Adolph Berle, and others who began to help FDR translate his big idea "the president's job is to care" into an economic policy. This would involve both having the government step in to help those caught in the Great Depression through no fault of their own, and regulating big businesses' treatment of labor.

Now that he was president, he would expand his Brain Trust to go beyond the original group and bring in people who were more familiar with Washington, including the most talented senators and members of Congress. This also involved people who he had made a close connection with as governor of New York—the first female Secretary of Labor Frances Perkins, the Secretary of Commerce Harry Hopkins, and New York Senator Robert F. Wagner, all of whom were "progressives."

The legendary success of FDR's first 100 days was less the result of his presidential power or being a solo legislative genius, and more due to his richly collaborative relationship with the Senate.

Senator Robert Wagner told FDR, even before he was elected, that a group of Republican senators had been dreaming up ideas for a "New Deal" for a long time and were very proactive in trying to take them forward. FDR was eager to meet the group, and it didn't matter to him whether they were Democrats or Republicans. The group included not only Robert Wagner himself, but also Republican Senators Robert La Follette and George W. Norris.

FDR without the slightest hesitancy invited them all over to the White House for martinis and to brainstorm ideas for the New Deal. He personally mixed the martinis himself, and it was said that although they were not the kind of martinis you would have at the Willard Hotel, they were martinis. FDR would then throw out a problem like: How do we restore confidence and optimism? How do we put people back to work? How do we make sure home mortgages are not foreclosed on? As people started talking, FDR would draw them out, talking a lot less than he listened. And that team came through brilliantly.

In the next 100 days (105, but who is counting?), FDR's administration shepherded 15 major bills through Congress to restore the economy and create a new economic order. Professor Patrick Maney, a political and presidential historian, has pointed out that while FDR lifted the nation out of a state of doom and gloom with his inaugural speech, the vast majority of the New Deal legislation came not from FDR alone, but from his richly collaborative relationship with this progressive group of senators, who had been brainstorming such legislation for some time.

It was the most intense period of lawmaking ever undertaken by Congress — a "barrage of ideas and programs," historian Arthur Schlesinger Jr. observed, "unlike anything known to American history." "At the end of February," Walter Lippmann wrote that when the special session adjourned, "we were a congeries of disorderly panic-stricken mobs and factions. In the hundred days from March to June, we became again an organized nation confident of our power to provide for our own security and to control our own destiny."

Those hundred days were only the start of a process that ended in transforming American society. As Arthur Schlesinger Jr. put it, "Who can now imagine a day when America offered no Social Security, no unemployment compensation, no food stamps, no Federal guarantee of bank deposits, no Federal supervision of the stock market, no Federal protection for collective bargaining, no minimum wage, no Federal refinancing for home mortgages, no Federal commitment to high employment or to equal opportunity - in short, no Federal responsibility for Americans who found themselves, through no fault of their own, in economic or social distress?"

HUMAN CONNECTIONS

*FDR understood that a president's real power comes from
making deep human connections with the people.*

It is important to point out that FDR's new "Contract with America" was something based on his innate goodwill toward others, not just on Democratic partisanship or ideology. The famous British economist John Maynard Keynes emerged from a meeting with FDR in the transition period of his first presidency keenly disappointed by his complete lack of interest in economic theory. In their conversations, Roosevelt had lamented that it was not human progress for rich and poor to be looked at as variables of an economic theory or units in statistics.

FDR had a superb ability to make human connections during his first 100 days as president, even with people he did not know. The story is told that a soldier who went on a tour of the White House said to Frances Perkins, Secretary of Labor, that he felt like Roosevelt knew him, liked him, and wanted to help him.

One of his first orders as president was that if people called the White House looking for help, someone on his staff was to talk to them in a genuinely kindly manner and find some way to provide them assistance.

Once when FDR was driving in New Bedford, Massachusetts, a young girl suddenly broke through his secret service guard and rushed up with a note for FDR. When the police threw her back into the crowd, Roosevelt said, "Get the note from the girl." Her note read, "I wish you could do something to help us girls…We have been working at a sewing factory… and up to a few months ago, we were getting our minimum pay of $11 a week…Today, the 200 of us girls have been cut down to $4 and $5 and $6 a week." To a reporter's question, the president replied, "Something has to be done about the elimination of child labor and long hours and starvation wages." With the help of Labor Secretary Frances Perkins, he set in motion a process for doing exactly as the girl had asked.

On another occasion, after the establishment of the Civil Works Administration (CWA), which provided jobs for unemployed manual laborers, an artist who had gone to school with Roosevelt wrote to him and suggested he do the same with artists as well. And that launched the whole Federal Art Project. By the end of its first year, 5000 artists were employed, which later doubled, culminating in hundreds of thousands of artworks—sculptures, paintings, murals in public buildings—and inadvertently fostering some of Modern Art's most groundbreaking artists.

Years later, the painter Norman Rockwell is purported to have said that Roosevelt had almost no knowledge or judgment in painting and did not get much enjoyment out of going to art galleries or museums, but he had done more for artists than any president in the history of the country. Roosevelt told people that artists were very important people in society, talked about how enjoyable it was to have them around, and fed them when they were down.

After FDR's death, thousands of people called and wrote Eleanor Roosevelt saying that in the worst days of the Great Depression, they had called the White House to speak to FDR and, in many cases, were not only put through, but received immediate help.

Chapter Four

Build Your Own Team of Rivals

The most important thing you can do in your first
100 days is to build a team.

In 1860, Abraham Lincoln, a prairie lawyer, stunned the country by winning the Republican Party's nomination for president, assuring his election. Lincoln suddenly had to run one of the biggest countries in the world with no executive experience in managing anything larger than a small general store in Springfield, Illinois. He was also facing a nation-encumbering crisis over the great question of slavery. He wanted to hire the smartest and strongest people in the country, and so he turned to his rivals.

The nation was not only surprised by his election, but also equally surprised by the fact that he appointed his rivals to the Cabinet—the former governor of New York William Seward as Secretary of State, the former governor of Ohio Salmon Chase as Secretary of the Treasury, and a famous judge Edward Bates as Attorney General.

The rivalry did not stop with their appointment, however. As mentioned previously, William Seward thought himself infinitely more qualified than the president and maneuvered to push Lincoln into the background as a figurehead, believing that he (Seward) would be the real commander-in-chief, operating in the shadows and making all the decisions. It was one month into the term when Seward wrote his famous April 1ˢᵗ memorandum admonishing Lincoln for not making any policy advances and making his own recommendations. Lincoln did not strongly react to Seward. However, he did assert that the Cabinet could not do his job for him—he would seek their advice, but he alone made the policy.

During Lincoln's first 100 days, Seward and other Cabinet members conspired against the president and threatened to resign if they did not get their way. Lincoln cleverly parried these attempts and kept them on board by being gracious and forgiving, and not emotionally reacting to their disloyalty.

There was a great squabble at the outbreak of the Civil War about whether to rearm Fort Sumter, which was under siege by the South, with a threat of bombardment of Charleston Harbor. Lincoln chose to rearm the fort as a symbol of federal authority, while most of his Cabinet fiercely dissented.

Yet, he was able to win them over, not only through his magnanimous personality, but also his willingness to foster robust dialogue with lots of room for dissenting views, as well as the force of his arguments. The Cabinet members were impressed by how confident Lincoln was in his judgment, while humble in his demeanor. It was the turning point for accepting his authority as president.

There is a story about a visitor to the White House who attended a dinner with Lincoln and his Cabinet toward the end of the first 100 days. He asked the assembled group, "How are the President and the Cabinet getting along with each other?" Mr. Seward stood up, raised a glass of champagne, and said, "We are all Lincoln men." The rest of the Cabinet then stood up and raised their glasses. One of them said, "Three cheers for the President."

I tell the story about Lincoln in the interlude, but I believe it's worth mentioning again here in this chapter on teams because it contains so much value for any newly elected official, political appointee, or public manager.

HIRE EXCEPTIONAL PEOPLE

With the death of President Franklin D. Roosevelt on April 12, 1945, Vice President Harry S. Truman suddenly became president. He was so daunted by the immediate challenges he faced that he told reporters, "I feel that the moon, the stars, and the planets had fallen on me."

He would have to oversee the defeat of Nazi Germany and Japan, manage the US's leading role in the post-war, new world order, and guide the American economy's transition from making planes and bombs to making cars and suburban homes. He would also have to maintain the unity of a powerful but divided Democratic Party.

Yet Truman's most daunting task was following in the steps of his predecessor, a man who was already being called one of the greatest presidents in American history, a man who had ended the Great Depression with the New Deal, remade American governance, and ruled the Democratic Party during his unprecedented twelve years in office.

Being president in FDR's shadow would be a tall task for Truman, or any president for that matter. Truman lacked Roosevelt's stature, charisma, and public speaking skills. However, the new president did have other qualities that he could bring to bear. The public related well to Truman, thinking of him as honest and plain-spoken — "one of them". Truman also seemed to relish making politically difficult decisions. His extensive reading about the great leaders of history, his experience in Missouri politics, and his two terms in the Senate made him a good judge of people's character.

Truman's sudden rise to the most powerful job in the world left him little choice but to retain most of FDR's men in his Cabinet to maintain stability. Yet, the new president had little confidence in this group. By the spring of 1946, within less than one year in office, he had replaced many of those officials with men of his own choosing. As it turns out, Truman's appointees were largely undistinguished and would contribute little to his presidency. However, one Cabinet appointee would go on to be recognized as an exceptional person and leave a lasting legacy.

WHAT DOES AN EXCEPTIONAL PERSON LOOK LIKE?

"Get me the best in the world" -Arthur Blank,
Founder of Home Depot, instructing his HR on hiring.

After firing FDR's Secretary of State James F. Byrne when their relationship soured, Truman had to decide on a successor. The man for this job would have to be able to be a real leader who commanded respect in the United States and abroad. He would have to lead the European economic recovery, providing humanitarian aid to millions, as well as manage the bone-chilling prospect of the looming Cold War.

President Truman asked a few key Cabinet members and Clark Clifford, his most trusted advisor, to act as a selection committee in interviewing candidates. Truman was determined to appoint someone who had not only held a lot of big jobs and gained a lot of experience, but who was also truly an exceptional person who could make an impact, rather than someone who could just fulfill the function.

One of their meetings was with General George C. Marshall, who had previously been the Army Chief of Staff. Truman and his staff had done a "deep dive" on Marshall before the meeting, perhaps looking for the kind of anecdotal information that does not wind up on resumes, and found out he was an exceptional person.

As a cadet at Virginia Military Institute, Marshall was not only good in academics, but he also excelled at football and was always talking about playing as a team and making personal sacrifices. When he was a freshman, during the hazing period, an over-enthusiastic sophomore ran a bayonet right through Marshall's body. Marshall came near to dying in the hospital, but when he recovered, he never reported the sophomore. The sophomores, in gratitude for his silence, called off hazing for the rest of the year, and Cadet Marshall became the unquestioned leader of his class.

As a young officer during World War I, Marshall was mentored by the legendary General "Blackjack" Pershing. Marshall's brains and complete dedication to his boss's goals helped him become Pershing's most highly valued strategic planner. He was instrumental in the United States winning the Allied Hundred Days Offensive, which led Germany to call for an armistice.

When WWII rolled around, Marshall became the Army Chief of Staff, where he also excelled. Dwight D. Eisenhower, who was one of his assistants at the time, said in the meetings of the combined Chiefs of Staff, "He [Marshall] quickly established himself as the dominant figure. His vision was so clear, his grasp of complex issues so instinctive and precise, and his convictions so strong, that he was almost invariably the leader in discussions and in resultant decisions… his complete absorption in the task at hand was apparent to all."

Marshall was the Mastermind behind D-Day and the Allied Invasion of Normandy, and it was Dwight D. Eisenhower who executed it. British Prime Minister Winston Churchill would describe Marshall as the "Organizer of Victory." Truman would say of Marshall's role as Army Chief of Staff, "Millions of Americans gave their country outstanding service. George C. Marshall gave it victory."

Marshall was not just a man of toughness, but also of compassion. As the general in charge of burying fallen troops in Europe, he wrote, "The cost of war in human lives is constantly spread before me." He could see it "written neatly in the many ledgers, whose columns are gravestones." He could also see it firsthand in the gaunt faces of local citizenry whose homes had been bombed, jobs lost, and loved ones killed during the war. He advocated later, "The maintenance of large armies for an indefinite period is not a practical or a promising basis for policy. We must stand together strongly… find another solution."

In this story, what may be pertinent to you as a leader is that when Truman decided that General Marshall was the man he wanted to hire for the job, his Secretary of Defense, James Forestall, saw a potential problem and spoke up: "Mr. President," he said, "If you appoint George Marshall, in two or three months, people are going to start to say that he would make a better president than you."

President Truman's response showed that both confidence and humility are the necessary ingredients of great leadership. "He would make a better president. But I'm the president, and I want to have the best people possible around me." 6 He needed an exceptional leader for this role and was not threatened by hiring someone who might be smarter and stronger than he was.

Your ability as a new leader to make your vision a reality starts with hiring exceptional people in key roles and being unwilling to settle for less. I have told this story about Harry Truman and Marshall to give you a sense of the leadership commitment it takes to scour the earth for exceptional people, as well as a sense of what an exceptional person really looks like.

When selecting people for your "team of rivals," the proof is in the pudding. If you talk to five or ten people who previously worked with the person you are considering hiring, for example 'Joe' as your chief of staff, would they all unanimously say, "Yes, Joe is a really exceptional person," or would they say, politely, "Joe, well he is okay"?

A good question to keep in mind is not whether someone went to Harvard, held a job in the previous administration, or played a key role or was chief of the party in your state, but whether the person has a track record of doing something which made a difference that mattered. This will tell you whether that candidate is qualified to be more than just a good assistant and will back you up on most things. It will tell you whether the candidate is a real leader who, when given a responsibility, is likely to accomplish something that will leave a legacy for both of you.

If you look at the Truman presidency, one of the things that he is most remembered for is the Marshall Plan to bail out Europe. If you look at the Nixon presidency, the thing he is most remembered for, besides Watergate, was his partnership with Secretary of State Henry Kissinger in opening up China. The same is true on a state or city level. Michael Bloomberg's legacy as Mayor of New York was largely the result of getting the right team in place.

MAYOR BLOOMBERG'S TOP FIRST 100 DAYS' PRIORITY: ASSEMBLE THE STRONGEST POSSIBLE TEAM

Most people in leadership roles play on one stage. Michael Bloomberg has played on three: CEO of a Fortune 500 company, three-term mayor of New York City, and former presidential candidate. Michael Bloomberg, like most leaders, is not a perfect human being. He mispronounces words, laughs at his own self-deprecating jokes, as if he is trying to please his mother who says he's too cocky, and has been accused of making sexist jokes that women find offensive. That said, his extraordinary ascent as a leader and team builder makes a great story which anyone in their first (or "next") 100 days can learn from.

Michael Bloomberg is an entrepreneur whose innovations in business, in city government, in climate change, and in philanthropy have made him a global leader on many of the issues America and the rest of the world are facing.

What is the secret of Michael Bloomberg's leadership DNA code? One clue is that, while growing up in a Jewish working-class family in Medford, Massachusetts, he read a story about a visit Ralph Waldo Emerson paid to John Quincy Adams in his later years. Emerson asked Adams how he thought the country was doing. Adams said, "I would by God that there was more ambition in the country...the laudable kind, ambition to excel." From that point on, Bloomberg excelled at almost everything he did.

As a 12-year-old, he became one of the youngest Eagle Scouts in history. To help pay his way through Johns Hopkins University, he worked in a parking lot, running to fetch cars rather than walking, and took out government loans. After college, he attended Harvard Business School and in 1966 was hired by the financial service firm Salomon Brothers for an entry-level job.

Bloomberg rose through the ranks at Salomon, overseeing equity trading and sales before being tapped to head the firm's information systems. When Salomon was acquired in 1981, Bloomberg was fired because he was "too independent a thinker." Rather than find this a reason to be depressed, he looked at it as an exciting opportunity. According to Bloomberg, "getting fired was the best thing that ever happened to me because it gave me the opportunity to try something else." The next day he got the idea for a technology company that would bring greater transparency and fairness to the financial system. He launched a small start-up in a one-room office.

Bloomberg spent the next twenty years as CEO of his global firm and amassed a personal fortune of $50 billion. One secret to his success was building a strong leadership team and replacing private offices with a situation-room-like atmosphere that was much less a hierarchy than an idea meritocracy with a free exchange of ideas. Today, his company is still immensely profitable and employs some 20,000 people in 120 countries.

By the late 1990s, feeling professionally restless, the billionaire businessman told friends that four jobs on earth could tempt him away from his company: president of the United States, secretary-general of the United Nations, president of the World Bank, and mayor of New York.

But Bloomberg realized that who we select for president of the United States is important, but that person's power is limited due to constitutional checks and balances and unhealthy competition between parties. Further, he began to have an intuitive sense that the national economy no longer really exists, there is only a global economy and a constellation of regional economies with major cities, like New York, at its core.

When he first started sending out trial balloons about becoming mayor, no one took him seriously. Said one pundit, "kinda goofy." Said another, "There is no leap of logic whatsoever, that could make Michael Bloomberg New York's next mayor."

Then-mayor Rudy Giuliani agreed with the pundits. "You're going to lose," he told Bloomberg flatly during a meeting at the mayoral residence, Gracie Mansion. "The city is weary of a Republican mayor like me and will look for more of a liberal Democrat." The warning was of no use. Bloomberg ran as a Republican in a Democratic town, only weeks after the 2001 September 11th disaster where 3000 people died. New Yorkers were looking for a proven chief executive and leader who could restore shattered public confidence and reinvigorate the city and its economy.

Mike Bloomberg won the election, and over the next twelve years, the ungovernable was governable. Instead of just dining at his house on East Seventy-ninth Street with his billionaire friends or clinking glasses with celebrities at charity functions in the garden at the Museum of Modern Art, he did many of the things most New Yorkers do. He took walks in Central Park and rode the subway to work without heavy security, so people could get close to him.

> *I do not have anything in common with the people who stand on escalators. Why would you want to waste your time? You have an eternity to rest when you die. -Michael Bloomberg*

SUCCESS DOES NOT BEGIN WITH STRATEGIC PLANS OR POLICIES; IT BEGINS WITH PEOPLE

Mr. Bloomberg, on his 100th day as mayor, spoke to the New York City Partnership and Chamber of Commerce on the same floor at Goldman Sachs where he labored for many years. He told the thousand or so executives who cheered when he entered the room that he had spent his first three months doing something seemingly underwhelming.

Bloomberg said that success did not begin with strategic plans or goals, it began with people in both the public and private sectors. "Ever since FDR, reporters like to write stories about what a new president or governor or mayor got done during his or her first 100 days in office. I was no exception. Leading up to my 100th day, the press asked me: 'What have you accomplished so far?'"

Most elected officials use it as an opportunity to release a laundry list of things that the media duly covers. "I had a different answer." Bloomberg said, "We built a team." Reporters replied, "Yeah, we know that. But what have you done?" Bloomberg replied, "We built a team."

He said that they kept asking him the same question, and he kept giving the same answer. They could not understand why he thought that this was a great accomplishment. But from his time in business, Bloomberg knew that the single most important element of success is assembling the strongest possible team: smart, driven, creative, and effective managers who are capable of building out their own strong teams.

According to Bloomberg, "Great leaders understand that great achievements are never accomplished alone. They share credit when the team succeeds, and accept responsibility when things fall short. They get rid of 'I' and 'me' and replace them with 'we' and 'us'. They find the smartest people and do whatever they can to hire them. You want the very best playing on your team. If not, they may wind up playing against you."

Bloomberg also offers some advice for new leaders of an incoming administration that is pertinent to building an 'A' team. Don't just hire people based on your gut instinct, jobs held, or friendships, he advises, but hire a search firm to make a 360-leadership assessment of the leaders you are intending to hire. Then you hire a chief of staff who can help you fill those roles with great people.

He says new leaders need to think in terms of both staffing to make the vision a reality and staffing for stability. It is important to select exceptional people for your cabinet or immediate team of direct reports who have the right stuff to drive your strategy of hope and change.

Bloomberg set about his vision of hope and change, "transforming" the city of New York by hiring former CEO Dan Doctoroff as his deputy mayor and Amanda Burden as the City Planning Commissioner. He asked Doctoroff to focus on redeveloping Ground Zero after the 911 disaster. He also asked him to focus on redeveloping the neglected areas of the city with his Five-Borough Economic Opportunity Plan that focused on educational programs and tax incentives designed to help create new jobs and attract companies. It is believed these policies helped to create 300,000 jobs, many of them high-tech related, as well as jobs on the middle and lower end of the spectrum.

Doctoroff, like Bloomberg, had an incredible work ethic and oversaw 289 separate projects and initiatives, including the rezoning of 6,000 city blocks and the creation of 130 million square feet of residential and commercial space, and 2,400 acres of new parks. He found many city-owned abandoned properties along the city's waterfront and turned them into habitable spaces.

Bloomberg and his team also celebrated the progress in mid-Manhattan, but he described the transformation of Lower Manhattan as "an enormous team effort," one that depended upon "city, state, and federal governments working collaboratively, investing together, and forming partnerships with the private sector."

HIRE EXCEPTIONAL PEOPLE FOR EVERY KEY ROLE

You want people on your team who stand out from the crowd like a ton of diamonds. They are often what Bill Campbell, the Secret CEO Whisperer of Silicon Valley, called "aberrant geniuses," who invent the next great thing, yet who are willing to make the sacrifices and are capable of playing as a team. As CEO friend Greg Goff of Andeavor, a Fortune 50 company, told me, "You want people in both business and government who are disruptors not just adaptors."

While I was coaching John Young when he was the Assistant Secretary of Defense in Acquisitions with an annual budget of $350 billion for new weapons programs, he said "I want people to be willing to run the Pentagon like a business." That meant delivering weapons systems that were on time and under budget.

KEEP THESE QUESTIONS IN MIND WHEN HIRING PEOPLE FOR YOUR STAFF OR ADMINISTRATION:

- *Character is destiny.* Does the candidate have a reputation that combines commitment, loyalty, and doing the right thing?
- *EQ (emotional intelligence quotient) is more important than IQ.* Does the person not only have brains, but also the skills and attitudes needed to establish positive relationships?
- *Talk back to the boss.* Is this person a sycophant or can you count on them to be candid with you?
- *Drive.* Does the person have a track record of making vision a reality and being relentless in the pursuit of goals?
- *Decisiveness.* Is the person a real leader or just a good assistant? Can they make a final decision without talking to you?

GUIDING PRINCIPLES FOR BUILDING A HIGH-PERFORMANCE TEAM

1. IT TAKES A COMBINATION OF GOOD CHARACTER AND GOOD TEMPERAMENT TO GET PEOPLE ON YOUR TEAM TO FOLLOW YOU.

Everyone knows Abraham Lincoln had good character, which is why he believed slavery was an abomination. Yet, what made his brand of leadership so ingratiating to the members of his "team of rivals" was his extraordinarily good temperament. He would often write letters at night to members of his team who were sometimes disloyal, just to blow off steam, then leave them in his desk, unsent and unsigned.

2. GROUND YOUR WORK IN A SHARED PURPOSE.

It is a leader's job to create a shared purpose that elevates people above their everyday selves and is not just a plaque on the wall. Set an ennobling purpose that everyone is genuinely committed to and believes in one hundred percent. Bloomberg said that what allowed him to build up an extraordinary track record of accomplishment as mayor was the shared purpose of "transforming New York", which came down to helping individuals change their lives for the better. He was able to get people from politics, business, and labor unions to put aside their desires for private gain and work toward a common cause.

3. COME UP WITH A LIST OF SHARED GUIDING PRINCIPLES WITH YOUR TEAM.

Principles, says Ray Dali of Bridgewater Associates, are stress-tested recipes for success that can be used to set expectations for the team. There can be hundreds of principles for building a winning team, but here are a few that I have found to be highly reliable. It is a good idea for newly elected officials, political appointees, and public managers to sit down with their group and create their own list of guiding principles that build on this list.

Here is a list for starters:

- *Character is destiny.* Developing strong character includes integrity, honesty, doing the right thing, hard work.
- *"To care for the general welfare."* As it says in the Constitution, your job is to put serving the public interest above serving private interests or partisan affiliations.
- *Think backward from your vision.* Start with the vision and think backward to a strategy and implementation.
- *Show respect for hierarchy but create an idea meritocracy.* Good ideas can come from anywhere.

- *Constructive and challenging debate.* Treat everyone as a colleague. It is okay to disagree. Build shared understanding that leads to something new.
- *Radical open-mindedness.* It is important to find the courage to stare down government orthodoxies and be open to wild ideas.
- *Radical transparency.* The only way to make good decisions is to have complete transparency of information.

Harry S. Truman: Transformation in Office

Onboarding involves helping a new leader learn a new job and integrate into the politics and culture of the organization so they can be successful.

At one o'clock in the afternoon of April 12, 1945, Franklin Delano Roosevelt was relaxing in a chair near the fireplace at his cottage in Warm Springs, Georgia, reading the newspaper and composing a few letters. His cottage, referred to by reporters as the "Little White House," was perched atop Pine Mountain and had often been a welcome respite for Roosevelt over the past twelve years in office.

Roosevelt was in high spirits, despite a period of ill health and, a few weeks earlier, a bout of grueling negotiations at the Yalta Conference where the end of World War II had been mapped out. He was surrounded by several cousins, an artist named Elizabeth Shoumatoff who was painting his portrait, and his mistress, Lucy Mercer Rutherfurd—the one person most responsible for his good mood.

When Franklin's head drooped forward and he seemed unable to raise it, his cousin thought he might have dropped one of his ever-present cigarettes. She asked if there was something wrong. He raised his hand to touch his head and whispered, "I have a terrific pain in the back of my head." Those were the eloquent Franklin Roosevelt's final words. The president died just under 100 days into his fourth term.

"JESUS CHRIST AND GENERAL JACKSON"

Back in the Capitol, the afternoon was gray outside and the light fading as Vice President Harry S. Truman arrived close to 5:00 p.m. at House Speaker Sam Rayburn's private hideaway on the ground floor of the Capitol Building in a room jokingly known as the "Board of Education." After a day of work in the Senate, Truman was about to mix himself a drink of bourbon and water and enjoy a game of cards, when he was given a message to call Steve Early, the White House Press Secretary.

First he made the drink and then telephoned Early who told him to "come to the White House as quickly and as quietly as you can." "Jesus Christ and General Jackson!" Truman muttered as he put down the phone, color draining from his face.

Truman realized something important was up, so he ran to the Senate side of the Capitol to get his hat. He rushed through the marble halls with senators, congressmen, and Capitol Hill guards gawking at him as his pounding feet and wingtip shoes made a thunderous noise.

He got into the black Mercury limousine that had been waiting for him, unguarded by any Secret Service detail, wondering what was going on. When he got to the White House, he took the elevator to the second floor where he was met by Eleanor Roosevelt. "Harry," she said, "the President is dead." In a poignant moment that revealed Truman's character, he asked, "Is there anything I can do for you?" He said nothing about how this historic turn of events would impact him.

Eleanor Roosevelt leveled her gaze at him and said, "No Harry, is there anything we can do for you? You're the one who's in trouble now." Truman, often called the "accidental president", was sworn in two hours later. Speaking to reporters the next day, Truman expressed how he felt, "Boys, last night after I heard about the President's death, I felt like a Missouri farmer who just had a bale of hay dropped on my head." Later he remarked, "We have lost a hard-hitting chief and an old friend of the services. Our hearts are heavy. However, the cause which claimed Roosevelt, also claimed us. He never faltered—nor will we."

Curiously, Truman had nothing in his background, nothing in his education, and nothing in his job experience that remotely qualified him for the job. He had never been to college, never managed anything bigger than a haberdashery shop in Independence, Missouri, and never made enough money to own his own home.

He was a product of the Missouri political machine. Tom Pendergast, the Democratic Party boss who controlled Kansas City, liked Harry's plain speaking and helped him get elected as a Jackson County Court judge, an administrative role which launched his political career. Harry Truman demonstrated his commitment and loyalty to Pendergast and performed well in the job. As a result, the "Democratic organization" as he called it, placed his name on the ballot for national office, and he won the U.S. Senate seat.

Not many years after that, this obscure senator from Missouri became president of the United States, thrown into making world-shaking decisions. The story of Truman's first 100 days is often a "eureka" moment for almost any newly elected (or appointed) official who stumbles across it. It is a story of leadership transformation while in office.

THE ACCIDENTAL PRESIDENT

FDR had chosen Truman as vice president at his staff's suggestion, almost like a man chosen randomly off the street. His comment was "I hardly know Truman." But he went along with the idea. Roosevelt, who played things close to the vest and was often devious, kept Cabinet meetings to cheery, light banter and preferred meeting with people one-on-one. He had met with Harry Truman only twice since taking office for his fourth term, discussed nothing of substance, and did nothing that would help him to onboard into the office of the president, should that be required.

Harry Truman greatly admired FDR but deplored how he treated his vice presidents. He once commented that FDR acted like he was nothing more than a messenger boy to the Senate. Bess Truman, Harry's devoted wife, was deeply resentful of FDR's attitude toward Harry. She believed Roosevelt was aware of his own failing health and that not preparing Harry to onboard into his new job was the "equivalent of dereliction of duty."

On the way out of the brief Cabinet meeting at the White House that fateful first day as president, Secretary of War Harold Stimson pulled Truman aside to tell him about a secret project—a "new explosive of almost unbelievable destructive power." Truman was stunned that he had been kept in the dark about the Manhattan Project and the atomic bomb until then. Truman appreciated Stimson's nuanced briefings on the bomb, understanding that it would cause grave losses to the Japanese, but speed up ending the war, save American lives, and help dictate the terms of peace. It was not long before Truman was required to make the decision indicating approval.

SHOEHORNING HISTORY INTO 100 DAYS

The dramatic pulse-pounding first four months of Truman's presidency saw the collapse of Nazi Germany, Hitler's suicide in his bunker, the founding of the United Nations, the decision to bomb Hiroshima and Nagasaki, the execution of Benito Mussolini, the dawn of the Cold War and beginning of the nuclear arms race, as well as the Potsdam Conference, which led to the post-World War II economic boom. "Never had fate shoehorned so much history in such a short period."

J. B. West, the White House Chief Usher who served five presidents, wrote in the book *Upstairs at the White House* that Truman and his family "were the closest family I have ever seen in the White House." Truman would leave his office at 5 p.m. and join his family every night on the second floor around the dinner table. There the family would tell stories, make jokes, and play cards. West remarked that you can tell a lot about a man by the way he treats women, and it was clear that for Harry Truman, his wife Bess and daughter Margaret were the most important people in his life.

One time when Truman was at a Washington gathering, he started to play the song "Stardust Memories" on the piano, which he was good at. Suddenly, the glamorous actress Lauren Bacall jumped up on the piano and started to sing the song. Harry kept playing but was shy and embarrassed. When he got home the next day and the story was in the newspapers, Bess Truman was furious and told him, "Harry, you should play the piano in public no more."

Truman's name became associated with the campaign motto "give 'em hell Harry," due to his no BS, irreverent, and direct manner of speaking. In truth, Harry was mostly very kindly and never "gave anyone hell" during his time in office, except on one occasion where a reviewer from the Washington Post panned his daughter's singing performance at Constitution Hall. Harry wrote a letter to the reporter and said, "Someday I hope to meet you. When that happens, you'll need a new nose, a lot of beefsteak for black eyes, and perhaps a supporter below!" Instead of the public berating Harry for this, they loved it!

The question is, how did Harry S. Truman, with little preparation to be president and little help in onboarding into his new role, come to be what historians consider a great or nearly great president, and what can you learn from this?

A MAN OF CHARACTER AND PERSONAL VIRTUES

Born and raised in Independence, Missouri, Truman believed in the plain and simple Midwestern principles and virtues that he was immersed in as he grew up. The fabric of a man is demonstrated by his personal virtues. Truman was a man of character, a man of integrity, a man who spoke the truth. He said he was "constituted" to be plain-speaking, to do the right thing, to take responsibility for helping his neighbors, and he translated those virtues into simple principles that defined his presidency: "Progress occurs when leaders seize the opportunity to change things for the better," and "If you don't like the heat, get out of the kitchen."

Truman was also known for his humility. Unlike many leaders, he never fell into the trap of mistaking himself for the institution or being seduced by power. He said, "When you get to be president, there are all those things, the honors, the twenty-one-gun salutes, all those things. You have to remember it isn't for you. It's for the Presidency." Yet, according to his daughter Margaret Truman, this practice of humility never meant that Truman downgraded his work or his accomplishments in his own mind.

GREAT LEADERS ARE READERS

As a child, Truman had poor eyesight, wore glasses as thick as old Coke bottles, and once called himself a sissy who was much less interested in playing sports than reading history books. He was fascinated with the Founding Fathers and kept a copy of the Constitution in his back pocket throughout his presidency. He often referred to the Federalist Papers, which had been written by Alexander Hamilton, James Madison, and John Jay to explain and defend the new Constitution.

He not only read books about our greatest presidents but also read the books they read, such as "Plutarch's Lives." He read about the Roman generals Cincinnatus and Cicero in Latin for fun. He wrote in later years of his affinity for the ideals of Cincinnatus, the gentleman farmer who was one day asked to become a general in the Roman army and then proceeded to lead his people to victory. Cincinnatus, like George Washington centuries later, knew when and how to lay down his great powers and return to the humble life of the plow.

Truman said that one of the principles of a democracy was that any day a citizen might be called upon to serve their country by taking a position of great power and assuming office, only to then return to the humble life they had come from. Of Independence, Missouri, he said: "This is where I am from, this is what shaped my decisions as president, and this is where I will return."

During his time in office, he was able to draw many lessons from great leaders of history and how they dealt with specific situations. He studied how President Washington convinced his divided Cabinet to buy into the idea of a strong presidency and strong Federal Government, how Lincoln pressured congressmen to pass the Fourteenth Amendment saying, "I am your president, and I will have your vote," and how Teddy Roosevelt stretched his presidential powers to personally intervene in a massive coal strike that was paralyzing the nation.

One of the things that stood out from his study of great leaders is that they were extraordinarily self-disciplined, and he was determined to be that way as well. He lived by the code "The buck stops here."

Truman was one of the most decisive presidents, making decisions in his first 100 days in which there was no clear right or wrong. He made the decision to drop the atomic bomb in minutes, based on Stimson's recommendation that it was the "least abhorrent choice." He also decided without hesitation to go forward with the Marshall Plan to rescue and rebuild Europe after WWII, even though it would cost billions in today's money. Winston Churchill, upon seeing the Marshall Plan for the first time, said that Truman was a man of exceptional character.

ELEANOR AND HARRY—A MENTORING RELATIONSHIP

Many people who admire and respect Harry Truman may not know that the thing which most helped him with his own onboarding process was that he was receptive to coaching and mentoring. This came from the former president's wife, Eleanor Roosevelt, who had been her husband's thinking partner and sounding board for years. She would provide Truman the wise, situation-specific, nuanced advice about being president that one could never find in a textbook, especially in the first 100 days. She wrote to Truman during his first weeks in office and beyond.

Eleanor liked Truman but knew he would need help in stepping up to the job. "His family is gone [back to Missouri]," she reported to a friend after a White House luncheon. "I am sorry for him and he tries so hard," adding that she "wanted to do all she could to help." Truman knew so little about foreign policy, Eleanor told another friend, that she almost felt like crying. "I was appalled at how little he knew."

Truman knew that if he was to win acceptance as FDR's heir, he needed to please one person beyond all others: Eleanor Roosevelt. Truman did not approve of everything she did, as she was a controversial figure, but he appreciated her advice, listening closely to everything she had to say. One of her first acts of providing counsel was to send a possession that had long been on her husband's desk, a little Democratic donkey.

She told him the poor donkey represented standing up for democratic ideals, such as taking care of the forgotten man or woman. However, she added: "He looks a bit obstinate, as Franklin said he needed a reminder sometimes that his decisions had to be final and taken with a sense that God would give guidance to a humble beast. Once having decided something, the obstinate little donkey kept his sense of humor and determination, going against great pressure."

Truman wanted to carry on the Roosevelt legacy, yet still wanted his own team. In the first hundred days of his administration, Truman replaced two-thirds of the Roosevelt Cabinet. Eleanor, who did not always agree with her husband's selections, gave Truman mixed reviews on his appointments, and made suggestions which were accepted.

He confided to her during his first 100 days that "dealing with Winston Churchill is almost as challenging as dealing with Stalin or Mao Tse-Tung." She offered advice on how FDR dealt with these and other men in foreign affairs. She told him it was all about creating a friendly, informal, personal relationship with them, getting rid of that stiff atmosphere that usually exists between heads of state.

Eleanor Roosevelt also advised him on how, as president, he could effectively legislate with members of Congress based on her husband's example. She told him that he could create pull by going before the American people and leading a moral crusade on one of the greater issues of the day. She told him that he could make progress by picking up the phone and calling members of Congress, who would be stunned just to get a call from the president in the middle of their day.

She advised him at one point that it was time to get off his moral high horse and strike some backroom deals. She explained to him that FDR got most of his New Deal passed in Congress by withholding hiring thousands of political appointees from the congressmen's respective states until they went along with it.

LEADERSHIP TRANSFORMATION IN OFFICE

One of the most interesting stories of Truman is the one that reveals his transformation in office. Like all presidents and politicians, Truman was not a perfect human being: he had many faults and flaws. As mentioned, Truman was steeped in the Midwest virtues that shaped his character, yet he was also a product of the spirit, the era, the climate of his times, when racism was rarely examined or called into question. Born in the border state of Missouri in 1885 not long after the Civil War, he learned to "share the South's view of the War Between the States" and "acquired an abiding belief in white supremacy." His parents, according to Truman, were "a violently unreconstructed Southern family and Lincoln haters."

To understand what life was like in this era, when Truman got to the White House, his mother told him that in no uncertain terms would she sleep in the Lincoln bedroom and that she would sleep on the floor instead. So confident were the Southern Democrats that Truman was one of them, on the funeral train that carried FDR's body, one senator from South Carolina told a Southern friend, "Everything's going to be all right—the new President knows how to handle the n----s."

Yet at the same time, Truman was intensely loyal to the Constitution and the Union. His reading of history and of such documents as the Declaration of Independence, the Constitution and Bill of Rights led him to begin to question the assumptions on which he was raised. Through self-education and despite his family background and Confederate lineage, Truman even grew to cherish the Great Emancipator.

Truman once reflected, "It took me a while to realize what a good man Lincoln really was, with a great brain and even greater heart, and he educated himself to the point where he knew how government should work and tried his best to make ours work that way." Still, it was not uncommon for Truman to offhandedly use racial slurs, which showed up in many of his private conversations and correspondence.

A defining moment for Truman, however, was when he learned that an African American WWII soldier returning from Europe to South Carolina was taken off a train, beaten, and blinded with a hot poker. Truman was shaken to the core. "Whatever my inclinations as a native of Missouri might have been, as President I know this is bad. I shall fight to end evils like this." According to historian and author Kari Frederickson, "Truman had a special feeling for soldiers, and from that point on, he took a different track."

Truman formed the President's Committee on Civil Rights, which issued a historic report condemning all forms of segregation and asking for an end to discrimination and segregation in the armed services. As the first president to address the National Association for the Advancement of Colored People (NAACP), Truman gave a speech at the Lincoln Memorial: "It is my deep conviction that we have reached a turning point in the long history of our country's efforts to guarantee freedom and equality to all of our citizens."

"As Americans," Truman said, "we believe that every man should be free to live his life as he wishes... If this freedom is to be more than a dream, each man must be guaranteed equality of opportunity. The only limit to an American's achievement should be his ability, his industry and his character." Truman emphasized in the speech: "When I say all Americans, I mean all Americans."

Before making the speech, knowing that his family would not approve, he had written his sister saying that he believed in civil rights and would not be swayed. "Mamma won't like what I say because I wind up by quoting old Abe. But I believe what I say and I'm hopeful we may implement it."

Truman's evolving views on civil rights during his first term deeply divided the Democratic Party, with several Conservative Southern Democrats walking out of the 1948 Democratic National Convention. There was a fury in their rhetoric. The chairman of the Democratic committee wired Truman: "I really believe you have ruined the Democratic Party in the South," and a Baptist minister threatened, "If that report is carried out, you won't be elected dogcatcher in 1948." A Georgian senator said they had been "kicked in the teeth" by Truman and another declared that "all true Democrats" found the President's program "obnoxious, repugnant, odious, detestable, loathsome, repulsive, revolting, and humiliating."

Yet Truman was undeterred. On July 26, 1948, he signed two executive orders: one calling for the desegregation of the U.S. Armed Forces and the second forbidding discrimination in the federal civil services. Since the American Revolution, African Americans had served almost separately from white soldiers. Although it took six years after the signing of the orders to finally desegregate the military, the order became a model for the desegregation of the southern states and equal opportunities for African Americans. It also marked the first time a president had issued an Executive Order to impact civil rights policy.

Fifty years later, Colin Powell, who became the first African American Secretary of State, spoke about the impact of Truman's Executive Order: "The military was the only institution in all of America—because of Harry Truman—where a young Black kid, now 21 years old, could dream the dream he dared not think about at age 11. It was the one place where the only thing that counted was courage, where the color of your guts and the color of your blood was more important than the color of your skin."

Dr. Philleo Nash, an adviser to Truman, said of him, "He was a man of his generation, of his region, of his background and he moved with the times and literally learned in the job. And when the time came, he did what was right."

Chapter Five

Your First "Next" 100-Day Plan

Plans are worthless; planning is everything. -Dwight D. Eisenhower

In 2009, George W. Bush and Barack Obama walked side by side through the stately gold curtains of the Capitol Building's portico doors toward the inauguration platform. Bush leaned closer, almost as if he wanted to whisper in his ear. Obama said, "I didn't really know if he wanted to say something or what he really wanted to do was give me a punch in the mouth due to some of the stuff we had been saying about his administration." Instead, Bush put his arm around President-elect Obama, smiled warmly, and said, "Get ready for the ride of your life. And you'd better enjoy every minute of it because it goes by a lot faster than you think."

It is impossible to know how one presidency ends and another begins. Yet, as Martin Luther King once said, regardless of who is president, "the arc of the moral universe is long, but it bends toward justice." Obama said something that day that could have been said by George W. Bush or any president in the history of our Republic: "The time has come to reaffirm our enduring spirit; to choose our better history; to carry forward that precious gift, that noble idea passed on from generation to generation: the God-given promise that all are equal, all are free, and all deserve a chance to pursue their full measure of happiness."

Robert Caro, LBJ historian, summed up the poignancy of the moment well: "Abraham Lincoln struck off the chains of black Americans, but it was Lyndon Johnson who led them into voting booths, closed democracy's sacred curtain behind them, placed their hands on the lever that gave them a hold on their own destiny, made them, at last and forever, a true part of American political life." And it was just about 50 years later, "a mere blink of history's eye," that Barack Obama, an African American with a Muslim name, sat down behind the desk of the Oval Office. He found a letter from the former president, with advice that would be meaningful to the passing of the baton between any two leaders in office—whether in the nation's capital, the states' capitals, or city halls.

"There will be trying moments," Bush wrote. "The critics will rage. Your 'friends' will disappoint you. But you will have an Almighty God to comfort you, a family who loves you, and a country that is pulling for you, including me. No matter what comes, you will be inspired by the character and compassion of the people you now lead."

It is the morning after Barack Obama's inauguration. He strolls out of the Oval Office to his private dining room where he meets his Chief of Staff, Rahm Emanuel, for a tête-à-tête. Overlooking the room is a large painting of Lincoln's War Council, called "The Peacemakers." It was painted by George P. A. Healey with a suggestive rainbow shining above Lincoln's shoulder which seems to visually evoke the discussion that is starting to take place.

There is a bust of Franklin D. Roosevelt on one table and one of John F. Kennedy on another. There are some personal mementos, a poster of Martin Luther King Jr., a Life Magazine photo of the March on Selma, as well as a pair of Mohammed Ali's boxing gloves.

Obama and Emanuel sit at the table laden with freshly baked blueberry scones and whipped creamery butter. Obama, the first president in recent memory with a flat stomach and iron dietary discipline, will not be eating any of that. He grabs his favorite snack, three roasted almonds, instead. Unfazed, Emanuel picks up one of the scones and puts it on his plate.

Obama, like our greatest presidents, had a sense of history and was concerned about how his administration would be regarded by history. He leans toward Emanuel and explains that he wants to be a great president and earn the reputation of a transforming leader who brought about an enduring change that helped the American people be better off. He does not just want to be known as a transactional leader who made tradeoffs to win an election, stood his watch, but did not have any long-term vision or goals.

President Obama wanted to deliver on his grand campaign promise of "Change We Can Believe In." He told Emanuel that on election eve, when it dawned on him that he was really going to win, he started to think about his first 100-day plan. He asked himself what singular piece of transformational legislation he could get through Congress in his first 100 days. Then he had an epiphany.

He was going to push for a major national healthcare bill that would help millions of people who were one or two major illnesses away from financial ruin. For him, it was a deeply personal issue, not just a moral one. Before his mother, who was devoted to him, passed away from breast cancer at the age of fifty-three, he had struggled to help her pay the medical bills and get proper treatment.

Emanuel listened empathetically, like a good chief of staff and best friend, but his emotions already were running strong. He signaled his concerns with a nod and a wistful smile. "Other presidents have tried to do healthcare and fallen flat on their face," he argued. Obama had campaigned on the economy and the environment, not healthcare.

Obama met with Vice President Biden, Emanuel, and his other advisors later that day and told them about his plan. They all warned him about the political fallout from starting with healthcare. Emanuel had a sixth sense that, while it might be doable with the Democratic majority in the House and Senate, it could get him in trouble. "I begged him not to do it." 6 Obama listened, saying he realized it could drive down his numbers in the popularity polls by fifteen percent, but then he laughed and said, "I'm feeling lucky."

DO I REALLY NEED A 100-DAY PLAN?

Ever since Franklin Roosevelt coined the term "first 100 days" in the election of 1933 with a promise to end the Great Depression with his New Deal legislation, the first 100 days has become a yardstick of a president's accomplishments and a bellwether of future success. However, today the "first 100 days" has become a mantra that is not only used by presidents, but also by governors, mayors, and candidates of every description.

Dwight D. Eisenhower, who as a WWII general was instrumental in planning and executing the D-Day invasion, is often quoted as saying that "plans are worthless, planning is everything." When he became president in 1951, he explained his thoughts about his own first 100-day plan which you may benefit from.

The details of a 100-day plan designed in advance are often incorrect, but as Ike pointed out, it is the planning process that is valuable. "The planning process demands the thorough exploration of all options and contingencies. The knowledge gained during this probing is crucial to the selection of appropriate actions as future events unfold."

Ike also said that it is good for a new leader to already have a strategic plan, if you suddenly find yourself dealing with an unexpected crisis, like the 2008 economic crash or the Covid-19 pandemic. His advice: "The first thing you do is to take all the plans off the top shelf and throw them out the window and start once more. But if you haven't been planning, you can't start to work, intelligently at least."

Ike reasoned that the importance of planning is "to keep yourselves steeped in the character of the problem that you may one day be called upon to solve or help solve." Professor Henry Mintzberg from McGill University business school says that it is not enough to have an "intended" 100-day plan and strategy. You must be prepared to have an "emergent" 100-day plan and strategy as intentions and reality collide.

When President Kennedy was elected, someone handed him a speech which mentioned his 100-day plan, asking him to fill in the blank. Kennedy scratched the line out, saying that he did not want to be held to that mark, and scribbled in 1000 days. Ironically, Kennedy, despite his inspiring "Ask not…" speech, did not have a first 100-day plan, nor did he rack up a single foreign policy accomplishment or legislative victory during this period or even beyond. Today, the only thing his first 100 days is remembered for is the disastrous and humiliating Bay of Pigs invasion.

THE CONCEPT OF THE FIRST 100-DAY PLAN IS TAKING HOLD

In 2020, I created a Google alert "first 100 days in politics and government" and began to notice a deluge of articles in my newsfeed every day. It seemed that for presidents, governors, mayors, political appointees, and public managers, building a first 100-day plan was a big idea whose time had come.

When Joe Biden was running for president, he used declarations about what he was going to do in his first 100 days as a platform for winning votes, saying he would appoint an African American woman as vice president. He also promised to rejoin The Paris Agreement on climate change, as well as end deportations.

One of the more interesting "first 100 days" alerts I received was regarding Christine Lagarde, who started her first 100 days as the head of the European Central Bank wearing an owl brooch to a January 2020 press conference. Lagarde made clear her determination to run the Central Bank differently, as it hunted for a way out of crisis management mode.

Lagarde, the bank's first female president, told reporters the previous month, "I'm neither a dove (favoring generous support to the economy) nor hawk (backing tough love), and my ambition is to be this owl that is often associated with a little bit of wisdom."

I discovered many headlines where "Mayor Pete" Buttigieg described his plan for his first 100 days in office when he was running for the presidency. I had the opportunity to interview one of Buttigieg's friends and colleagues from the United States Conference of Mayors, Mayor Lauren McLean of Boise, Idaho, soon after she took office, and she enthusiastically shared her first 100-day plan with me. It included things like making Boise an economic opportunity zone for entrepreneurship and innovation, as well as building a new library and infrastructure improvements.

McLean's example shows how important it is to think in terms of an emergent strategy, as she was, like many US mayors, hit by the perfect storm of the pandemic, economic collapse, and racial justice demands. Her sincere and honest attempts to deal with the situation, such as requiring Boise citizens to wear masks, providing police support to guarantee Black Lives Matter protestors the right to assemble, and placing a halt on evictions, not only led to fistfights in front of City Hall, but a movement to recall her election. The recall was suspended months later, unable to get the required signatures.

Good 100-day plans are based on a winning aspiration that is connected to one (or very few) goals, that if achieved, can lead to a cascade of positive outcomes. Great examples are President Kennedy's goal of putting a man on the moon by the end of the decade and bringing him back safely to earth; President Johnson's goal of passing the Civil Rights Act in his first 100 days, President Reagan's tax cuts, and President Obama's Affordable Care Act.

USE YOUR 100-DAY PLAN TO ADDRESS A NATION-ENCUMBERING CRISIS

More than any other president since Franklin Roosevelt, more than Jack Kennedy, Ronald Reagan or Barack Obama, Joe Biden seized upon his first 100-day plan as an opportunity to bring America through a nation-encumbering crisis. His original first 100-day plan rested on restoring the American spirit—who we are and what we stand for—along with four pivotal priorities of 1) climate change, 2) beating the pandemic, 3) rebuilding, 4) racial justice— and he supercharged it.

Just the weekend before the inauguration, with his chief of staff Ron Klain, Biden made the decision to issue a blitz of executive orders that would help the United States stand tall again, after being knocked to its knees by multiple crises.

These involved a boatload of decrees, which the president has the power and authority to issue without Congressional approval, that would dramatically reverse many of Donald Trump's policies and much of his toxic legacy. The logic behind doing this was to take bold and unreasonable action to secure some early wins that would build momentum, rather than wait for Congress to wind its way through a second impeachment trial.

Some of the orders were based on symbols and some were based on substance. They included such things as rejoining the Paris Agreement on climate, rescinding the ban on people from Muslim countries, finding a way to reunite parents separated from their children at borders, extending pandemic-related notices on foreclosures and evictions, removing penalties on student loan payments, and issuing a mask mandate for the first 100 days.

He also announced at the same time an almost 2-trillion-dollar economic stimulus and relief package, signaling to Democrats and Republicans that whatever comes from it, he would be setting the direction and responding with a commitment to collaboration and cooperation.

CREATING YOUR ONE-PAGE FIRST (NEXT) 100-DAY PLAN

One thing I noticed from all the news stories on leaders with a first 100-day plan was that many were a hodgepodge of campaign slogans like Make America Great Again, aspirational vision statements like the Green New Deal, and goals without any clear strategy or coherent action plan attached.

I also came across some first 100-day plans put together for newly elected officials, political appointees, and high-profile public managers by "shadow leaders"—PhDs and consultants who work in Washington think tanks—that were almost one hundred pages long, and which put me to sleep within minutes of opening.

With all this in mind, I decided to provide you, the reader, with a vocabulary, set of guiding ideas, methods, and tools that would help you create a first 100-day plan. I also decided to provide a way for you to distinguish the difference between a good first 100-day plan and a bad one and understand why that is important. Finally, I thought it might help to point out some of the most predictable mistakes that leaders make when creating a 100-day plan.

THE KISS PRINCIPLE FOR YOUR 100-DAY PLAN

According to David Axelrod (campaign manager for Barack Obama) in a Masterclass with Karl Rove (campaign manager for George W. Bush), "The people who elected or hired you expect you to lead, not just to follow." The people want you to be the "remedy" to the problems they face, not the "repetition" of what your predecessor did, who either ignored the problem—as Herbert Hoover did in the Great Depression—or took actions that exacerbated the problem—like Donald Trump did during the Covid-19 crisis when he held big rallies where it was optional to wear masks. Rove believes that the process of creating a first 100-day plan is a way to remember why you ran for office to begin with and to translate your vision, grand strategy, or campaign promises into reality.

I have discovered in coaching leaders in their first 100 days that, once the thrill of getting the job subsides, they often become depressed when faced with the discouraging complexity of the situation they inherited or when they get bogged down in elaborate strategic planning and preparations. This can lead to weeks, if not months, of meetings that in the end lead nowhere except to death by PowerPoint.

In creating a first 100-day plan, I have found, it is best to apply the old KISS principle (Keep It Simple, Stupid). By that, I mean that you keep your first 100-day plan to one page (or two) with clear goals and priorities, a strategy that is general (not too specific), along with a bias for action.

In suggesting that you apply the KISS principle, I am not saying to make your first 100-day plan simplistic. Supreme Court Justice Oliver Wendell Holmes Jr., who held court on many landmark decisions on very complicated issues, once said: "The only simplicity for which I would give a straw is that which is on the other side of the complex." In other words, getting to simplicity from the other side of complexity can take a lot of thought from you and your team.

The One-Page Strategic Plan template you will find here is based on my experience that it is actually possible to put your entire plan on one page (back and front).

A ONE-PAGE 100-DAY PLAN

Plans are worthless, planning is everything. -President Dwight Eisenhower

Your name, title, term of office

Answer with the help of your coach, chief of staff, team

Start with the WHY
- Where you come from, family background, true values
- Why you decided to run for office or seek the job in the first place
- What are the issues you feel most optimistic or outraged about?

WHAT are the most important goals for you to achieve in your next 100 days?
- Immerse yourself in learning about the greater issues of the day (challenges/opportunities)
- Extract a vision from a looming crisis or immediate situation
- What are your most urgent and important goals?

What is your strategy for HOW to reach your most important goals?
- For each goal, gain insight into the problem, obstacle, or nut to crack
- Gain insight into a strategy that is a solution for overcoming it; general not too specific
- What are the coherent actions you need to take?

Whose help will you need over the next 100 days to reach your goals?

To make the complex simple in order to create a plan on one page, it requires of course that you have a good grasp of what makes a good first 100-day plan and that you spend enough time pondering your most important goals and priorities, as well as the strategies for reaching them.

It helps to do this with a person who can be a coach, thinking partner, or sounding board. Their role is to ask questions and draw you out so that you can come to a clearer understanding of your own ideas. There also may come a time in this process where you want to bring in your personal "brain trust," people who can lend different views or perspectives. Alan Kay, notable American computer scientist, has a well-known quote: "A change in perspective is worth an additional 80 IQ points."

It is also important to keep in mind the importance of feedback and iteration. In other words, get started and try something, get feedback, and then create another iteration that addresses the feedback and brings you closer to your final goals. Matt Taylor, industrial designer and founder of the DesignShop and the "group genius" process, says that it takes six iterations to get to genius. Each iteration takes half as long and doubles the output of the previous iteration.

FDR's One-Page 100-Day Plan

The story of FDR's leadership transition provides a good example for teasing out the guiding principles behind the one-page strategic plan that anyone can use. FDR was elected by a landslide against Herbert Hoover, who though a personally charitable man, did not see it as the government's role to help people during the Great Depression. FDR spent his first week in the White House in sheer terror because he did not really have a first 100-day plan that would deal with the Great Depression or offer Americans a New Deal. While taking a bath to relax and conversing with his son

James, he had an epiphany that amounted to a plan he could have put on one page.

His WHY was not just to occupy a presidential chair. The real reason that caused him to run for office in the first place, was that he believed that the president's job was not to be a bystander to the Great Depression, as Hoover had done, but to care about the American people—at a time when half the nation was unemployed and millions were standing in bread lines and relying on soup kitchens for meals.

His campaign was all about coming up with a New Deal that would bring about the introduction of a new order of things. He also believed in the power of the Federal government to help people caught in the web of circumstances who were not in a position to help themselves, by directly intervening in their everyday lives in their hour of need.

His WHAT was his singular goal of ending the Great Depression, and to do that, he had only three top priorities: 1) restore confidence and optimism, 2) put people back to work so they could pay the rent and put food on the table, and 3) provide relief in numerous ways.

When he was clear about the WHY and the WHAT, he started thinking about a strategy (or approach) for the HOW. To do what he wanted to do, he would need to overcome what he felt was his biggest problem—what to do when you don't know what to do. He came up with a strategy that was both general, and not overly specific: "I will try one thing, and if that doesn't work, I will try something else." In other words, experiment.

An understanding of the coherent actions he needed to take came out of the question: Whose help do I need in order to be able to deliver on my first 100-day plan? This involved picking great people that he could trust for his Cabinet and bringing together his "Brain Trust," a group of professors who were experts in their fields and known for being creative and innovative thinkers. He also developed a richly collaborative relationship with the senators and members of Congress who were already coming up with many New Deal ideas. He then jumped into action and proceeded to pass a torrent of New Deal legislation.

GOOD AND BAD FIRST 100-DAY PLANS—THE DIFFERENCE AND WHY IT'S IMPORTANT

Coaching leaders in politics and business in their first 100 days has given me the opportunity to see many versions of a 100-day plan. It is important for any new leader to know the difference between a good first 100-day plan and a bad one, and why it matters. The following diagram provides a list of guiding ideas.

Good vs. Bad 100-Day Plans

The Difference and Why It Matters

Good 100-Day Plans	Bad 100-Day Plans
• Emerges from your purpose and what you passionately care about	• Tries to be all things to all people
• Focuses on one or two pivotal goals you will drive in first 100 days	• Focuses on fuzzy vision statements and a laundry list of goals
• Shows insight into the problem and a strategy for reaching goal(s)	• Lacks insight into the problem or solution strategy
• Indicates where you will take immediate actions that will secure early wins	• Consists of too much elaborate planning and preparations, no early actions set

---

- *Create a plan that emerges from what you passionately care about and is deeply purposeful,* rather than trying to be all things to all people and failing in the process. A good example is what George H.W. Bush said in his inauguration address, "We as a people have such a purpose today. It is to make kinder the face of the nation and gentler the face of the world."

- *Start with developing a personal agenda that is focused,* as Barack Obama did with the Affordable Care Act. Identify your three or four top priorities and put first things first, rather than focus on fuzzy vision statements like Make America Great Again, or a laundry list of goals and vague priorities, or just standing your watch and reacting to events.

- *Gain insight into the problem or big "nut to crack,"* which often leads to a solution or strategy for reaching it. Take into account that the strategy is not the goal; it is the approach for how to reach the goals. As Governor Charlie Baker of Massachusetts has said, "We must have the courage to put partisanship aside and embrace the best ideas and solutions no matter which side of the aisle they come from." Don't just start with brainstorming and writing down a random list of things to do to reach the goal, without first gaining insight into the problem or a solution strategy.

- *Focus on getting going, starting right now, immediately—and securing early wins* that will build political capital, credibility, and momentum, rather than getting bogged down in the discouraging complexity of the situation which leads to too much elaborate planning and preparation and no early, easy-to-achieve actions that can jump-start progress towards goals.

THINGS TO DO AND PITFALLS TO WATCH OUT FOR IN CREATING A FIRST 100-DAY PLAN

1. MAKE SURE YOUR FIRST 100-DAY PLAN IS ANCHORED IN AMERICA'S ENNOBLING IDEALS AND ENDURING VALUES.

Donald Trump's presidency was over before it even began because of his Muslim ban. He lost massive personal and political credibility as president the moment he declared it and never really recovered. This is a good example of the fact that everything you do in your first 100 days has a disproportionate impact on everything that happens thereafter.

2. WATCH OUT FOR OVER- (OR UNDER-) REACHING YOUR GOING-IN MANDATE.

George H.W. Bush later reflected that when he became president, he struggled with the "vision thing" and looked at his job as standing watch and reacting to events. He said he did not have a popular mandate to bring about sweeping change and did not ask for one. He was defeated by Bill Clinton after one term in office, in part for underreaching what was possible. Clinton, on the other hand, had no problem with "the vision thing" and announced that he was going to pass a bill that would give everyone in America a healthcare security card. However, he wound up overreaching the popular mandate and failing because he brought forward a bill that made going to the doctor something that was full of red tape. Both Democrats and Republicans opposed it as just another big government tax and spend program.

3. GOING PUBLIC WITH YOUR 100-DAY PLAN SETS UP A "CREATIVE TENSION" BETWEEN GOALS AND REALITY THAT SEEKS RESOLUTION.

When George W. Bush was elected president, he and Chief of Staff Andrew Card created a very detailed 100-day plan but kept it a secret because he did not want to be held accountable. When his first 100 days rolled around, Bush said, "We've had some good debates, we've made some good progress and it looks like we're going to pass some good laws"—though he had mightily resisted what he considered the arbitrary milestone. At that point, the late journalist Daniel Schorr summed up G. W. Bush this way on NPR's *Talk of the Nation*: "If you say, what has he done in 100 days, not much." Today, there is a growing trend amongst elected officials to not only create a 100-day plan, but also to go public with it, and report out on what happened As Mayor Laurie Maclean told me, "When you go public with your first 100-day plan, it establishes a creative tension between your goals and the reality that you seek to resolve, knowing you will be held to account for it."

4. WATCH OUT FOR THE DON QUIXOTE SYNDROME OF FIGHTING WINDMILLS.

When Alexandria Ocasio-Cortez was elected to Congress, she put together a bill along with Senator Edward Markey known as the Green New Deal, which some experts said made total sense. The only problem was that Ocasio-Cortez soon began to look like Don Quixote fighting windmills, as it would require shutting down the oil industry, junking your Ford F150 truck, and cost trillions of dollars.

As Joe Biden pointed out in a presidential debate, however admirable the idea behind the Green New Deal was, the next president would not have the authority or change readiness in Congress or money to pay for it. In setting goals in your first 100-day plan, ask yourself: *Where can I exploit my existing authority, change readiness, and resources to secure an early win?* The response you want to your proposal, whether it is about climate change, economic renewal, or reinventing the police force, is for people to say, "this is what we have all been waiting for." Once you secure early wins, you then use them to spearhead a breakthrough to your larger goal.

5. Remember that Napoleon Bonaparte Syndrome
of fighting too many battles at once.

When Napoleon began his second (next) 100 days as Emperor after his daring escape from the Isle of Elba, he declared his vision of a European Union, as well as of making many democratic and economic reforms in France. Yet, he got involved in chasing so many goals and priorities, as well as in fighting battles with other kings on too many fronts, that he diluted his forces and was defeated at the Battle of Waterloo before his first 100 days were up.

Lyndon B. Johnson: The Man Who Would Be King

Lyndon B. Johnson's story is a spellbinding tale about an almost mythic character with epic strengths and flaws. With superhuman energy and an indomitable will, he ruthlessly climbed the ladder in service of his own personal ambitions. Then when he reached the top, he had a transformative experience where he connected his personal ambitions to his ambitions for the nation—and almost miraculously wound up having a transformative impact on society. This story, about one of the greatest politicians of the 20th century, reveals a treasure trove of lessons that can help any new leader win and wield power in their first 100 days.

Many people wonder how Lyndon Johnson got his name. He told the story like this: "I was three months old when I was named. My mother and father couldn't agree on a name, so they just called me 'baby.' The people my father liked were all heavy drinkers— pretty rough for a city girl like my mother. She didn't want me named after any of them."

"Finally, there was a criminal lawyer—a country lawyer— named W.C. Linden, who would go on a drunk for a week after every case. My father liked him, and he wanted to name me after him. My mother was reluctant, but she finally agreed to go along if she could spell it the way she wanted to."

"Later when I was campaigning for Congress, an old man with a white carnation in his lapel came up and said, 'That was a very good speech. I want to vote for you. The only thing I don't like about you is the way you spell your name.' He then identified himself as W.C. Linden."

LYNDON JOHNSON'S LINEAGE

Johnson's saga as a leader came from hearing wonderful tall tales and legends about his ancestors and their pursuit of the American dream, those who headed West to a wide-open land of unlimited opportunity where any self-reliant man or woman could reinvent themselves.

The men of the family were all well over six-feet tall, with enormous ears, enormous noses, and enormous ambitions. Their family history shows they all needed to lead and be in command of other men. They helped found the Lone Star State, fought off raiding "Indians," and drove cattle up the Goodnight-Loving and Chisholm Trails.

Johnson's process of becoming was also shaped by his father, Sam Ealy Johnson, a typical Texan with big hat, big boots, tales to tell, and a bottle of Tabasco sauce in his back pocket—because his food was never spicy enough. Lyndon idolized his father for his noble ideals, having served five terms in the Texas State Legislature doing something he had a wonderful expression for: "helping those whose lives were caught in the tentacles of circumstance."

Johnson also hated his father for his lack of realism in switching careers to become a rancher, and swiftly going bankrupt when he speculated in the cotton market. This resulted in his father and the whole family becoming a laughingstock, an object of ridicule, and left Johnson with insecurities he would overcompensate for throughout his life.

Johnson's life was also shaped by growing up in the Texas Hill Country, in a small town in the middle of nowhere, without electric lights, running water, or movies. It was not just dire poverty that marked him during his youth, but also loneliness. There were so few people around that even the flash of a jack rabbit's tale was a big event.

So, it was Lyndon Johnson's ancestry, his father, and growing up in the Texas Hill Country—one of the most desolate, poorest places in America—that caused him to ruthlessly thrust himself toward success.

He felt even as a young schoolboy that he was bigger than his circumstances and that a great destiny awaited him. One day he went to the front of the classroom and took a piece of chalk and wrote his name across two blackboards as the other children watched. On one blackboard he wrote "Lyndon." On the other blackboard he wrote "B. Johnson." You might think this was delusions of grandeur, but even then, Lyndon Johnson had the intention of writing his name across the pages of American history. In fact, when he was twelve, he told classmates, "You know, someday I'm going to be president of the United States."

LYNDON JOHNSON'S LEADERSHIP DNA

We are all a moon with a bright side and dark side. -Mark Twain

By the time Lyndon Johnson left the Hill Country of Texas and enrolled in Southwest Texas State Teachers College, his physical DNA had elevated him into a 6'3" lanky young man who flailed his arms when he spoke about anything he was passionate about.

His leadership DNA also elevated him into the kind of character who stands out in every crowd. His classmates noticed, even then, that Lyndon Johnson's leadership makeup had a bright thread and a dark thread that were inextricably woven together—both of which sent conflicting signals to his brain.

The dark thread was his ambition, a hunger for power and ruthlessness with which he sought it, and was often in conflict with his bright thread—his compassion, natural-born empathy, and visible concern for people caught in the tentacles of circumstances.

Lyndon Johnson was a dialogue of opposites. He could be noble and mercenary, visionary and vulgar, a bully and bootlicker, compassionate and cruel, honest and deceptive, your best friend and a betrayer, boastful and whining, hotly emotional and icily cold and calculating—all in the same few minutes.

The Darker Side. America's most iconic historians have in their celebrated biographies of Lyndon Johnson focused on his darker, seamier side. He is described as a "cruel genius," a "flawed giant" who not only wanted to win, but also needed to win, and whose insecurities often led to ferocious strategies and savage tactics.

As one example, Lyndon Johnson ran for class president during his time at Southwest Texas State Teachers College, holding Constitutional debates with other candidates to raise the vision and values of the class. Yet to win the election by a landslide, he blackmailed another student, and he physically ripped pages out of hundreds of college yearbooks containing unflattering remarks about himself.

Countless other stories are attributed to Lyndon Johnson's darker side, yet as the highly esteemed Lincoln historian David Herbert Donald has said, these biographies of Lyndon Johnson's darker side create a caricature, not a true portrait of an extraordinarily talented, yet tragic figure who had a big impact. What these biographies often leave out was Lyndon Johnson's own psychology, what he really thought about himself.

If Johnson were to come down from the Senate cloakroom in the great beyond, he would call, "Hey fellas, I know I had a dark side, but where is the rest of me?" He might say "Sure I wanted power, but that was inseparable from what I wanted power for."

The Bright Side. Johnson idolized Abraham Lincoln, Franklin Roosevelt, and many other prominent Americans, and wanted to be like them. Starting at an early age and throughout his life, Lyndon Johnson cast himself in heroic dimensions. He was "the grandson of Sam Houston and the Alamo," "the devoted son of a model mother," "the champion of the Hill Country," "the master legislator," "the conqueror of poverty, prejudice and disease," and most of all "the humble servant of the people."

The former governor of Texas John Connally Jr., who was one of Johnson's closest confidants, said that Johnson may have had a dark side, but his bright side was very bright. He personally saw him act many times in a manner that was noble, virtuous, and upstanding. Whenever Lyndon Johnson walked into a room, he was warm, generous, ebullient. It was obvious he really loved people and wanted to help them, even if he had to bend them to his will to do so.

His first real job was as a schoolteacher in Cotulla, Texas, a small border town near the Rio Grande in a school for children of Mexican-American farmers. He recalled, "When they came to school, I saw hunger in their eyes and pain in their bodies. Those little brown bodies had so little and needed so much. I was determined to spark something inside them, to fill their souls with ambition and interest and belief in the future." None of the other teachers cared whether these children could read or write or would have a successful life. This teacher cared, coming in early and leaving late, doing everything he could think of to help them.

Johnson cared about the "nigra" he met on a bus trip who had to pee on the side of the road because Jim Crow segregation laws prevented him from using public bathrooms. He cared about "grand-maw" who needed to see a doctor and could not afford to go to one.

The great destiny that was waiting for Lyndon B. Johnson, the champion of the Great Society legislation, people of color, the poor, or the elderly was never going to be solely the result of his "bright side"—his magnanimity, compassion, and kindness.

Nor was it going to be solely the result of his "dark side"—his blind ambition, hunger for power, and ruthlessness. His budding political genius lay in being able to weave both of these sides together like the double helix of a DNA molecule.

LYNDON B. JOHNSON'S ENTRY INTO POLITICS

Due to his ambition, compassion, and desire to play a bigger game in a larger arena, Lyndon Johnson decided to leave teaching and go into politics. He took advantage of his father's Texas connections in the state capital Austin and in Washington, D.C. to make his presence known, but it did not take long for people to see him as a natural-born leader and larger-than-life figure.

As one observer wrote about Lyndon Johnson, "He's a tall man, tall in the cord-lean frame of a man used to being fit. He is brown with the imprint of the Texas sun etched in his face and around his eyes. There is a gentleness in his manner, but there is no disguising the taut, crackling energies that spill out of him even when he is standing still. And no mistaking either the feel of strength, unbending as a mountain crag, tough as a jungle fighter."

Johnson had the right stuff but what he needed was an opportunity, and that opportunity came in 1931 when Richard Kleberg, heir to the King Ranch in Kingsville, won a special Congressional election to represent Texas. Johnson, just twenty-four years old, got himself into Kleberg's office in San Antonio one day with a combination of audacity and humility and implored Kleberg to let him join his staff. Johnson carried a letter of recommendation with him in his pocket from Sam Rayburn, future Speaker of the House and friend of his father.

Kleberg had little interest in performing the day-to-day duties in Washington. Instead, he appointed Johnson as his legislative secretary and delegated all things to him. Johnson attacked the job with furious energy, studying Congressional protocols and making sure not one constituent's letter went unanswered.

People soon discovered that the young Lyndon Johnson had a talent for politics. His political genius first revealed itself in his response to a deluge of mail that concerned thousands of Texas ranchers and homeowners worried about going bankrupt as the Great Depression set in. No one else in Washington or Texas could figure out what to do about it. Johnson, a mere Congressional aide, took responsibility without being asked—and figured it out. He came up with an ingenious financing plan that involved bullyragging banks and putting pressure on federal and state agencies.

Johnson knew he needed a wife and a helpmate. He met Lady Bird while attending Georgetown University Law Center for several months. During their first date, he asked her to marry him (and many dates later, she agreed). He was beguiled by this Texas southern belle, whose feminine mystique and lilting accent disguised just how smart and strong she really was.

She had a calming influence on him and soon became his closest confidant, helping him deal with the tangle of his ambition, compassion, and "Vesuvius eruptions" when things did not go his way in Washington. Yet she never intruded on what he was thinking or in his business of politics unless invited.

CHOOSE YOUR MENTORS WISELY

When Johnson walked into the Congress on his first morning as Kleberg's legislative secretary, he saw a man it would have been easy to overlook. Short, stocky, balding, with a grey business suit, there was nothing in his appearance that would grab your attention. He was leaning on the railing in the rear of the House, as if he were a tourist visiting the capital.

When Johnson saw him start to greet members coming in for the day, it began to dawn on him that it was "Mr. Sam," Sam Rayburn, whose letter of recommendation had helped him win his job. Rayburn would button-hole one member as he walked by and talk to him earnestly for a few moments, and then tell a funny story to another. Johnson got it in his mind that day that the faster, more effective way for him to gain power and influence was to see if he could get Sam Rayburn to be his mentor. He was successful in doing so.

Johnson found out that despite Sam Rayburn's spending most days between 9 a.m. and 5 p.m. surrounded by staff members and congressmen seeking favor, he was a single man, and his nights and weekends were very lonely. He very much wanted a wife and child. Rayburn wrote to his sister, "God, what I would give for a tow-headed boy to take fishing!"

Johnson invested in the relationship with Rayburn in a way that went well beyond a monthly meeting or a weekly call. He would invite Rayburn over to his house every Sunday for dinner. When Lady Bird, who Johnson was dating at the time, came to town, she developed a great fondness for Mr. Sam, saying he was the "best of us—the best of simple American people" and learned to cook his favorite dishes—like chili and cornbread with homemade peach ice cream.

When the dishes were cleared, the two men would spend the day reading the Sunday papers and talking for hours on end, with

Johnson seeking his advice. Rayburn would say things like "Don't try to go too fast. Learn your job. Don't ever talk until you know what you're talking about."

Rayburn came to depend on Johnson, and in turn, Johnson would often say over the years in Rayburn's presence that he was "just like a Daddy to me." After a few years as Kleberg's legislative secretary, Johnson called on Rayburn and asked for a favor. Johnson wanted President Roosevelt to appoint him as the Texas State Director of the National Youth Administration. He was twenty-six years old and only a secretary to a member of Congress, and the White House would have normally thought it crazy to appoint someone so young as the head of a multimillion-dollar federal agency.

Rayburn, who was known for never asking anyone for anything, interceded on Johnson's behalf with Tom Connally, the senior senator from Texas. In his memoirs, Connally said, "It was an astonishing thing. Rayburn would not leave my office until I agreed to do it." Connally went to the White House, but they refused his recommendation and announced another appointee who was formally sworn in. Upon hearing the news, Sam Rayburn went to the White House. It is not known what he said, but as a result, the White House announced that a mistake had been made, and Johnson was appointed. Johnson's political career was on its way.

His long-time lawyer and close friend Edward Clark later talked about how Johnson had a remarkable ability to quickly make a good impression on older men who possessed power. "I never saw anything like it. He could start talking to a man… and in five minutes he could get that man to think, 'I like you, young fellow. I'm going to help you.'"

Bobby Baker, a Washington insider who became one of his closest advisors, said that Johnson "seemed to sense each man's individual price and the commodity he preferred as coin… with an ability, shocking in the depth of its penetration and perception, to look into a man's heart and know his innermost worries and desires." He could size up a man's strengths, vulnerabilities, and how to win him over with a customized response in a minute.

In much the same way, Johnson later created a mentoring relationship with Richard Russell Jr., the most powerful man in the Senate, as Rayburn was in the House. It is said that Johnson would wind up betraying both Sam Rayburn and Richard Russell when they could no longer help him or stood in his way, although this is debated by some who were around during this time.

FIRST 100 DAYS IN CONGRESS—LEVERAGING OTHER PEOPLE'S POLITICAL CAPITAL

Johnson was stunned when he woke up April 1, 1937 (two years into his role as Texan Director of the National Youth Administration) to pick up the Austin newspaper which reported that the congressional representative from the 10th Congressional District, James P. Buchanan, had suddenly died of a heart attack. He decided on the spot to jump into the race and called a "skull session" of his friends and allies from the NYA to plot a strategy. He was a relative unknown in the district, and someone in the group said the people would most likely ask "Lyndon who?"

Johnson's brainstorming with his friends led to an epiphany. Although he had no political capital with the electorate in that district, that did not mean he could not borrow other people's political capital. He would campaign as "FDR's man in Texas." He told people on the campaign "I am one-hundred percent with FDR." Lady Bird, who had grown up in a wealthy family, used her inheritance to help him finance his campaign.

If you watch Lady Bird's home videos of Lyndon Johnson's campaign stops, you can see with your own eyes his bright side. You can see that Lyndon Johnson not only loved politics, but also loved people and wanted to help them. Racing by automobile, he would barnstorm into every Texas crossroad town, talking with the local politicians and with every single voter he could find. He worked long hours every day and demanded that every person who worked for him do so too. Full of warmth, generosity, and almost maniacal energy, he would hug and kiss every woman and man in his path as he walked to the courthouse steps to give his speech.

He held his arms out wide as he spoke as if to embrace the bedazzled crowd. He made the people in the crowd feel he was one of them, talking about how he had grown up in the Hill Country where everyone was so poor, they didn't know that they were poor. He believed, like his daddy and FDR, it was the government's duty "to do right by the people." He swore he would fight to help them if elected.

His strategy paid off and at just twenty-eight years old, he won the election. His 3,000-vote plurality came primarily from the farmers and the ranchers in the most remote areas whom he had visited one by one. As Robert Caro said in his book about Johnson, he "had visited these people. And they (now) sent him to Congress."

As a freshman member of Congress, Johnson showed early on his innate political instincts and ability to create the kinds of relationships that would build his political capital. At the beginning of his term, with the help of Texas Governor Allred, he had the opportunity to meet and be photographed with President Roosevelt when the president boarded the train in Texas for a return trip to Washington fresh from a fishing vacation in the Gulf. Johnson was then invited to share the president's private railway car and ended up spending the day with him as they rode through Texas. By the end of the trip, Roosevelt told Johnson that if he needed help he could call "Tommy" Corcoran and wrote out the telephone number. Corcoran recalls the president's word when he returned, "I've just met the most remarkable young man. Now I like this boy, and you're going to help him with anything you can."

Johnson also gained access to an after-hours drinking group composed of his mentor, majority leader Sam Rayburn, and his peers in power. This access made Johnson invaluable to the New Deal insiders in the White House, a group of brilliant, young political players, with power and influence. Johnson cultivated these relationships, which included backyard cookouts and informal dinner parties, evenings together laughing and telling stories. He learned that information and relationships were all-important in Washington.

It was this cultivation of relationships which brought Johnson one of his proudest achievements: bringing electricity to rural Texas. His friendship with Tommy Corcoran helped him succeed in "getting a dam for his district that was in political and legal trouble, and subsequently rural electrification aid for which the district was not technically eligible." When Johnson would see Corcoran, he would say, "the next time you see the President, remind him about my dam." Corcoran reminded Roosevelt so often that finally one day Roosevelt said, "Oh, give the kid the dam."

Johnson was able to deliver on a promise he had made to himself long ago as a boy to bring electricity to the Hill Country of Texas. He would become known in Texas, not for his bright side or dark side, but for the man who brought the lights to the Hill Country of Texas.

LYNDON JOHNSON'S RISE—MASTER OF THE SENATE

Lyndon Johnson's ambition often conflicted with his compassion to help others. He had not been in the Congress very long before he began itching to climb the next rung of the ladder and run for the Senate.

He and Lady Bird, using what was left of her inheritance, bought low-cost radio and television time. She was a great businesswoman and had already earned a million dollars to put in the campaign war chest. He would combine this with the money he received from Brown & Root, an industrial services company, on the promise of continuing federal contracts and tax breaks. Johnson lost in his first bid for the Senate in 1941, but succeeded in the second bid in 1948 when he redoubled his campaign efforts.

He gave 350 speeches in two months by flying around Texas in his helicopter. He would drop thousands of circulars over the huge State Fairgrounds before landing to greet the throngs of people. When he finished his speech, he would throw his Stetson hat out over the crowd with a flourish and get back into the helicopter. He would also travel in his big Cadillac Seville to campaign rallies in hundreds of small towns. One day a cop stopped him for speeding. When he walked up to the car and saw Johnson, he gasped, "Oh, my God!" Johnson replied, "And don't you forget it" as he sped away.

This was the election that Johnson allegedly stole from Coke Stevenson, a very popular senator, who was stupefied when on election eve, he discovered he had lost tens of thousands of votes he should have won. Some people in Texas nicknamed Johnson "Landslide Lyndon" for winning by only a handful of votes, but instead of taking offense, he loved it and adopted it as his nickname.

When he got to the Senate, he plunked himself down and observed what was going on. It was not just the senators who ran the place, but also the Senate pages and staff. He heard that his old friend Bobby Baker "knew where the bodies were buried."

There were a lot of questions Johnson could have asked Baker, like: How do I make my maiden speech? How do I introduce a bill? Yet, the most important question he wanted to ask was: Who is the most powerful person in the Senate? Baker told him that it was Richard Russell, a gentleman and Southern Conservative from Georgia. He decided to play the role of the "professional son" with Russell when he found out that he, like Rayburn, was a bachelor without children. He got past Russell's defenses by asking him to be his mentor, casting himself in full agreement with Russell's Segregationist policies.

He ingratiated himself with Russell by walking around Washington with him on weekends and going to baseball games. He studied up on Russell's legislative accomplishments and flattered him by calling him the "old master." Russell was the chairman of the Finance Committee, one most freshman senators were not that interested in, but Johnson requested to be on it and soon became a member.

Johnson idolized FDR and wanted to extend the New Deal in America, as well as do something about civil rights, but he never breathed a word about it to Russell. Instead, he totally aligned himself with Russell and the Southern Conservatives, who were the chairs of almost every committee in Congress.

His early efforts to prove to Russell that he had similar feelings on matters of government included Johnson's maiden speech which he began with the words, "We of the South…" where he said he would fight against prejudice… prejudice against the South by Northerners. He said that a civil rights bill might express noble ideals but would only inflame passions and divisions between the races. He told Democratic liberals that he was all for civil rights but would have to wait until the time was right.

He spent many hours talking to and learning from Russell in order to master the Senate's Byzantine protocols and arcane rules. This would prove an important key in Johnson's being able to steer major bills through Congress without running amok. As a result, with Russell's support, Johnson was allowed to rise in the Senate and become the Democratic Whip after just one year. His political genius revealed itself again later in figuring out how to become Majority Leader of the Senate.

Johnson also kept up his relationship with Sam Rayburn, in part because it would help him build a political brand with Russell and other senators of being someone able to "deliver the House" on major pieces of legislation. He called Sam Rayburn his political "daddy," just as he came to do with Richard Russell, yet never allowed the two of them to meet with him at the same time, juggling when the two would be invited over for Sunday brunch or dinner.

Soon Johnson was determined to become master of the Senate, and one of his main goals was to disrupt the seniority system which had left Southern Conservatives in their 70s and 80s in charge of almost every committee. They stood in the way of not just civil rights legislation, but of almost every progressive bill being released onto the Senate floor. The Southern Conservatives had also figured out a way to use the Senate's arcane rules, including the filibuster, to stop any bill they did not like. Johnson developed a strategy to dismantle the seniority system, not like a Machiavellian lion making speeches on television denouncing them, but more like a wily fox behind closed doors.

He offered to serve the elderly Richard Russell, Robert Byrd, and others who had held their jobs as Chairman for decades, as their informal floor manager for most of the bills that came out of their committees onto the floor, relieving them of long days and the labor of doing it themselves. Furthermore, their paternal fondness for Johnson made his offers of assistance seem like the offers of a loyal young friend, eager only to help. Johnson was not exaggerating when he told Historian Doris Kearns Goodwin that these elderly senators were as grateful for the offers "as for a spring in the desert."

During his years as both Majority and Minority Leader, Johnson played a strong role in recommending who would be made chairman of committees, seizing the opportunity to fill the seats of fifteen who died during this time. He also played a strong role in recommending on which committees freshman senators like Jack Kennedy, Hubert Humphrey, and Stuart Symington would be assigned (fourteen in all), placing them in his debt. This was also in part a strategy to loosen the grip of Southern Conservatives by getting progressives on their team whose passions he could modulate until the right time.

Another piece of the puzzle of how Johnson became master of the Senate was that he realized "he who controls the purse strings, controls the world." He started raising money for members of Congress in both houses—Democratic and Republican alike—through his Texas oil baron connections. He carried a list of senators and congressmen in his pocket. His thumbprint had smudged the names of the people he favored as well as the ones he was furious with. He would say "no sir" (no money) to his staff regarding people who had slighted him in a minor way or disagreed with him. No one got any money without giving something back. Some senators said his motto was: "Ask not what you have done for Lyndon Johnson, but what you have done for him lately?"

He became the coach and mentor of a moderate group of Republicans and Democrats in favor of progressive legislation. He kept the group unified by emphasizing shared purpose on behalf of all Americans, strongly advocating a bipartisan approach. He believed that finding the middle ground was the essence of legislative leadership, often repeating "Come now, let us reason together…" They would pick a progressive issue where it was possible to make some headway and then march to common ground.

Johnson was soon to become a towering figure in the Senate to whom everyone paid homage. Johnson had breakfast in the Senate cafeteria every day, holding court with whoever wanted to see him. According to Robert Caro, he was not only the youngest but the greatest Senate Leader in history. His colleagues called him Leader. "Good morning, Leader." "Could I have a minute of your time, Leader?" Great job there, Mr. Leader." "Mr. Leader, I never thought you could pull that one off."

Johnson led from his bright side and his dark side in ways that got him labeled as not just the Master of the Senate, but also as a "flawed giant" and "cruel genius." Yet in the long eyes of history, the proof is in the pudding. Johnson was able not only to transform the institution, but also to make things happen that were not supposed to happen.

President Eisenhower called him one day to ask for his help in passing his Civil Rights Act of 1957, a bill that Ike was not that passionate about, having refused to call out the National Guard to help integrate schools. This call had a certain irony, as previously Johnson had not only voted against civil rights, but actively worked against it.

Yet none of this meant Johnson was against civil rights. He took up Ike's challenge, calming his Southern segregationist colleagues by saying that if we pass the "Nigra bill" it will get it off the table in the Senate, and "keep the Nigras voting Democratic for 200 years." Johnson went into the Senate and drove the Civil Rights Act to passage, breaking a 24-hour Southern filibuster by Strom Thurmond, something everyone said would be impossible. He looked at it as his most important accomplishment in the Senate. He knew that although it was a weak bill, it would be a spearhead for a stronger one.

THE VICE PRESIDENCY—A POSITION THAT DID NOT MATTER

Johnson took it for granted that he would be the presumptive presidential candidate in 1960. He had the right combination of charisma, vision, and not just political power but also the skills of a master legislator. What Johnson did not realize, however, was that in 1960, you did not campaign for the presidency in the Senate, you campaigned for it on television. While Johnson was busy moving bills through Senate committees, John F. Kennedy was flying around the country in a small plane with Ted Sorensen, his speechwriter.

Kennedy would appear on TV every night in a charming and disarming way with flashes of wit, humor, and rhetorical eloquence. Johnson lost out to Kennedy in part because his larger-than-life personality did not translate to TV. Johnson thought that when he got on camera, he needed to tone himself down, to appear statesman-like.

Johnson lost the presidential race before it even began, but Kennedy knew he needed Johnson as his vice president to win the election because Johnson was from Texas, a Republican-leaning state, and no Democrat was going to win the presidency without winning Texas. Johnson was disappointed he was not going to be president but accepted Kennedy's invitation.

Yet, according to Jackie Kennedy, both John F. Kennedy and his brother Robert F. Kennedy felt threatened by Johnson's latent political power, and unwittingly they began to marginalize him. Robert Kennedy, like his brother was a Boston Brahmin, and thought of Johnson as a big Southern hillbilly, and set out to humiliate him. He never called him "Mr. Vice President", as was custom, but "Lyndon", which Johnson despised. He also called him "Rufus Cornpone", and Lady Bird Johnson "his little porkchop." Johnson was sent on more foreign goodwill tours than any vice president in history. He was totally kept out of the inner circle, even though Kennedy's domestic programs were stuck in the Senate and going nowhere.

Here you have the Master of the Senate, the greatest legislator, the greatest dealmaker, and the greatest passer of legislation in 100 years, yet he was kept in the waiting room for many meetings, excluded from participating or even giving advice. Johnson recalled later that never in about two years had O'Brien, the head of Kennedy's congressional liaison staff, so much as stopped by his office to ask for any advice.

Robert Caro comments on Johnson's days as vice president: "He was always so sad-looking that they called it a hangdog look.

The long Texas strides were short and hesitant now. He realized that he had really been put in a position that didn't matter." His former aide Bill Moyers felt that Johnson had become "a man without purpose… a great horse in a very small corral."

THE TRANSITION ON THE FLIGHT FROM DALLAS

"He's gone," said special assistant to John F. Kennedy, Kenny O'Donnell, coming out of a small hospital cubicle to the soon to be thirty-sixth President of the United States standing nearby. "And right then," said Homer Thornberry, also a member of the Texas congressional delegation speaking of Johnson, "he took charge."

Lyndon Johnson became president at the crack of a gunshot. He later said, "An assassin's bullet has thrust upon me the awesome burden of the Presidency." Johnson's entourage left the hospital and raced to the airport. Colonel Jim Swindle had been alerted to prepare for immediate takeoff. He was fixing to start the engines after disconnecting the mobile air conditioning system.

"Mr. President," said Malcolm Kilduff, the Press Secretary for the Dallas trip, as he informed him that the Cabinet members who had come to Texas were already on a plane to Washington. It was the first time anyone had ever called Lyndon Johnson that, but when he answered, Kilduff could tell from the tone of his voice it was a president answering, steadfast and in command. "He reacted immediately," Kilduff remembered. Immediately and undeniably.

Robert Caro points out in his book *Passage to Power* that those aides closest to Lyndon Johnson were immediately struck by a sudden change in his looks and bearing. Now the hangdog look was gone. The drooping jaw was firm and "set." Looking back, Lady Bird recalled that his face had become "almost a graven image of a face carved in bronze."

Johnson, almost always the master politician, was as big as the moment. As he stood in the cabin of Air Force One, he had a gut feeling that many Americans struck with the loss of President Kennedy might feel he was not the legitimate heir to the throne in this Camelot presidency, but a usurper, who had seized the moment.

Imagine Lyndon Johnson preparing to take the Oath of Office in the cabin of the plane. He is arranging for everybody to stand where he wants them. One witness was still missing, the most important one. He told Judge Sara Hughes, who would officiate the taking of the oath, that Mrs. Kennedy had wanted to be present and they would wait for her.

He then asked aides O'Donnell and O'Brien, "Do you want to ask Mrs. Kennedy if she would like to stand with us?" When they did not respond at once, the glance he threw at them was the old Johnson glance, the eyes burning with impatience and anger. "She said she wants to be here when I take the oath," he told O'Donnell. "Why don't you see what's keeping her?"

After speaking to Mrs. Kennedy, Larry O'Brien found a prayer book on the side table in the dead president's cabin, a book bound in calfskin and embossed with a crucifix. He took it to be a Bible. In Air Force One's crowded stateroom, where a shell-shocked Mrs. Kennedy stood beside Johnson, O'Brien handed the book to Judge Hughes, who held it out for Johnson to place his hand on. The oath sworn, President Johnson said: "Now let's get airborne."

THE TRANSFORMATION IN
THE WHITE HOUSE

On the flight back to Washington, President Lyndon Johnson might have felt that he was a character in Carlos Castaneda's book *The Teachings of Don Juan* who had just swallowed peyote and started hallucinating about shifting from a Mexican peasant with a striped poncho to a Toltec Ruler with a crown.

He may have thought about a recent meeting with a friend in the Senate, who had asked him to use his influence with the Kennedys to get a bill passed. Johnson confided that he lived in a wretched state of powerlessness and advised his friend to give up trying to get anything done through him because his career was over. He had said, "I'm finished."

His sudden ascent to power, however, would not only allow him to find a seat for himself in the Oval Office, but also to find his greatness as a leader, starting with going through a process of leadership transformation in office.

Up until this point, Lyndon Johnson's bright side (nobility, natural-born empathy, kindness) more often than not took second place to his dark side (ambition, hunger for power, ruthlessness). The moment he stood in the cabin of Air Force One and took the oath of office, all of that changed. He began to connect his personal ambition in service of his own desire for power, to his ambition for the nation and to making a difference in other people's lives.

He told presidential writer Hugh Sidney of Time Magazine that during his first weeks in the White House, he had trouble sleeping, especially when he walked into the East Room one night and saw the huge picture of George Washington, and then a statue of Abraham Lincoln nearby. He talked about experiencing eerie, haunting, and transforming feelings that elevated him above his everyday self.

He discussed his feelings with Jack Valenti, invited to be Johnson's advisor during this period. Valenti later commented, "It's as if there is a curious up-soaring of mind and spirit that seems, as if by godly osmosis, to invade the veins of a man the moment he becomes President."

Johnson said, "I am going to build the kind of nation that President Roosevelt hoped for, President Truman worked for, and President Kennedy died for."

On his first night as president back at his home "The Elms" in Spring Valley, the same day President Kennedy was assassinated, President Johnson started sketching out on a yellow notepad his goals and priorities for the next few months. Said Valenti, who was there that night, "He knew with stunning precision the mountaintop to which he was going to summon people." He did not call it "The Great Society" yet, but that is what he was sketching out in detail. He talked about a tax cut, a civil rights bill, a college loan bill, and an affordable medical insurance bill for the elderly.

He realized that this was an historic moment, and he was determined to seize it. The martyred President seemed to grow in popularity every day, and Johnson discussed how this was creating an opportunity to drive his legislative legacy forward in Congress.

This historic moment was also due to the fact that, since the March on Selma and the violence that erupted there, enormous pressure was placed on the White House to do something on civil rights. He needed to act without delay, as he recognized that there was a fierce urgency now.

WELL, WHAT THE HELL IS THE PRESIDENCY FOR?

Johnson looked at FDR as a hero whose moral crusades and track record of performance he could seek to reach and exceed. He pressed congressional liaison Larry O'Brien to help with getting bills passed in his first 100 days. He wanted to have "done more than they did in Roosevelt's hundred days."

He told his staff later that first week, "I'm going to get Kennedy's tax cut out of the Senate Finance Committee, and we're going to get this economy humming again. Then I'm going to pass Kennedy's civil-rights bill, which has been hung up too long in the Congress. I'm going to pass it without changing a comma or a single word." He then laid out his other Great Society programs.

Everyone in the room was stunned. They started to immediately push back on him, saying things like, "Mr. President, civil rights is a noble cause, but it is a lost cause, given the situation in the Senate. It might be foolhardy to burn your political capital right at the beginning on civil rights." Johnson stood up and delivered one of the most famous lines in American presidential history, "Well, what the hell's the Presidency for?" His advisers were stunned and pushed back again, not wanting to rile him, imploring him to go for some low-hanging fruit and talk about civil rights later.

President Johnson was unwavering: "We have talked about civil rights enough. We have talked about it for 100 years or more. It is time to write it in into the books of law." He reasoned the Civil Rights Act would be a spearhead for passing his entire Great Society program.

As James Reston wrote in the New York Times, "President Kennedy's eloquence was designed to make men think; President Johnson's hammer blows are designed to make men act." By the time President Johnson was done, he would write many pages into the books of law.

THE GREAT PERSUADER—HOW LBJ PASSED THE CIVIL RIGHTS ACT

Richard Neustadt, founder of Harvard's Kennedy School of Government and advisor to Presidents Kennedy, Johnson, and Clinton, said that "presidential power is the power to persuade." The president can accomplish things just by virtue of the inherent power and influence vested in the office or through executive orders.

In reality, whether you are the president, governor, or mayor, this is true of anyone in politics or government: *your power is not just a matter of the office you hold, but also your ability to persuade others to get things done.*

Mastering the fine art of persuasion is the way you gain power and influence with people who have different visions and values. It is the way to entice constituents to vote for you, as well as to entice colleagues to cross the aisle and bargain with you.

Lyndon Johnson earned a reputation as the Great Persuader early in his career. Leon Jaworski, a lawyer who came to fame as Richard Nixon's Watergate Prosecutor, said of Johnson, "this man makes the greatest, most persuasive speeches to a small group of anyone I have ever known."

In his inaugural address, President Kennedy said "Let us begin." President Johnson built on the growing popularity of Kennedy after his death and said "Let us continue," which helped to drive his entire legislative agenda.

Yet Johnson realized long before he became president, that the power of persuasion is not just about what you say, it is just as much about what you do. The story of how LBJ in his first 100 days passed the Civil Rights Act reveals a whole playbook of strategies in the art of persuasion that anyone can learn from.

It is important to emphasize that for a "new" leader, the first 100 days is an exciting time and stressful time. When Johnson left the Oval Office and went up to the family residence after a long day, the first thing he did was ask his staff, "Where's Bird?" He relied on Lady Bird for her calming influence and to help him lead from his bright side rather than his darker side.

John Connally Jr., his friend and confidant, once said that history would have been very different had no Lady Bird intervened when Johnson flew into one of his rants, rages, or moments of sobbing self-pity. She would calmly say, "now Lyndon."

A NOBLE AND MIGHTY PURPOSE

President Johnson went on TV and said about the plight of Black Americans: "Their cause must be our cause. Because it's not just Negroes, but really it is all of us who must overcome the crippling legacy of bigotry and prejudice."

An individual who rises to a position of power, who takes a stand for a noble and mighty purpose that resonates with the hearts and minds of a people, and goes after it with a sense of urgency and energy, can have tremendous powers of persuasion.

Lyndon Johnson had been allowed to rise in the Senate, not because of a noble and mighty purpose that beat in his heart, but because it was said he had a "knack" for making people who were on both sides of the fence on an issue think that he was on their side.

Nowhere was this more strikingly in evidence than with civil rights. When he spoke to Northerners, like Senator Paul Douglas of Illinois, he spoke in a barely discernible clipped Texan accent about making Lincoln's Emancipation Proclamation real. When he talked to Southerners, like Richard Russell, his friend and mentor, he talked in a long-voweled Southern drawl and said we "need a nigra bill" to calm them down.

Robert Caro has a wonderful way of explaining this: "When a man is climbing, trying to persuade others to give him power, concealment is necessary... But as a man obtains more power, camouflage is less necessary. The curtain begins to rise. The revealing begins."

When Johnson delivered that famous line, "Then what the hell is the Presidency for," he was no longer a man trying to convince people on both sides of the fence that he was on their side. From that point on, he began to work with a noble and mighty purpose, and a strong sense of urgency and energy. His power of persuasion with the American public, Democrats and Republicans in Congress, and the news media multiplied exponentially. It became a visceral, tangible, palpable force that would not be denied.

One of the first things he did was call his old mentor Richard Russell to say, "Dick, I love you and I owe you. But I'm going to tell you something. I'm going to run over you if you challenge me on this civil-rights bill. I aim to pass this bill. This bill is going to pass. And no one is going to stand in my way."

THE TRIUMPH OF WILL—IF IT'S TO BE, IT'S UP TO ME

Before President Kennedy's fateful trip to Dallas, his whole domestic agenda, which included a much-needed tax cut to stimulate a faltering economy, a civil rights bill, and an education bill, had all been stuck in the Senate with no prospect of going anywhere. When Johnson became president, he made Kennedy's agenda his own and threw his superhuman energy, indomitable will, and political skills into moving it forward. Within days of Johnson's becoming president, things started moving.

Once, while walking around his ranch in Texas, Johnson said, "The best fertilizer for a piece of land is the footprints of its owner." He applied this doctrine to conducting the presidency. Johnson did not delegate the tax cut bill or civil rights bill to his congressional liaison, to the Speaker of the House, or the Senate Majority Leader. He took off his suit jacket, rolled up his sleeves, and dove into the legislative process himself.

One of the big stumbling blocks he had to overcome was the fact that the civil rights bill was being held captive in both the House and Senate. Howard W. Smith, Chairman of the Rules Committee in the House, was holding JFK's badly needed tax cut and social welfare programs hostage in his committee, as long as there was a civil rights bill on the table.

Johnson went on a personal moral crusade to get Smith and the House of Representatives to get the Rules Committee to release the bill through a "discharge petition," so it could be voted on in Congress. This required a majority of the members of Congress to sign the discharge petition, and he was about twenty-five votes short.

He asked Larry O'Brien for a list of House members who were vulnerable to pressure. He then jumped into action, ordering the White House switchboard to get him their phone numbers and he began calling them up one by one. The members, who never before had received a call from the President, were not only pleasantly surprised, but taken in by Johnson's charming yet forceful style. One observer commented, "Johnson loved the telephone… it was almost miraculous what he could achieve in that context."

Johnson was famous for persuading people with what is called "the Johnson Treatment." He used his intimidating personality, as well as his imposing physical size to lean into people and invade their space to emphasize his point when he met them in person. Washington Post columnist Mary McGrory described Johnson's persuasive tactics as "an incredible, potent mixture of persuasion, badgering, flattery, threats, reminders of past favors and future advantages." All of this was based on his superb grasp of human nature.

A story is told that while trying to lobby a senator who he knew had a grandiose personality, Johnson told him that "next to me, your President, and Robert Kennedy, the Attorney General, you are the most important person in Washington, and I must have your vote on the Civil Rights Act to get the others on board."

Another story is of a member of Congress from Missouri who told Johnson that if he voted for the civil rights bill, the Kansas City Star would tar and feather him politically. Johnson replied sharply, that if he did not vote for the bill, the next time he wanted a bridge built, he could call the Kansas City Star.

The pressure worked. Not two weeks into Johnson's presidency on December 4th, Howard Smith indicated that he would release the bill from Committee, rather than have it taken away from him, and begin hearings that would be completed by the end of January, allowing the bill to be sent to the full House. On February 10, 1964, the bill passed in the House 290 to 130. Now it was on to the Senate.

MOBILIZING THE RIGHT PEOPLE

Lyndon Johnson knew that to get the civil rights bill passed, he had to take into account what Abe Lincoln had said: "Public sentiment is everything. With public sentiment, nothing can fail; without it nothing can succeed."

Johnson's goal was, in Martin Luther King's words, "To create a mighty and irresistible tide of public opinion," starting with giving speeches on the topic every chance he got. He began the first 100 days of his presidency by saying "Let us continue," and he accelerated it by saying, "We shall overcome," the theme of a very popular civil rights protest song.

He sought to get public opinion on his side, not just by giving speeches and press conferences, but by mobilizing the right people. He called Katherine Graham, owner of the Washington Post, and asked her to run daily editorials about passing the civil rights bill—editorials which would both stimulate public opinion and put pressure on Congress.

He invited Dave McDonald, the President of the United Steel Workers Union, to have his team lobby for the bill all over the country. He invited Martin Luther King Jr. over to the White House many times to collaborate with him on civil rights issues and asked him to join him on many phone calls.

He handed King a list of names and phone numbers of the senators and congressmen whose votes he needed and asked him to "get on the horn" (phone) and help bring them on board. He also asked King to use his power and influence to find a way to reach out to the hundreds of thousands of people involved in the civil rights movement and do everything possible to mobilize every human being he could.

BUILDING COALITIONS

Johnson not only needed to make his mark in history, he also had a great need for people. He started to invite movers and shakers to the White House every breakfast, lunch, and dinner, with the goal of building a coalition that would help pass the Civil Rights Act.

The guest list was eclectic—Ben Bradlee of the Washington Post, Supreme Court Justice Abe Fortas, Roy Wilkins of the NAACP. It also included such notables as Southern Democratic Segregationists Richard Russell and Robert Bird, as well as pro-civil-rights Republicans like Everett Dirksen and John Lindsay.

Johnson would often buttonhole people before or after these meetings and give them a dose of the Johnson Treatment. There is a famous picture of LBJ, a towering figure leaning over Abe Fortas seeking to physically intimidate and psychologically invade his space. Ben Bradlee recalled feeling that "a St. Bernard had jumped up on you, licked your face for an hour, [and] had pawed you all over leaving scratch marks."

It was almost as if he cast a spell on the target, leaving them in a hypnotic state where they couldn't disagree and often couldn't respond. It may not have been pretty, but it played a key role in passing the Civil Rights Act of 1964.

Johnson would sit at the head of the table, talking about the proposed Civil Rights Act in a very deliberate, but low-key way. He would say things like "Emancipation was a declaration, but still not a fact in this country"—and this needed to be addressed in the

20th century. As always, he would say there is nothing that cannot be accomplished if men would only reason together.

One of the people he most often watched out of the corner of his eye was Republican Majority Leader Minnesota Senator Everett Dirksen, known to be in favor of civil rights, but who had not yet taken a strong stand on it. Dirksen was the key to building a coalition between Republicans and Northern Democrats who could get the bill over the line.

During this period Johnson often complained to Dirksen that the Republicans, "the party of Lincoln," were standing in the way of civil rights due to their fear of Committee Chairmen in the Senate and Congress who were Southern Democrats.

In one of these White House meetings, Johnson brought out a piece of paper he carried around with him in his pocket that was a summary of a Census Bureau report showing that the lifetime earnings of an average Black college graduate were lower than that of a white man with an eighth-grade education. When he found a newspaper article that said segregation was not decreasing, but increasing, he clipped it and sent it to Dirksen, writing in black magic marker, "Shame, Shame, Shame."

President Johnson was one of the first Washington politicians to get a car phone, which he loved to use. The day after sending that clipping, Dirksen called Johnson, reaching him in his limo. Dirksen boasted, "I'm calling on my car phone." Not to be outdone, Johnson said, "Can you hold on a minute, Ev? My other phone is ringing."

After getting back to the White House, Johnson still was not sure if he could count on Everett Dirksen to deliver the Republican side of the Senate. He asked his staff, "Where's Bird?" who he came to depend on more and more. She suggested he call Senator Humphrey, who was the other senator from Minnesota, and Johnson's floor manager in the Senate. He called, asking Humphrey, "What is Dirksen going to do?" Humphrey said, "I think he is going to deliver the Republican vote." Johnson said, "I didn't ask you what you think. I need to know."

The President said, "You and I are going to get Ev. It's going to take time. We're going to get him. You make up your mind now that you've got to spend time with Ev Dirksen. You've got to let him have a piece of the action. He's got to look good all the time. Don't let those [liberal] bomb throwers, now, talk you out of seeing Dirksen. You get in there to see Dirksen. You drink with Dirksen! You talk with Dirksen! You listen to Dirksen!"

Johnson demanded constant updates from Humphrey and Senate Majority Leader Mike Mansfield, always pushing them to be more aggressive. He wanted his civil rights bill to be as strong as the Emancipation Proclamation, and he wanted it passed without changing a single word. He did not want anything in the bill watered down by brokerage and dealmaking.

CLEARING THE SENATE

Johnson invited Chairman of the Finance Committee Senator Harry Byrd of Virginia, who was a wily segregationist, to the White House for a very elaborate lunch to uncouple the 1964 White House Budget and Tax Cut bill from the Civil Rights Act. As vice president, Johnson had strongly advised Kennedy to hold back on a civil rights bill until the tax cut had cleared Congress. Kennedy, who was not a master legislator, did not listen, and now both bills were stuck and the tax bill was a hostage. By holding it in committee, the South pressured the administration to give up on civil rights legislation.

Yet Johnson and Byrd were old friends, and during a lunch laden with Southern specialties, they came to a shared understanding: if Johnson submitted a budget below $100 billion, Byrd would release the tax bill. Johnson then personally bullied department heads to reduce their appropriations requests and delivered a budget of $97.9 billion.

The Finance Committee passed the tax bill on January 23, 1964. It was not spoken, but President Johnson had enticed the South to a bargaining process that involved a tax cut and a smaller budget in exchange for a civil rights bill.

Mike Mansfield, the low-key Senate Majority Leader, then maneuvered the Civil Rights Act out of Committee, and on March 26th, the Senate agreed to begin debate on the floor, and the Southerners began their expected filibuster. The battle lines were drawn.

The only option the pro-civil-rights group now had was to get the necessary votes for a seldom used cloture motion, which is the only procedural means available in the Senate to forcibly end debate on a filibuster and bring about a vote on a bill or resolution.

The President, with Hubert Humphrey as his floor manager, began to personally round up the 67 votes that were needed to break the Southern filibuster headed by his former mentor, Richard Russell, a dyed-in-the-wool segregationist.

Second, a bipartisan legislative team of senators and staff with a sense of shared purpose, led by Majority Whip Hubert Humphrey and Minority Whip Thomas Kochel, worked collaboratively to develop a plan to defeat a highly-organized filibuster.

Third, they enlisted the help of Minority Leader Dirksen. This presented Everett Dirksen with a dilemma. It was a presidential election year and, as one historian commented, Dirksen was asked to "deliver Republican votes in support of a Democratic president who could not bring along enough of his own party to seal the deal."

Dirksen met with the entire Republican Caucus to emphasize that civil rights was an American issue, not a Democratic or Republican issue, not even just a Negro issue. He also sat down with Humphrey and the bipartisan group and on a chalkboard they collaborated on no fewer than twenty-nine amendments to the draft of President Kennedy's Civil Rights Act of 1963.

Johnson called Humphrey over to the White House and grabbed his arm so hard it felt he was going to tear it off and beat him to death with it. He was concerned they were watering the bill down with horse-trading. Yet Humphrey said, "Mr. President, we've got a much better bill than anyone ever dreamed possible. We haven't weakened this bill one damn bit; in fact, in some places we've improved it."

The debate of the Johnson civil rights bill occupied the Senate for sixty working days. On the day of the pivotal vote on cloture, visitors packed the galleries. Outside the Capitol, queued among the news cameras and microphones, hundreds more gathered, hoping for a glimpse of the dramatic proceedings inside the Senate Chamber. "It was a scene reminiscent of the Senate during the first half of the 19th century."

Dirksen, who had a powerful deep resonant voice and natural wisdom that reminded people of the Founding Fathers, said, "America grows. America changes," he stated. "And on the civil rights issue, we must rise with the occasion. That calls for cloture and for the enactment of a Civil Rights Bill." Noting that the day marked the 100th anniversary of Abraham Lincoln's second presidential nomination, Dirksen proclaimed in words that echoed Victor Hugo, "Stronger than all the armies is an idea whose time has come.... It will not be stayed or denied. It is here!"

The secretary called the roll. Mr. Aiken—aye. Mr. Allot—aye. Mr. Anderson—aye. Mr. Bennett—no. And so, it began, members and visitors alike listening with bated breath for the outcome of the most consequential cloture in Senate history. Mr. Church—aye. Mr. Clark—aye. Mr. Eastland—no. All around the chamber, everyone was keeping tabs. Mr. Thurmond—no. Mr. Walters—no. Mr. Williams—aye. It was Williams who provided the 67th vote. The final tally was 71 to 29. With cloture evoked, there would be 100 hours of debate before the vote, one hour for each senator.

Finally, on June 19, 1964, the Senate convened to vote on the civil rights bill. It passed by a vote of 73 to 27. On July 2, the House approved the Senate bill, avoiding conference, and that evening President Lyndon Johnson signed the bill into law. As Dirksen had stated, nothing is as powerful as an idea whose time has come.

For Lyndon Johnson, the passage of the Civil Rights Act of 1964 was the result of a hero's journey that started back when he left the Hill Country of Texas and went to Washington as a Congressional aide. It was a hero's journey where he grew through the many adversities along the way and which culminated in a boon to America.

The Civil Rights Act was also a spearhead for a breakthrough that would create the opening for Johnson to pass his Great Society programs. This not only included the Civil Rights Act, but also the Voting Rights Act, the Immigration Act, the College Loan Act, and Medicare, (amongst others). It also included a Small Business Act designed to encourage entrepreneurship and innovation that led directly to the venture capital industry and to Silicon Valley.

History does produce undeniably great presidents; it is not an unbroken parade of fools. Lyndon Johnson might have been one of the great ones, if he had bet all his presidential chips on the Great Society—civil rights, federal aid to education, Medicare, Medicaid, immigration reform. Instead, he tragically stacked the balance of his chips on the war in Vietnam, and spent his last days in the White House feeling like an outcast as he listened to protestors chant, "Hey, hey LBJ, how many kids did you kill today."

Still, when the high court of history meets, the final verdict may say that, while Lyndon Johnson's period of almost divine intervention didn't last long, it lasted long enough for him to have a transformative impact on American society and help millions of people become better off.

Chapter Six

Shared Purpose, Collaboration, and Compromise

During a nation-encumbering crisis, great leadership does not just matter, it matters ten times more. Washington, Lincoln, and Franklin D. Roosevelt are examples of great leaders who emerged in rising to the occasion of a nation-encumbering crisis.

Today, America's leadership is being stress-tested as a result of the pandemic, the resulting economic crisis, and a moral crisis concerning racial injustice. America also faces a hyper-partisan and polarized political environment, skewed by "fake news" and "alternative facts" where, as of May 2021, sixty-five percent of Republicans believed or suspected the 2020 election was stolen and were still supporting a recount in Arizona.

For those of you who are about to begin your first (or next) 100 days, the question of what makes a great leader has never been more crucial. Many books have been written about the characteristics of great leaders. Yet in our quest to find presidents worthy of becoming part of the iconography of Mt. Rushmore, or senators and members of Congress who would make the top ten list in American politics, the most important ingredient has been lost to history.

SEARCHING FOR THE DA VINCI CODE
OF GREAT LEADERSHIP

In delving deeper into the question, I felt a little bit like the alter ego of the protagonist Robert Langdon in one of Dan Brown's books—*The Da Vinci Code, Angels and Demons,* or *The Lost Symbol.* His character, a Harvard Professor of History (symbology) who looks like Harrison Ford in a tweed suit, has a magnificent obsession to follow obscure historical trails set by secret societies (the Freemasons, the Illuminati, the Priory of Sion, black ops security forces). This often leads Langdon to an "aha" moment where he discovers a secret message buried in the past that not only saves lives, but also provides insight into the dilemmas we face today.

I have spent a lifetime searching for the Da Vinci Code of great leadership, including following obscure historical trails, such as the Freedom Trail in Boston, the seat of the American Revolution, and seeking the answer in meandering between the Library of Congress and statues and monuments in Washington, D.C. I have also read thousands of pages of history in the process of writing this book.

My explorations and experience have revealed four truths about great leaders (and leadership) that might be the key to pressing the reset button on American politics—and could be our last line of defense in preserving our democracy.

First, great leaders, like Washington, Lincoln, and FDR, come from diverse backgrounds, yet all seem to possess the same family of human traits that are worthy of emulating in your first 100 days. It is these traits that give leaders a special presence in any room and help them make the ascent to power and to establish positive relationships with both supporters and opposers—traits which include ambition, empathy, humility, listening, and self-reflectiveness.

Secondly, they are moral leaders, not mere power wielders. As FDR said, "The presidency is not merely an administrative office.

That is the least of it. It is pre-eminently a place of moral leadership." American history clearly shows that our greatest presidents are those who take the entitlements guaranteed by the Declaration of Independence and the Constitution to a few white men born into wealth and privilege—and extend those entitlements to all citizens of the United States.

Third, as my friend and mentor, political historian James MacGregor Burns once told me, "Great leaders are not dreamers. They interpret the nation's aspirations and bring them to pass by knowing when to be like the proud and mighty lion, who takes a stand and is not afraid to get into a fight, and when to be the wily fox, who disguises their true intentions so as not to get caught in snares."

The fourth truth, I believe, has been largely lost to history. According to the template laid down by the Founders dating back to the Constitutional Convention, ours is a system of government based on the permanent separation of powers. *It is also based on civility and mastering the secrets of shared purpose, collaboration, and compromise.* This is in reality the only way to get things done for the betterment of all, when working with colleagues who have conflicting visions and values.

THE FORGOTTEN LEGACY OF FDR'S FIRST 100 DAYS

Sometimes all it takes is a tiny shift of perspective to see something familiar in a totally new light. -Dan Brown, The Lost Symbol

Following the 2020 election, I had two voices in my head, one that spoke with the rousing voice of an idealist. It said that the first 100 days of the new administration could be an opportunity to press the reset button both by restoring the centuries-old unwritten rules of civility that had been ripped up in the US Senate and

House of Representatives, and by employing the power of shared purpose, collaboration, and compromise.

The other voice spoke with a natural skepticism and left me with nagging questions: Is it possible for people like President Biden, Nancy Pelosi, and Chuck Schumer to collaborate with Mitch McConnell, Kevin McCarthy, and other Republican leaders around the greater goal of getting us out of the nation-encumbering crisis we are facing today? Is it possible for members of the Senate or the House to lead a push in this regard, given that people who collaborate in American government these days are not treated as heroes but often as traitors to be taken out back and hung? Are there any examples of collaboration in American history?

I began to go on my own version of a hero's journey, my own version of Dan Brown's Robert Langdon in search of who might reveal the answers to these questions. I was lucky enough to find an answer when I stumbled across an article with the provocative headline: "The First 100 Days: 'A Standard That Not Even Roosevelt Achieved.'"

It was written by the highly esteemed professor Patrick Maney, former Chairman of the Department of History at Boston College and author of the book, *FDR's Forgotten New Deal*, as well as various articles.

FDR was amongst our three undeniably greatest presidents. He restored confidence and optimism during the darkest days of the Great Depression. Yet, according to Maney, the legend that he singlehandedly crafted a 100-day plan and drove its passage through Congress "is vastly overblown." Further, it puts pressure on leaders to achieve instantaneous greatness and has crippled our ability to operate in a collaborative way.

I called up Professor Maney for an interview to find out more. To set the stage for the conversation, I talked about my view that American historians place too much emphasis on the "great man" theory of history, and not enough on the "great group." As British historian and essayist Thomas Carlyle said, "The history of the world is but the biography of great men." Yet, the founding of the country was not accomplished by a single extraordinary leader, but rather by an extraordinary constellation of leaders.

For over 100 years, most of the books written about Washington, Lincoln, and FDR portray them in a way that is consistent with the "great man" theory, where leaders single-handedly save the day. Yet these books leave out these leaders' ability to think and work together with those with whom they differed.

Today, our three undeniably great presidents are finally starting to be portrayed as achieving their greatness through their ability to build a shared purpose and to inspire people to collaborate and compromise. Washington is today remembered not just for being the Father of his country but also for getting Hamilton, Jefferson, and Madison to think and work together. Lincoln is remembered for his Team of Rivals.

I asked Professor Maney about his ideas on FDR's fabled first 100 days and especially his relationship with Congress. Without hesitation, he explained that FDR's relationship with Congress "was richly collaborative." Yet this has been lost to history.

When FDR gave his inaugural address on March 4th, 1933, he echoed complete confidence. He unhesitatingly accepted the leadership of the great army of the American people, and then with a cheerful note of optimism delivered that unforgettable line, "The only thing we have to fear is fear itself." As mentioned before, he spent his first nights in the White House in sheer terror because, contrary to legend, he did not really have a 100-day plan. His goal was to end the Great Depression, and his strategy was known as "experimentation"—to try one thing, and if that does not work, try something else.

However, FDR also had a companion strategy that went along with this: to assemble a "Brain Trust" of people to help develop ideas, as well as to tap the views of the best and brightest in

Congress. With his congenial nature and impeccable social skills, he invited senators and members of Congress over to the White House almost every day, where he personally mixed them martinis. According to Professor Maney, they weren't good martinis, but they were martinis.

The personable and kindly Professor Maney said he investigated FDR and the New Deal, not from the presidential side, but from the Senate's side, and discovered in his research that when FDR arrived at the White House, he inherited an extremely collaborative Congress that he was eager to work with in a bipartisan way to meet his promise of "Action, action, action now."

Respected historians like Arthur Schlesinger Jr. heap praise on FDR as an extraordinary leader, who in his first 100 days passed fifteen pieces of major legislation. Yet most of these were the result of FDR's collaboration with the Senate and the House. In fact, while FDR deserves to be credited with bringing unlikely collaborators together and tapping the power of multiple minds in crafting his legislative agenda, of the fifteen heralded pieces of New Deal legislation, only three originated in the White House.

Maney discovered a historical trail in his research that led him to conclude that the source of much of the New Deal legislation came from the influence of two prominent Republican Senators: Robert La Follette and George W. Norris.

Robert "Fighting Bob" La Follette was the charismatic senator from Wisconsin and recognized as the founder of the Progressive Movement. He was ambitious but not without empathy. He fought against political bosses, business trusts, and special interest groups that cared little for the forgotten man or woman of America. He supported environmental protection and championed the labor unions' right to strike.

It turns out that during his term as governor of Wisconsin, he created the precursor to FDR's Brain Trust. He brought unlikely collaborators together for brainstorming sessions on the greater issues of the day, with the idea of coming up with innovative solutions.

He invited professors from the University of Wisconsin—fifty-seven at one point—to draft bills that would help the citizens of the state be better off. One innovation he implemented to fight powerful party leaders beholden to big business was his public reading of the "roll call" in districts in which legislators had voted against his reform proposals.

George W. Norris is perhaps the consummate example of the kind of senator or member of Congress we need today. FDR called Norris "the very perfect, gentle knight of American ideals." He was known both for standing up to the "wrong and evil" of party leaders who served big business rather than the everyday Americans—and for the insurgency in the Senate against them.

It was Senator Norris who brainstormed and sponsored the Tennessee Valley Authority Act which created millions of jobs and, along with Senator John L. Rankin, sponsored the Rural Electrification Act, which brought electric lights and running water to millions of Americans who had never had them.

For Congressional leaders today who are afraid to collaborate with the other side for fear of the political consequences, the interesting aside is that in 1957 both Senators La Follette and Norris—along with Henry Clay, John C. Calhoun, and Daniel Webster—were recognized by the Senator John F. Kennedy Committee as the five greatest senators ever to serve the nation.

Bob La Follette was so admired and respected that he was the Progressive Party's 1924 presidential candidate against Calvin Coolidge. George Norris was re-elected to the Senate five times between 1913 and 1943. Any newly elected person thinking about whether to take the hero's journey and lead an insurgency against powerful party bosses and work toward a bipartisan government today should read the biographies of these men and reflect on their examples.

In speaking with Professor Maney, I felt as Thomas Paine said, "the scales fell from my eyes," and one of the big ideas of this book was validated. America's greatest presidents, senators, and members of Congress were not only great leaders, consistent with the great man theory, but were also capable of creating great groups. Their ability to bend history in the right direction was not just the result of having a majority in Congress, but also due to their mastery of the secrets of creative collaboration.

When I asked Professor Maney about FDR's forgotten relationship with Congress and how this has given future presidents the wrong mental model of leadership and crippled their ability to succeed, he said simply that it has been lost to history. However, it could just be an example of what one historian referred to as "bad leadership makes bad history." I thought to myself that this book will endeavor to rewrite our future history based on learning lessons from the past that we can apply successfully today.

BUILDING A TEAM OF RIVALS IS NOT ENOUGH

I have always thought of President Barack Obama as a great puzzle. He was the first Black president in American history. He is charismatic, good looking, and smart. George F. Will, one of the staunchest Republicans, said that Barack and Michelle Obama are the kind of people you would like to serve with on the board of your local school PTA.

A great orator, Obama said he wanted to be president, not just of blue states or red states but of the United States. He promised a bipartisan presidency and to work in a collaborative way with the Republican Congress. He read Doris Kearns Goodwin's Team of Rivals and hired Hillary Clinton, his rival for the presidency, as his Secretary of State and Robert Gates, a Republican, as his Secretary of Defense.

Yet, he struggled greatly in being able to collaborate with Republicans and, following his initial successes in his first 100 days, he became one of the most polarizing presidents in recent memory and got road-blocked for the next eight years. How did this happen? It would be easy to blame this on Republicans, but that begs the question.

One clue to solving the puzzle comes from Ralph Waldo Emerson who said that "who you are speaks so loudly that it drowns out what you are saying." The ability to collaborate doesn't come from speeches or reading the right books or even scouring the world for the best practices; it starts with who you are and the way you think and interact with others, especially those with whom you differ.

Malcolm Alter, author of *The Promise*, a book on Obama's first 100 days, says Obama took office in the White House with confidence (almost over-confident). He had to become an instant president to deal with two major crises he inherited—the global financial crisis that could have led to another Great Depression and the wars in Iraq and Afghanistan.

Unlike President George W. Bush, who had an open-door policy to the Oval Office and enjoyed "thinking out loud" conversations that resulted in thinking and working together with his team, Obama strongly discouraged drive-by meetings and did not like his thinking process to be interrupted. According to David Axelrod, his former campaign manager and Senior Advisor when he was president, Obama was slow to give praise, and the only way his staff knew he was satisfied was when he said "next."

He was audacious in delivering on his vision of hope and change during his first 100 days, yet when he started getting pushback from Mitch McConnell and the Republicans on the Affordable Care Act and bank bailouts, that primitive defense mechanism we all have in our brain seemed to take over. He unwittingly defaulted to the "king of the rock" strategy and forgot about his promise of a bipartisan presidency. Shortly after being confirmed as president, he told both Houses of Congress, where the Democrats had a majority, "Elections have consequences. We won, you lost. Get over it." Unfortunately, the "king of the rock" strategy leads people to feel they have no voice in the process and no way to influence it other than trying to pull you off your rock.

Obama, with Nancy Pelosi's guiding hand and a Democratic majority in both houses, then fought to get the Affordable Care Act through Congress. It was a piece of transformational legislation that, despite its flaws and there were many, brought healthcare to almost 30 million people who had never had it before. Then the problems started.

One day his chief of staff Rahm Emanuel walked into the Oval Office and said Mitch McConnell was "ticked off." He handed Obama a copy of the National Journal quoting McConnell as saying, "The single most important thing we want to achieve is for President Obama to be a one-term president." Obama sighed.

People asked Senate Majority Leader Mitch McConnell why he would make such a bold, cynical, almost unpatriotic statement. "It was the way he jammed through the healthcare bill and stimulus." 6

"People say the White House and the Congress would work better together if President Obama and I talked more or had a supper and beer together occasionally." McConnell explained that he would normally like to do that but that "Professor Obama talks down to people. He acts like the kid in your class who exerts a lot of effort to prove he is the smartest one in the room."

Obama would call McConnell up, and the conversation would take just long enough to deliver his soliloquy. "Yes, Mr. President." "No, Mr. President." "Goodbye, Mr. President." "Indeed." McConnell said John Boehner was famous for putting the phone down when the President called while he was having another meeting. McConnell said, "I never put the phone down, but I did watch an inning of baseball."

To be sure, McConnell and Obama hold deeply philosophical and political differences. Yet, from the start of the Obama presidency, McConnell had insisted that he would work with the man in the Oval Office, if only he would follow the example of President Ronald Reagan and House Speaker Tip O'Neill, political opposites who found a way to get along and collaborated on legislation to save Social Security.

The breakdown that happened between Obama and McConnell shows that each valued collaboration with the other side. Yet, it also highlights that each of us come to office with a bright side and a dark side and unconsciously move back and forth between the two. That's why I continually emphasize the importance of coaching and mentoring in the first 100 days and beyond.

It also shows that there is a difference between knowing "what" and knowing "how." It is obvious that our leaders need help in learning how to collaborate with each other, especially when stakes are high, opinions differ, and emotions are running strong. Again, the one thing that can make a difference in this kind of situation is masterful coaching and feedback. Without that, there may be very little light at the end of the tunnel.

LEADERSHIP TRANSFORMATION IN OFFICE: HOW IS THE ANSWER

During the 2020 Democratic Party presidential primary debates, most of the candidates—including Joe Biden, Kamala Harris, Pete Buttigieg and Elizabeth Warren—talked about what they would do in their first 100 days. CNN correspondent Dana Bash said, "Most of you have a 100-day plan for everything." Then she turned the question around and asked, "Do you have something in your 100-day plan for how you will handle your first meeting with Mitch McConnell?" Elizabeth Warren made an awkward attempt at an answer saying she would try to create pull from the outside by marshaling public opinion on issues, while pushing from inside the Senate and the House. The rest of the candidates appeared as if the question had never occurred to them.

It seemed to me that all the candidates focused on the "what"—goals and policies on things like the green revolution, Medicare for all, gun control, and so on. None of them seemed to focus on the "how"—how they were going to work with Republicans who would be dead set against their ideas.

The point of view of this book is that the "how" lies nested in a template the Founders laid down in the Constitution itself. The only way American government can work with its permanent separation of powers is through shared purpose, collaboration, and compromise. This was not just an ideal for the Founders but one that they lived through as they spent a sizzling hot summer in a hall in Philadelphia tasked with the drafting of a constitution for the United States of America—one that they could all put their signatures to.

Your job as a leader is to bring people together around a shared purpose that is big enough for everyone to subordinate their egos to, one that can provide a bridge between both sides and the various points of view.

Collaboration is different from everyday teamwork, cooperation between departments, or communication. It often involves bringing unlikely collaborators together from different sides of the political fence and exploring the various diverse views and perspectives until you begin to build shared understandings which lead to a surprising, thrilling, breakthrough solution. It is about adding one plus one and getting three, as happened in Jimmy Carter's Camp David Accords or Ambassador George Mitchell's Northern Ireland peace breakthrough, or in the repeal of Apartheid laws in South Africa.

It is important to note that before there is a breakthrough, the situation always looks impossible. In all of the situations mentioned here, it looked like the two sides would never find common ground and a path forward, until they did.

Thus, the last piece of the puzzle is the ability to put foolish pride behind you and be willing to compromise. I am not talking about the kind of 11th hour weak compromises that senators and members of Congress patch together to keep the government open. I am talking about a strong, healthy compromise where adding one plus one does equal three. An example of this is President Johnson's passage of the 1964 Civil Rights Act which happened with the help of Southern Conservatives.

DON'T BE JUST A REPUBLICAN OR A DEMOCRAT, BE A PROBLEM SOLVER

When Congressman Josh Gottheimer, a New Jersey Democrat, was elected to the US Congress in 2017, he wanted to do something to make a difference in his first 100 days in an unusual way. He wanted to focus not on what bills need to be passed—but on how members of Congress think and work together.

Gottheimer, like most Americans, was disgusted with the fact that Congress seemed to be hijacked by a few extremists from both parties who prevented progress from being made. He came up with the idea of starting a bipartisan group whose members drew their identity not just from being a Republican or a Democrat but also from being "problem solvers" committed to breaking the partisan divide and solving our nation's complex problems.

This led Gottheimer and Tom Reed, a Republican from New York, to create the Problem Solvers Caucus, a group made up of twenty-five leading Democrats and twenty-five leading Republicans, all committed to "marching to common ground" on the issues that matter most to Americans. Says Gottheimer, "There are many areas where we can work together to achieve strong outcomes including infrastructure, healthcare, and cutting taxes. Retreating to our respective wings will never be the answer."

According to Gottheimer, the group had been much more successful than people realize, in part by using the methods advocated here: shared purpose, collaboration, and compromise. "I was especially proud when our bipartisan Break the Gridlock package was adopted into the House rules earlier this year [2019]. That package included commonsense reforms to make Congress work better and prevent small groups of extremists from obstructing for the sake of it."

The group had been instrumental in getting Donald Trump to sign into law the Great American Outdoors Act preserving our national parks, getting foreign influence out of our elections, stopping parents from being separated from children at our borders, and weighing in on infrastructure improvements.

The Problem Solvers Caucus built personal credibility, political capital, and momentum based on these early wins, and by the time the 2020 election had approached, was ready to take up a major issue.

By any yardstick, the week of October 7th in 2020 was filled with bizarre, disruptive, and disturbing news, with the president of the United States obviously still recovering from Covid-19 yet insisting on resuming public activities—and a potentially deadly kidnapping plot directed at a prominent governor was uncovered.

Earlier in the week, President Trump declared he would not sign any Covid-19 stimulus legislation before the election. He ordered Treasury Secretary Steve Mnuchin and Republicans to stop negotiating with House Democrats. Airline stocks went into a tailspin and millions of Americans worried that there would be no stimulus checks and PPP might dry up. Most Americans were thinking, "Can't you guys just work together and figure this out, sit down in a room like normal people and try to solve the problems?"

The bipartisan Problem Solvers Caucus unveiled its "March to Common Ground" framework to help break the gridlock on the Covid-19 relief package and encourage negotiators to get back to the table. A few days later, Trump said informal talks were "starting to work out." It turns out that the primary reason was that the bipartisan Problem Solvers Caucus came up with a plan of their own, largely behind the scenes.

This work had started earlier in August, when the Senate failed to pass a second Covid-19 bill. The Problem Solvers got together on Zoom video and started working long hours. They worked Labor Day weekend and through the month of September. The focus was on getting together around the shared purpose of getting the country through this crisis, and to collaborate and compromise. It involved splitting a $587 billion dollar difference between Republicans' desire for fiscal restraint and the Democrats' desire to provide help to people in need.

By October 17th, the media reported that President Trump was just inches away from signing the package. Then the rush to confirm his Supreme Court nomination before the election took over, and the package was again delayed.

HOW TO COLLABORATE BETTER: PRINCIPLES AND PRACTICES TO KEEP IN MIND

When writing my leadership book Mastering the Art of Creative Collaboration, I scoured the world for the best practices on the subject. To gain insight into collaboration, I interviewed Shimon Peres of Israel on the Oslo Peace Accords, the chief scientist at the original Mars project, several Silicon Valley entrepreneurs, and the head of a philanthropic organization dedicated to ending hunger and empowering women.

When I finished this research, I began holding CollabLabs with leaders in politics, business, education, and sports to help people discover the genius within their group. The collaborative sessions were usually focused on jointly solving complex problems with people who saw the world differently, and they often led to exciting, thrilling, breakthrough solutions.

The following are the principles and practices we discovered doing this work. The goal here is to help you in your first 100 days, if you have a vision of hope and change and want to learn more about how to collaborate with people who have conflicting visions and values. This work is based on the notion that the greatest breakthroughs of the 21st century will not come from the great leader or solo genius who lays down their vision and inspires people to execute. They will come from great groups mastering the secrets of creative collaboration.

The following principles and practices will give you a place to start.

1. COLLABORATION DOESN'T JUST HAPPEN. IT TAKES LEADERSHIP.

Washington, Lincoln, and FDR were all strong leaders, but they achieved their noble goals and aspirations through creative collaboration with people with whom they differed. At meetings, they talked less than they listened, combined divergent views and perspectives to come up with creative ideas, and encouraged experimentation.

2. SEARCH FOR A SHARED PURPOSE OR GREATER GOAL THAT EVERYONE CAN SUBORDINATE THEIR EGOS TO.

Great leaders create a shared sense of purpose that can elevate people above their everyday selves and partisan differences. One of your most important jobs as a new leader is to articulate goals that represent the things that all Americans want, focusing on where it is possible to march toward common ground: climate change, a Covid-19 vaccine, infrastructure improvements.

3. BRING UNLIKELY COLLABORATORS TOGETHER IN ONE PLACE.

Choose people less interested in whether the person sitting next to them is a Republican or Democrat than they are in solving the problem. In fact, seek out people who see the world differently. When you have all of the ideas on the table culled from the diverse views you represent, you come up with very different solutions than if everyone thinks in the same way. Democracy works better when we hear everybody's voices.

4. SPEND LOTS OF TIME IN DIALOGUE, FOCUSED ON
COLLABORATIVE PROBLEM-SOLVING.

Size up the greater goal, come up with a one-sentence definition of the problem, then brainstorm solutions. The idea is to come up with something great by connecting the dots between people and ideas: One plus one equals three.

5. SET UP SHARED WORKSPACES THAT HELP PEOPLE
THINK AND WORK TOGETHER.

The most widely shared space of all time is a napkin where people sitting around a table express their ideas, but whiteboards and collaborative software also work. Capture people's ideas in a shared space and then feel free to make a comment or edit each other's work.

6. CREATE A "RAPID PROTOTYPE" OF THE SOLUTION
YOU WOULD LIKE TO PUT FORWARD.

Now it is time for serious play. Bring the group together to create a rapid prototype. For example, a framework for a second Covid-19 Cares Act, a one-page strategic plan for achieving both law and order and police reform, a blueprint for a new high school.

7. GET FEEDBACK AND ITERATE.

I have learned that each iteration of a rapid prototype takes half as long as the previous iteration and doubles the output.

Today, we hear many people in the government talking about the Constitution and what the Framers intended when they wrote it. But as mentioned before, somewhere along the line we lost awareness of the process which allowed this great document to be created. It pays to remember how the Constitutional delegates— an extraordinary combination of people with conflicting visions and values—shuttered themselves in a hall for a summer, locked the windows, and with a purpose that was greater than each of them created something that George Washington called "The Miracle of Philadelphia."

Who Will Be Our Next Profile in Courage?

At some future date, when the high court of history sits in judgment on each of us as public servants...our success or failure...they will ask first, were we truly men of courage? -John F. Kennedy

Long before making his famous "Ask not..." inaugural speech, John F. Kennedy said that he would rather write a Pulitzer Prize-winning book than be president of the United States. This interlude is not about his presidency nor anyone else's, but about a topic he nailed in his book *Profiles in Courage,* which did win a Pulitzer Prize.

Kennedy's *Profiles* book tells the stories of eight United States senators—unsung heroes—who under enormous political pressure found the courage to stand up to those in power who were making the world a darker place, to vote their conscience versus vote their party, and to put aside winning by walking across the aisle to collaborate with the other side for the greater good.

I have sought to make this interlude a clarion call to every American in the aftermath of the Trump impeachment trials, the attempted coup d'état and January 6, 2021 insurrection on the

Capitol, the first (and only) since the British burned Capitol Hill in the War of 1812.

Donald Trump's ability to attract millions of people by speaking to their dark side, and not their bright side, put senators like Mitch McConnell, Lindsey Graham, Chuck Grassley, and the Republican caucus in a trance they could not wake up from until it was too late.

The political pressure they felt to stay in Trump's good graces and win the next election resulted in their failing to find the courage to uphold the sacred principles of our constitutional democracy in order to serve the needs of the American people or—most importantly—to look themselves in the mirror and tell the truth.

I have written this book for every elected official, political appointee, or public manager who is struggling to find the courage to stand up to a leader who is playing "king of the rock", to help them find their voice when America's ennobling ideals are on the line, and to find the right balance between good citizenship and partisanship.

Today, many are asking: Who will be the next profile in courage? I am hoping that it is you. This interlude is intended to inspire, empower, and enable you on your hero's journey.

Courage is the noblest of virtues for it is the one that guarantees all the others. -Winston Churchill

THE (FIRST) TRUMP IMPEACHMENT HEARINGS

It was December 5th, 2019. As I drove through Philadelphia in a white blur with snow swirling across my windshield, I listened to the Speaker of the House start to quote from the Declaration of Independence on NPR Radio. Nancy Pelosi announced that the House of Representatives would begin drafting articles of impeachment against President Trump.

The House Speaker revealed her emotion. "Sadly," she said in a hoarse voice, "but with confidence and humility, and with allegiance to our Founders and a heart full of love for America, today I am asking our chairman to proceed with articles of impeachment." Speaker Pelosi sounded full of regret.

I looked through my frosty windshield as I made a detour and drove toward Independence Hall with the Great Clock of History towering above the entrance, the red brick building where the Founders spent a sweltering hot summer with the windows locked shut for the sake of secrecy, drafting the Constitution and the Articles of Impeachment that referred to the "abuse of power" and "high crimes and misdemeanors."

A few weeks after Pelosi's announcement, Jonathan Turley, a George Washington University Law Professor and Republican witness against the impeachment, spoke. He told the House Judiciary Committee that he, like most of the country, was caught up in the madness of the moment (both anger and insanity). It was madness that surrounded Donald Trump's presidency, the madness of a hyper-polarized, volatile, political context—the madness of the Congress not doing America's business and having to deal with the whole grueling impeachment process.

"I get it: You're mad," he testified. "The president is mad. My Republican friends are mad. My Democratic friends are mad. My wife is mad. My kids are mad. Even my dog seems mad—and Luna is a Goldendoodle and they don't get mad. So, we are all mad… Where has that taken us and where will it?"

Turley had serious questions about whether the abuse of power was an impeachable offense and whether Donald Trump's attempt to extort the president of a foreign government to interfere in a United States election by providing dirt against Joe Biden and his son was really a high crime and misdemeanor. People listening to the hearings were not only outraged, but their reaction was so virulent that Turley went back to his office to discover several death threats on his answering machine.

Many members of Congress, primarily from the Republican party, had already made up their minds to acquit the President before the trial had taken place, even though they privately expressed moral certainty that the President was guilty of the abuse of power, high crimes and misdemeanors. Many Americans in both parties were asking "why?" and President Kennedy's book took me beyond looking for answers to the question and brought me to a moment of true insight.

Political "moral" courage is the one essential ingredient to change the world. Yet it is the kind of courage most hard to come by. -Robert F. Kennedy

POLITICAL PRESSURE VERSUS POLITICAL COURAGE

John F. Kennedy had long been interested in the topic of political courage, starting with writing his senior thesis at Harvard, later published as a book—*Why England Slept*. It was a study about Neville Chamberlain's decision to appease Hitler, who had just invaded Poland (Chamberlain called the war "fake news") and the failure of British politicians in his own party to find the courage to voice their opposition, thereby leaving London unprepared for the Nazi Blitz.

After Kennedy showed great physical courage in battling to save himself and his men who were floating around in the South Pacific, he ran for office as a war hero. He was elected to Congress in 1946 and the Senate in 1952. This gave him a personal and direct experience of the difference between the physical courage, demonstrated by the men and women who put on the cloth of the nation in battle, and the political "moral" courage needed to take a stand that a difference can be made, not abandoning one's conscience to win votes.

When Kennedy took a leave of absence from the Senate in 1954 to recover from back surgery, it gave him the opportunity to practice what we call "pause leadership"—to step back, and he wrote *Profiles in Courage*. This work started with scouring the Library of Congress for examples of legislators who, despite great political pressure, had demonstrated the kind of courage needed to change the world.

The list included John Quincy Adams, who in his first week as senator decided to put *being an American first* over his political party (the Federalists party) and vote with Thomas Jefferson on the Louisiana Purchase, the biggest expansion of the Federal government in history. The list also included Daniel Webster from Massachusetts, Thomas Benton from Missouri, Sam Houston from Texas, Edmund Ross from Kansas, Lucius Lamar from Mississippi, George Norris from Nebraska, and Robert A. Taft from Ohio.

Kennedy also had great admiration for Massachusetts politician Leverett Saltonstall, the "Senator's Senator," for the courage he showed in advancing legislation that would help Americans be better off by walking across the aisle to collaborate and compromise without walking away from principle. "Salty," as he was called, would sit in markup sessions on bills, listening to everyone and scribbling on a yellow pad. Then he would present his doodles and ask, "How would this work?" His hand touched thousands of bills.

Kennedy said in *Profiles in Courage* that once you have an appreciation for the pressures most senators and congressmen are under, that make them struggle to find the courage to think and act according to the dictates of their own consciences, you will have a much greater appreciation of those who do so. He said there are three kinds of pressure that cause politicians to lose political (moral) courage and abandon their consciences.

First is the pressure to be liked, something politicians are as susceptible to as anyone else. Second is the pressure to not disappoint the president or other members of your own party who have helped get you elected or directly contributed from their own bank accounts to your campaign coffers. The third pressure is to be re-elected by voting in a way that pleases your base of support.

I believe that these three pressures played a significant role in the Trump impeachment trials, as well as in the aborted attempt to overthrow the 2020 presidential election, and the mismanagement of the Covid-19 response that led to the loss of over 400,000 American lives before the new president's inauguration, January 20, 2021.

MITCH MCCONNELL AND LINDSEY GRAHAM—FROM TRUMP DETRACTORS TO TRUMP ENABLERS

Donald Trump was a rogue president who was smart enough to figure out that in-your-face tweets, provocative stances on a Muslim ban, and building "a big, beautiful wall" would only take him so far. He knew that to succeed, he would need the help of conventional Republicans in both the Senate and the House, and he started to build symbiotic relationships with people who would benefit from being in his orbit and vice versa.

Mitch McConnell and Lindsey Graham may have entered politics with sincere and honest intentions. Yet, they went from being Trump detractors to Trump supporters as a way of dealing with the kind of pressures that Kennedy talked about.

Mitch McConnell beat Senator Walter Huddleston in 1984 for the Kentucky Senate seat that the incumbent Democrat had held for three terms—a surprise win in a state which at the time rarely elected Republicans. The race was won largely on a last-minute ad McConnell ran, which featured a pack of bloodhounds running around looking for his opponent, who had missed numerous votes because of his paid speech schedule. Eventually, Mitch McConnell, who Democrats have called "the grim reaper," worked his way up the hierarchy, and in 2014 became the Senate Majority Leader and successfully prevented most of Obama's legislation from reaching the Senate floor—or even being discussed.

McConnell's and Trump's personal styles probably could not be more different. Trump is an extrovert, McConnell an introvert. Trump plays to win in the short haul, each month, each week, each day, each hour. McConnell is a shadow warrior who plays the long game. Yet when Trump won the 2016 election, McConnell, who was a conventional Republican, decided to make the most out of it.

McConnell never has had a great need to be loved by everyone, but he had been under long-term pressure to maintain his job as Senate majority leader, even as early as 2008, where he thought his re-election would be at its best a pure toss-up. With Trump, he also saw an opportunity to appoint a generation's worth of conservative federal judges. When the Trump impeachment trial rolled around, McConnell, who some say is a "cynical political genius," did not waste two minutes in picking sides, perhaps not seeing any other option for continuing his reign. When the House voted to impeach Trump the first time, McConnell said that the Founders had made impeachment difficult for a reason, and the reason was it could be a strictly partisan exercise. Asserting that this was the case now, he decided to overlook Trump's morally corrupt leadership and moved to acquit Trump.

It is worth noting that in an impeachment "the Senate sits as a High Court of Impeachment to consider evidence, hear witnesses, and vote to acquit or convict the impeached official," and each senator is required to swear or affirm that he will "do impartial justice according to the Constitution and laws."

Yet, prior to the impeachment proceedings, in a late-night interview with Fox News host Sean Hannity, McConnell all but guaranteed a Trump acquittal saying there was "zero chance" that the President would be removed from office, and he promised "total coordination" with the White House and Trump's defense team. Those comments enraged Democrats, as they prepared to advance the fourth ever set of presidential impeachment articles toward a Senate trial for which, they said, the results seemed to be already rigged.

Trump also groomed conventional politician Lindsey Graham to be on his side, although they got off to a rough start in the 2016 presidential campaign with Graham calling Trump a "kook," "crazy," "unfit for office" and a "race baiting, xenophobic, religious bigot... not qualified to hold any public office." Trump pointed out that Lindsey Graham was not worthy of being a Republican presidential candidate in part because he collaborated with moderate Democrats. It is important to consider that John McCain, a real American patriot and moral leader, had mentored Graham. It was under his guiding hand that Graham had championed many successful bipartisan efforts on issues like healthcare, immigration, waterboarding, and more.

After winning the presidency, however, Trump decided to overlook Graham's campaign bullbaiting because he was under pressure to get things done in Congress. He charmed and disarmed Graham by extending him invitations to come join him in Mar-a-Lago for the weekend and be his golfing buddy. "We have gotten close," Graham said. "I personally like him," he added, "I play golf with him." Asked what the secret of his success with the president was, he said, "I try to begin every meeting with a compliment."

Lindsey Graham enjoyed basking in Trump's golden halo with adoring women wearing red hats, and admiring men carrying Trump flags and banners when he would visit their state. He said of his relationship with the president, "being in his orbit, I think, has been good for me and good for him."

"There's a funny meme going around," Pressley Stutts, a Tea Party leader in Greenville, S.C., noted. "It says, 'President Trump, he's even made Lindsey Graham great again."

In 2020, Graham was under pressure not only to be liked, but also to be re-elected, and he wanted to have strong Republican credentials with Trump's base. In the 2014 election, he had been primaried and almost lost his seat in the Senate and did not want to face that prospect again.

Graham said, "I have stepped up, and I am getting rewarded for it by conservatives," when in fact he was a victim of self-deception and stepping down, morally speaking. He was soon to become Trump's wingman on the judiciary committee when the ultra-Conservative Judge Kavanaugh was under consideration for a Supreme Court appointment. Graham also became the top vote-getter in turning down the lamp on the Statue of Liberty with the administration's anti-immigration stances, as well as Trump's "political hitman", often dispatched to campaign against the moderate senators he had previously worked hand in glove with on bipartisan social and economic issues.

When Donald Trump's first impeachment rolled around, Graham conferred with McConnell and dismissed it "as pure partisan nonsense," bypassing and making allowances for the President's moral corruption and abuse of power to unfairly win an election. He then took on the behind-the-scenes role of acting as a whip to secure every Republican vote in the Senate in a vote of acquittal.

When people started asking how Lindsey Graham went from Trump skeptic to Trump sidekick, he had little to say, "What happened to me?" the senator asks. "Not a damn thing." I am guessing that Lindsey Graham had doubts about the President and may have felt guilty about his categorical dismissal of the impeachment charges, yet on some level, he could not bring himself to disappoint his friend and disagree on this or other things.

I looked at the newspapers around the time of the impeachment and discovered that Lindsey Olin Graham had given a speech the week before at a luncheon in South Carolina where the master of ceremonies fired up the crowd with a raucous round of Lindsey Graham Trivial Pursuit. "What is the senator's middle name?" she asked the ballroom of Republicans in Greenville, S.C. "What's the name of the bar the senator's family owned?" Graham had grown up hanging around his parents' beer-and-pool joint, the Sanitary Cafe, in working-class South Carolina where he played the "good kid" to the regulars.

Graham took the stage with all his Southern charm and, not wanting to appear too high and mighty, continued the banter.

Then in just a couple of minutes, Lindsey Graham, a US Senator and former presidential candidate showed his stand was based on his "friendship" with the President, who he never failed to disappoint, along with blind loyalty to the Republican party, capable of the abuse of power and high crimes and misdemeanor at least at a certain level. His voice became softer, but his tone sharpened to a knife's edge, "To every Republican, if you don't stand behind this president, we're not going to stand behind you." One bystander observed that the room fell silent. The speech by this powerful senator got a lot of airplay back in Washington, among both Senate and Congressional colleagues considering how to vote on impeachment.

The truth is that at the end of the day, most senators and members of Congress, once they become part of the most exclusive club in the world located on Capitol Hill, are afraid of not being re-elected and losing their jobs.

ADAM SCHIFF, HOUSE FLOOR MANAGER

I may be saying this perhaps to be neighborly, not partisan, but I was impressed with Congressman Adam Schiff, the House floor manager during the first impeachment trial. Congressman Schiff grew up down the street from me in Framingham, Massachusetts in a section called Pinefield in a track house his parents bought for $16,500 on the GI bill.

Like me, he went to Hebrew School at Temple Beth Shalom five nights a week where he studied for his Bar Mitzvah and liked studying the Talmud, way before his family moved to California and he became a lawyer and politician. The Talmud is a Jewish book of wisdom and law. His friends from his early days said that Schiff, even in classroom debates, had a very strong sense of morality and pointing out right from wrong.

During the trial, he implored every Republican within earshot to show "moral courage" as they considered whether to remove President Donald Trump from office for abuse of power and obstruction of Congress. He emphasized that political "moral" courage doesn't come from disagreeing with our opponents but from disagreeing with our friends, and with our own party.

> *Moral courage is not disagreeing with our enemies, but our friends. - Adam Schiff*

"The House chose this road," McConnell commented after the introductory remarks by Democrats had been made, emphasizing that they would have to meet a very high bar for removal. "It is their duty to investigate. It is their duty to meet the very high bar for undoing a national election."

The door was then opened for the Democratic witnesses to come forward.

LT. COLONEL ALEXANDER VINDMAN: "HERE, RIGHT MATTERS"

I could not help but think about President Kennedy's *Profiles in Courage* as I listened to the testimony of three key witnesses, all US citizens, one the son of immigrants, and the other two who arrived as children. These witnesses were US Ambassador to the EU Gordon Sondland (a Trump campaign contributor), US Ambassador to the Ukraine Marie Yovanovitch (a career diplomat), and Director for European Affairs for the NSC Lt. Colonel Alexander Vindman, who worked at the White House and was in regular contact with Donald Trump. I thought to myself, would it not be poetic justice if their testimony brought down Donald Trump, who had threatened to turn off the light on top of the Statue of Liberty and to create walled cities at every border?

Vindman stood out to me in the hearings because while exuding an air of strength that comes with wearing a military uniform, he somehow struck me by no means as weak, but rather as vulnerable, a public servant accustomed to being in the background, who had to testify before the high and mighty in the Halls of Congress with the cameras on him. He is a first-generation European Jewish immigrant, born one generation after Hitler and Stalin. The stories his parents told him about the pogroms against Jews still bore their imprint in the recesses of his mind.

Still, he was not to be taken lightly at all. When Ranking Member Representative Devin Nunes, Republican from California, addressed him as "Mister," Vindman corrected him, politely but firmly, "Ranking member, it's Lt. Colonel Vindman." He demonstrated that the uniform was not just a symbol of being employed by the military, but a symbol of an honorable individual who is worthy of respect.

Vindman began his opening testimony saying he had called his father that morning from the lobby and said, "Dad, my sitting here today, in the US Capitol talking to our elected officials is proof that you made the right decision forty years ago to leave the Soviet Union and come here to the United States of America in search of a better life for our family." When his father voiced concern,

Lt. Colonel Vindman said, "Do not worry. I will be fine for telling the truth."

When pressed by a congressman about telling his father not to worry, he replied without hesitating, "this is the country I have served and defended, that all of my brothers have served. And here right matters." The audience broke into spontaneous applause. At another point, Vindman reflected on the fact that he would not have been able to speak so freely in many countries around the world.

In his opening statement Lt. Colonel Vindman also explained that as the top expert on Ukraine on the NSC, he was on the July 25th call between US President Donald Trump and Ukrainian President Volodymyr Zelensky. During the call, Trump urged Zelensky to launch investigations into former Vice President Joe Biden and his son Hunter, digging down on a debunked conspiracy theory about the 2016 US presidential election, making it clear that without it, he would not release the urgent funding that they needed in order to defend themselves against the ongoing Russian invasion.

Lt. Colonel Vindman told lawmakers that he followed procedure and went to NSC Legal Advisor John Eisenberg to register his strong concerns, as "he considered the president's demands of the Ukrainian leader as inappropriate… it could have significant national security implications for the United States." The whistleblower got the transcript of the call and reported it to the Washington Post, which led to the event spiraling into an impeachment inquiry.

Vindman was bull-baited and bulldozed by Representative Nunes who, lacking any moral ground to stand on, resorted to high school debate tactics to throw the witness off his game. He suggested Lt. Colonel Vindman was part of a Democratic conspiracy to label Trump a Russian spy and that Democrats have a coordinated campaign with the whistleblower to do what they have wanted to do since 2016—throw Trump out of office.

Only a few weeks after the impeachment hearings were over, Trump fired Vindman, who was escorted from the White House by an armed guard.

Courage will not come if we wait for some other person or some other time. We are the ones who we have been waiting for. -President Barack Obama

THE RE-INCARNATION OF MITT ROMNEY

When historians one hundred years from now are looking for good examples of a presidential candidate or a senator who was a profile in courage during the Trump impeachments, the contested 2020 election, and the siege of Capitol Hill, I believe they will find one in Mitt Romney, senator from Utah. Romney lost to Barack Obama in the 2012 presidential election due to his being down a couple of quarts of charisma and being seen as too much of a square. Romney was a hybrid Republican candidate who believed in both fiscal responsibility and helping people be better off. He hired many women in his Cabinet as governor of Massachusetts, built a strong economy by creating economic opportunity zones, and passed a precedent-setting Massachusetts Health Bill which became the basis for Obamacare.

When he lost the presidential election, Romney showed great resilience in recovering and running for senator from Utah, where he maintained his strong Mormon roots. He now seemed to become "a man in full." People close to him say he grew through the adversities of his loss to Barack Obama.

On the day in 2020 when Senator Mitt Romney left Utah for Washington to vote up or down at the first Trump impeachment hearings, he faced all the political pressures Kennedy talked about that can make leaders lose their moral courage. He was your typical "great guy" who wanted to be liked by the American people, especially after being rejected by voters in 2016. He had received phone calls from President Trump, Mitch McConnell, and Lindsey Graham pressuring him to take the party line.

Mr. Romney went public with an alarm on Sunday before the impeachment vote, saying in the Salt Lake City Tribune that he found President Trump's conduct of bribing a foreign government to investigate and dig up dirt on a political rival was deeply "troubling in the extreme."

Donald Trump immediately struck back with a series of gun-punching tweets starting with one that showed a picture of Romney on election eve 2012 with a gloomy look on his face after he realized he lost to Obama. Others called Mr. Romney a "loser," "fool," and "pompous ass." A television ad airing in the state, paid for by the conservative Club for Growth group, slammed Romney as "slippery," "stealthy," and a "Democrat secret asset" wasn't helping his polling numbers.

Mitt Romney felt strangely alone as he walked through the Salt Lake City airport with his backpack to catch his flight back to Washington to vote on impeachment. A Trumpian heckler he saw at the newsstand warned that if he voted the wrong way on impeachment that week, the next time he ran for reelection, he would be "primaried."

During the flight to Washington, Romney thought about his father George Romney, former governor of Michigan who he idolized as a boy and still paid homage to. The senior Romney was principled, independent, and a rabble-rouser. George Romney had once stuck his index finger in Richard Nixon's chest at a rally during inauguration week and unceremoniously told him to get out of Vietnam.

On July 4th, 1963, Governor George Romney drove his car to the rich Republican Grosse Pointe neighborhood without any escort and marched in a civil rights protest over segregated housing. When reporters from the Republican Grosse Pointe Press asked what he was doing there, he said, "I am here because the issues involved in this march today [on Democratic principles and civil rights] are so fundamental that they are above the partisan level." He then appointed a civil rights commission and an equal opportunity housing board in Michigan.

More than fifty years later, when Mitt Romney was confronted by the heckler in the airport who threatened that he was going to get primaried, the senator felt strong in his resolve to put his principle of fulfilling his Constitutional duty above party loyalty, but he also felt vulnerable.

Trump Administration former National Security Agency Chief John Bolton, author of the whistle-blowing book *The Room Where It Happened,* said in a CNN interview, "I don't believe Donald Trump has ever read the Constitution, and if he did, I don't think he understood it."

Romney, by contrast, had spent the weekend before the impeachment vote poring over the Constitution and The Federalist Papers, written by Alexander Hamilton, James Madison, and Supreme Court Justice John Jay. It was in the Federalist Papers No. 66 that they talked about the potential threat of a president's abuse of powers and the nature of impeachment based on "high crimes and misdemeanors."

When Romney stood on February 5, 2020 to make his speech on the impeachment vote, he talked about going through the dark night of the soul, wrestling with wanting to be considered one of all the president's men, thought of as a loyal member of the Republican party, and the dictates of his own conscience. He said he had weighed heavily the many political consequences that would result from his vote.

The following are Romney's words.

The Constitution is at the foundation of our Republic's success, and we each strive not to lose sight of our promise to defend it.

The allegations made in the articles of impeachment are very serious. As a Senator-juror, I swore an oath, before God, to exercise 'impartial justice.' I am a profoundly religious person. I take an oath before God as enormously consequential. I knew from the outset that being tasked with judging the President, the leader of my own party, would be the most difficult decision I have ever faced.

I was not wrong.

The historic meaning of the words 'high crimes and misdemeanors,' the writings of the Founders and my own reasoned judgment convince me that a president can indeed commit acts against the public trust that are so egregious that while they are not statutory crimes, they would demand removal from office.

The people will judge us for how well and faithfully we fulfilled our duty. The grave question the Constitution tasks senators to answer is whether the President committed an act so extreme and egregious that it rises to the level of a "high crime and misdemeanor.

Yes, he did.

The president asked a foreign government to investigate his political rival. The president withheld vital military funds from that government to press it to do so. The president's purpose was personal and political. Accordingly, the president is guilty of an appalling abuse of the public trust.

What he did was not 'perfect'— No, it was a flagrant assault on our electoral rights, our national security interests, and our fundamental values. Corrupting an election to keep oneself in office is perhaps the most abusive and destructive violation of one's oath of office that I can imagine.

Romney closed with:

> I acknowledge that my verdict will not remove the President from office.... My vote will likely be in the minority in the Senate. But ...I will tell my children and their children that I did my duty to the best of my ability, believing that my country expected it of me.
>
> I will only be one name among many, no more or less, to future generations of Americans who look at the record of this trial. They will note merely that I was among the senators who determined that what the President did was wrong, grievously wrong.

SCHIFF'S CLOSING SPEECH: "IS THERE ONE AMONG YOU WHO WILL SAY, 'ENOUGH!'?"

Schiff began his fiery closing speech in the attempt to use his powers of persuasion to change what seemed like an all too predictable outcome from the start. "Every single vote, even a single vote, by a single member, can change the course of history," he said. "It is said that a single man or woman of courage makes a majority. Is there one among you who will say, 'Enough'?"

"We must say enough—enough! He has betrayed our national security, and he will do so again," Schiff told the Senate. "He has compromised our elections, and he will do so again. You will not change him. You cannot constrain him. He is who he is. Truth matters little to him. What's right matters even less, and decency matters not at all."

"You are decent," he added. "He is not who you are."

Mitch McConnell, Lindsey Graham, and other senators had made it clear that they indeed intended to vote to acquit President Trump, and that they would not even allow relevant witnesses to be heard. Yet after Schiff's passionate closing speech calling for the president's impeachment, they and many of their colleagues felt compelled to give their fellow lawmaker some begrudging admiration and respect. Senator James Inhofe, a conservative Republican from Oklahoma, said the following morning in the Capitol, "I have to say this, Schiff is very, very effective."

As I listened to Mitch McConnell's closing remarks before the vote on Donald Trump's first impeachment, I recalled that during the 2016 Republican presidential primaries, many people sounded the alarm on who Donald Trump really was and warned us that he would take the country to a bad place. There were people who predicted that his presidency would end up where it did at that particular juncture in American history.

These people I am talking about were not just Democrats, like Barack Obama, Hillary Clinton, or Joe Biden. These people were Republicans, many of whom were sitting in the Senate Chamber that day. I had heard many speak back in 2016 on national TV with a level of sincerity and heartfelt concern you do not very often hear from politicians.

Lindsay Graham, Trump's new best friend (and converted enemy), said during those primaries, "If you want to make America great again, tell Donald Trump to go to hell. It's a defining moment for the Republican party and the conservative movement."

Senator Rand Paul of Texas said, "I'm thinking how we got the race for the most important office in the free world to sink to such depths. How could anyone in the Republican party think that this clown is fit to be president?"

Nikki Haley, the former governor of South Carolina who Trump later appointed as Ambassador to the United Nations, said during a Republican primary rally with Marco Rubio looking on and nodding, "We need to fight to remove Donald Trump from the Republican ticket if only because he refuses to disavow the KKK."

Senator Mike Lee of Utah said during a campaign appearance after Trump had almost sewn up the nomination: "You sir are the distraction. Your conduct sir is the distraction. Mr. Trump, with all due respect, I ask you to step aside. Step down and allow someone else to carry the banner of the principles of our democracy." Mike Lee was one of the senators who, facing political pressure, lacked the courage to vote "yes" on Trump's first impeachment.

Senator Ted Cruz, who House Speaker John Boehner once referred to as "the devil himself," rose to the occasion and said, "We're on the verge of having someone take over the Republican party who is a con artist. He doesn't know the difference between truth and lies. He lies practically every word that comes out of his mouth."

Senator Marco Rubio summed things up in a campaign appearance with almost psychic power: "There is only one presidential candidate who has violence at their campaign rallies, Donald Trump. Leadership is not about going to an angry and frustrated people and making them even angrier. That is not leadership, that's called demagoguery."

He added, "Mark my words, four years from now, or two years from now, or one year from now, Republicans all over the country are going to be trying to figure out how they fell into this. If we are going to be a party of fear and get people to vote for us by making them afraid, then we are going to spend a lot of time in the wilderness. It's unchartered territory, I don't know how it is going to end."

The 2020 (first) impeachment vote was cast in the Senate on abuses of power—52 to acquit, 48 to impeach—and we have all seen where that ended.

It ended with Trump at a press conference holding up a copy of the Washington Post that said "Trump Acquitted" for presidential abuse of power in trying to rig an election and, as a result, he was so emboldened by the whole process that within days he began purging the White House and diplomatic service corps of those who had testified against him.

It ended with Trump seeking to overthrow a legitimate election of Joe Biden as president by calling up the Georgia Secretary of State Brad Raffensperger and bullying him to find him 11,000 votes or face criminal charges.

It ended with Trump telling his followers that the election was stolen from them, urging them to "fight" and "fight like hell," to "take back our country," just before a violent mob stormed the Capitol as Congress was set to confirm that President-elect Joe Biden had won the 2020 election.

It ended with Vice President Mike Pence being swiftly removed from the Senate chamber during the electoral vote count and taken to a secure location, with some Trump supporters chanting "Hang Mike Pence," and erecting makeshift wooden gallows with a dangling noose.

It ended with House Speaker Nancy Pelosi being pulled off the House floor and taken to an undisclosed location with one rioter threatening to put "a bullet in her noggin on Live TV" and with her office being ransacked while young staffers hid in an adjoining room under tables, in darkness, and silence, terrorized for two and a half hours.

ANCHORED IN AMERICA'S ENNOBLING IDEALS AND ENDURING VALUES

The moral of the story? The leaders who were profiles in courage, like Representative Adam Schiff, Lt. Colonel Vindman, and Senator Mitt Romney, did not act that way because they possess a special DNA code that helps them deal with political pressure that others do not have. Their heroic acts were the result of being anchored in America's ennobling ideals and enduring values, and a personal choice they made to "say something and do something" rather than be complicit in their silence.

This is something that you as a newly elected leader, political appointee, or public manager in your first, or next 100 days must keep in mind. It is a time when you have not yet had the opportunity to build up the confidence you need, to stand up to morally corrupt leaders who are playing "king of the rock", or party leaders that insist you must go along, and you are likely to feel vulnerable.

Yet remember, as President Kennedy said, "To be courageous requires no exceptional qualifications, no magic formula, no special combination of time, place, and circumstance."

"In the end," he said, "any man or woman does what they must in spite of personal consequences, in spite of obstacles, and dangers, and pressures." Kennedy added, "and that is the basis of all human morality."

Chapter Seven

Secure Early Wins:
Start Small to Win Big

Chances are that when you got the news you had won the election or were appointed to a government post, you were so excited about the opportunity in front of you to make a difference that you were not only ready to give everyone in sight a bear hug, but also ready to do cartwheels. Yet the chances also are that soon after taking office, you will wake up one morning and find yourself facing a wall that looks like it is hundreds of feet high that you will have to get through to get something or anything done.

Someone, whether it is the president, governor, mayor, (or whoever) is always playing the "king of the rock" game and someone else is trying to pull them off and expecting you to help. Those on both sides of the political fence—Republicans or Democrats, Liberals or Conservatives—cannot seem to agree on anything. Instead of being treated as a hero when you attempt to collaborate with the other side, you are treated as a traitor who should be taken out back and hung.

This final chapter is about a breakthrough strategy for cutting through the whole discouraging complexity of the situation and using your first 100 days to secure small early wins that achieve rapid results and become the spearhead for a larger breakthrough.

Securing early wins has many benefits. They allow you to go beyond an aspirational vision, like Make America Great Again, or grand strategies like the Green New Deal, and focus on concrete goals that can be achieved in 100 days or less, through catalytic breakthrough projects. It is a way to focus on what you can accomplish with existing political power, resources, and readiness for change. Your ability to deliver rapid results makes it possible to demonstrate to voters that they have made the right choice in voting you in.

YOU DON'T NEED TO ACHIEVE INSTANT GREATNESS IN YOUR FIRST 100 DAYS

The idea that you must achieve instant greatness in your first 100 days, and that it is the only time you must bring about transformational change, just does not square with the facts. We have mentioned before about Abraham Lincoln's first 100 days where he focused on taking charge of his team of rivals and attempting to secure some early wins, such as making the decision to defend Fort Sumter and his call to arms for 75,000 men. It was not until eighteen months later, September 1862, after much soul searching, discussion, and reflection, that Lincoln began the second 100 days of his presidency, driving transformational change by issuing the preliminary draft of the Emancipation Proclamation. He promised that by the end of his next 100 days, he would absolutely and forever abolish slavery in the United States.

Leadership transition expert Michael Watkins says that securing early wins creates a virtuous circle of personal credibility, political capital, and momentum that will allow you to start driving major change. If you get in trouble with someone in a position of power or fail in securing early wins, it creates a vicious circle (downward spiral) of diminishing personal credibility, political capital, and momentum.

Pete Buttigieg, former Democratic presidential candidate, is an example of someone who secured early wins in his first 100 days as the mayor of South Bend, Indiana that created personal credibility, political capital, and momentum for driving further change. Buttigieg was a Harvard Business School graduate and McKinsey-trained consultant who believed in "data-driven decisions." When he was elected mayor of South Bend, the city was listed as one of the top ten dying cities in America with its high unemployment, many signs of urban blight, and a four-lane speedway running through downtown. "What is particularly troubling for this small city," said an article in Newsweek Magazine is that "the number of young people declined by 2.5 percent during the previous decade, casting further doubt on whether this city will ever be able to recover."

Mayor Steve Luecke was stepping down at age sixty-one, after fifteen years in office, and City Hall was about to undergo a generational change. Buttigieg, then twenty-nine, jumped into the ring. "I think the fact that I'm young is precisely why I can move the ball forward and break some old habits."

Buttigieg won the election and rolled up his sleeves and got to work in his first 100 days. His first instinct was not to push an aspirational vision statement or grand strategy, but to say, "Hey, we're covering what we're in charge of." He wanted to secure some early wins, making City Hall a "data portal" to opportunities and issues hidden in plain view. He not only did a deep dive on the city's current budget and plans but also stopped and talked to people on the street to get their ideas and find out what bothered them. Buttigieg argues, "If there's a problem, you don't get to say it's fake news and pretend that the pothole isn't there… you gotta go out there and deal with it."

Looking out his office window one day, he got the idea for scoring an early win that would not only help lift the depressing black cloud that seemed to hang over the city, but also get rid of "the contagion of blight." It was called "1000 Houses in 1000 Days." This involved both demolishing and repairing one thousand ugly, decrepit, often abandoned buildings that lined both entrances to the city, something he was sure would improve property values. He learned that the previous mayor of the city had given up on the city and was giving away city-owned property almost for free. He had sold the Hibberd Building, once the home of a successful printing company, for only $1.

Buttigieg offered incentives to developers to improve the city's façade downtown, as well as to entrepreneurial citizens to start small growth-oriented businesses, whose business plans he personally volunteered to review.

There was pushback from the conservatives who believed he wanted to increase value without thinking of the consequences, especially to low-income residents. One critic said that the mayor had to realize that South Bend had a history, "It's not like you're putting on your Superman cape and blue suit. People were here before you were." Yet eventually he got a green light with his data-driven argument. There was also pushback from Blacks and Latinos who lived in houses and apartments in these areas. Yet, when Buttigieg secured federal aid to help them make repairs on their homes, he turned many around.

Buttigieg said in his book that securing an early win by hitting such a target convinced citizens of South Bend it was possible to do difficult things and bring the city back to life and restore the civic confidence that had been missing for decades. He admits sometimes being less visionary than technocratic and said that "we didn't get everything right," being so strict on code enforcement that under-privileged people were sometimes driven from their homes. Yet overall, the project was wildly successful with South Bend citizens and had an eighty-six percent approval rating.

Buttigieg, carrying his greater goal of a renaissance for South Bend within him, searched for other early wins that would build on the momentum of this one. For example, one day after driving into work and getting out of his car, he had to brace himself to compensate for the strong blast and whoosh of winds from cars flying by. He remarked to his secretary how much he hated the fact that the main drag going through the city was basically a four-lane raceway.

He came up with a breakthrough project called "Smarter Streets." He eliminated one-way streets and narrowed the streets and widened sidewalks in the downtown areas and other places to slow down traffic coming and going. They also installed bicycle routes, trees, and on-street parking, all designed to keep people downtown after work.

To realize his vision for South Bend and to drive transformational change, Buttigieg continued to build on the momentum gained by his previous early wins. He discovered through his City Hall data portal—often the South Bend Tribune—that this small city of 100,000 people had a much higher lead poisoning ratio than the scandal-plagued city of Flint, Michigan, which is about the same size. South Bend's problem stemmed, not from the drinking water, but from lead paint.

Kathy Schuth, executive director of a South Bend neighborhood group, organized a parents' meeting on lead paint in January 2017 where the mayor spoke. The previous administration had done little besides sending in an occasional city health inspector and let the landlords do the rest. Buttigieg, according to Schuth, "took a second look and said this is a big problem. And there are ways the city could play a strong role."

Buttigieg proved to be effective at building a shared purpose and getting both Republicans and Democrats to collaboratively solve problems. Jake Teshka, the one Republican on the South Bend City Council, said that Buttigieg won his backing for his initiative requiring city inspections of rental units—over his initial objection.

"He brought in the Real Estate Investors Association, tenants' rights groups, folks from the far right, far left, he brought them to the table," Mr. Teshka said. "We got down and dirty with it and the mayor was supportive through the entire thing."

"There was a lot of resistance," to Buttigieg's goals and plan, said Mark Neal, a former city controller. "People said the streets are perfectly fine." Some called it "Buttigieg's folly" because he was spending a lot of city money, $25 million.

To bring people onboard, Buttigieg had to develop as a leader in building a shared purpose and learn to become more of a collaborative person. He could not just make McKinsey-style PowerPoint presentations and cite data with numbers attached. He had to learn to become a more patient listener, not just because he needed to listen to people's ideas to round out his own, but because of what being a good listener says about you—that you respect people enough to genuinely care about what they think.

The result of growing as a leader while he grew the city was that he was eventually able to bring everyone on board and get support for securing all his early wins: "1000 Houses," "Smart Streets," the lead paint initiative, and more.

This led to turning old commercial buildings into residential lofts, a makeover of a shutdown Studebaker car factory, a new Marriott Aloft Hotel in the city's tallest building that most people probably thought would have been torn down. There was more than $100 million in private investment, according to the City, that helped South Bend emerge from the Great Recession. Today, about 1,000 people live downtown compared to virtually zero when Buttigieg took office in 2012.

Buttigieg, despite having to grow through much adversity, was re-elected by a landslide, a plurality of more than seventy-five percent, and was soon in the running for the Democratic nomination to be president in 2020.

FAIL TO SCORE EARLY WINS AT YOUR PERIL

Lori Lightfoot is an outstanding leader and person in many ways. She was elected Mayor of Chicago in 2019, the first Black woman and first lesbian ever to hold such a job. She started her first 100 days with a vision, "One Chicago based on equity and inclusion." She wasn't afraid to stand up to authority. She told Donald Trump when he threatened to bring in the National Guard to quiet BLM protest rallies and use guns on protestors, "I will encode what I really want to say to Donald Trump…it's two words: It begins with F and ends with U," and in response to Trump's comments at the presidential debate, she tweeted: "keep Chicago out of your lying mouth."

She had never held an elected office before running for mayor, and people saw her as uniquely positioned to bring about sweeping change in a city racked by political corruption, enormous financial burdens, a dysfunctional police department, and racial segregation. Even before being elected, she wrote a 100-day plan that touched many of these issues, including crafting a one-year strategic plan budget for the nearly bankrupt city. She got together with every department head to set a standard and raise the bar.

She got outside City Hall and traveled to the wealthier North Side and to the more racially segregated East and South Sides, talking with constituents and listening loudly. She even broke down in tears at a press conference reflecting on her first 100 days about having talked to teens in poor racially segregated neighborhoods.

Yet soon voters started to complain at neighborhood rallies. The executive director of United Working Families gave her a D grade in her first 100 days, "We are holding Mayor Lightfoot to the promises she made as a candidate. She hasn't failed yet, but it's a far cry from what the people of Chicago were promised when they voted for her in April." People wanted to see some evidence of a tangible accomplishment, which they did not see. Mayor Lightfoot's response at a press conference on her first 100 days, when asked about this was, "My job is not to please every single constituency."

It is easier to play Monday morning quarterback and make a judgment of an elected official in a very complex situation than it is to enter the arena and be marred with blood and sweat. Still, I wish I could have been Lori Lightfoot's coach and accompanied her that day. If so, on the way back to City Hall, I would have coached her on the importance of securing an early win and having something to show.

THE BREAKTHROUGH STRATEGY: GO FOR RESULTS NOW

I wrote a book in 1995 called Masterful Coaching on how to become an extraordinary leader in the process of realizing an impossible future for yourself and your organization. That book gave me the opportunity to coach leaders at the highest level in business, government, and the military.

In doing research for that book, my first goal was to inspire and empower people to go on a hero's journey to develop a vision for an "impossible future" that represented "playing a big game in life" versus settling for less and playing small. The second goal was to provide people with a way to make their vision of an "impossible future" a reality, which was still somewhat of a mystery to me.

One day I stumbled across a book called The Breakthrough Strategy by Robert Schaffer, which provided some clues to unraveling it. Intrigued, I called Bob Schaffer up to gain further insight into the whole topic. Bob, who is the founder of Schaffer Consulting, struck me as being a very warm, salt-of-the-earth kind of person and, at the same time, a very bright and original thinker with some game-changing ideas.

To paraphrase Bob, the best way for a leader in their first 100 days to make vision into a reality is to apply the breakthrough strategy. This starts with thinking backward from your vision to a general, not too specific strategy. And then, like Mayor Pete, focus on going for an early win where you can achieve a success that will lead to a widening circle of successes.

The "breakthrough strategy" is all about bypassing elaborate planning and preparations and securing a "rapid succession" of early wins that delivers rapid results. Or as Schaffer puts it, "Get going right now, immediately, and produce a success that becomes a widening circle of successes."

SECURING EARLY WINS:
START SMALL TO WIN BIG

You may be wondering whether you should focus your first 100 days on seeking to secure big early wins that bring about transformational change, as President Johnson did with the Civil Rights Act, or should you seek a series of small early wins that build personal credibility, political capital, and momentum.

The answer is "it all depends." You need to think backward from your winning aspiration, develop a strategy, and then do a good diagnosis of the situation in order to decide where to play and how to win, and whether you are going after a large or small early win.

Take the time to reflect on the following questions. You may have a vision such as a Green New Deal, Medicare for All, or building a wall to achieve border security, but do you have the political power to make your vision a reality? Are you taking office during a nation encumbering crisis, such as President Biden faced in 2021, that demands a major change? Or is it a time of stability? Are you a master politician like Lyndon Johnson, or a greenhorn? Is there a danger of overreaching or underreaching your mandate?

Barack Obama is an excellent example of a president who came into office with a vision, a drive to create transformative change, and a plan to secure some big early wins. Yet he may have unwittingly overreached his mandate with the Affordable Care Act and the American Economic Recovery Act that bailed out banks. While he was able to bring healthcare to millions who had never had it before, one side effect was that he lost both houses of Congress in the next election.

By contrast, I think Buttigieg is an excellent example of a leader who had perhaps a bit less vision, but who was able to bring about transformative change through a rapid succession of small successes. Instead of his mandate shrinking during his time in office, it expanded because of his achievements.

There are many who think that going for a small early win is like grabbing the low-hanging fruit, and it smacks of creeping incrementalism. But in fact, starting small often results in winning big and can produce exponential returns. As Robert Schaffer points out, "Each small early win becomes a spearhead to a larger breakthrough."

MOVE BEYOND A STATE OF POWERLESSNESS

Ninety percent of the stories we read in the newspapers about leaders in Washington are about the same five people. They are written about people like Joe Biden, Nancy Pelosi, Chuck Schumer, Mitch McConnell, Kevin McCarthy—who not only have a vision they want to realize but are also able to wield enormous political power. We often forget the remaining 500 or so leaders elected to the Senate or House of Representatives who, despite their sincere and honest intentions to make an impact, live in a wretched state of powerlessness due to having their intentions thwarted.

The newly elected leader who comes to office full of enthusiasm soon begins to realize that their power is limited by various factors. The president, governor, or mayor is from the other party. Whoever is Speaker of the House or Senate Majority Leader not only has a different vision from you, but also has different values. For example, the Chairman of the Rules Committee does not even allow your proposal to be put on the floor.

As a leader, the breakthrough strategy offered here will help you make sure that possibility triumphs over resignation. It will help you make the shift from a wretched state of powerlessness to the feeling that you have some power in the world. It will help you to recognize that there are always more options than you currently see for moving the ball forward on your goal.

Adopt a "can-do" attitude. Instead of looking at your vision and grand strategy and policy proposals, and telling yourself "It can't be done," ask yourself "What can I do?" Instead of focusing on trying to amass more authority or resources, or to create new readiness for change, focus on what you can accomplish by exploiting the existing authority, resources, and change readiness.

Set yourself up for success by designing breakthrough projects where, instead of people rolling their eyes in disbelief and saying this is the dumbest thing in the world, people look you in the eye and say with unrestrained enthusiasm, "This is what we've all been waiting for."

Instead of giving up on the idea that building a shared purpose, collaboration, and compromise are at all possible and sitting back and waiting for the next election, see what you can do to build a coalition amongst colleagues on both sides of the fence and march toward common ground.

START SMALL TO WIN BIG: GUIDING PRINCIPLES AND PRACTICES

As a newly elected official, political appointee, or public manager, the "breakthrough strategy" is something that you need to embrace if you want to be effective. The first step is to understand a handful of guiding ideas, and then put them into practice.

1. THINK BACKWARD FROM YOUR VISION TO A STRATEGY.

The strategy should be general, not too specific. (If the problem is too much partisanship, the solution is a Problem Solvers Caucus.) Keep in mind that the whole idea of the "breakthrough strategy" is to bypass elaborate planning and preparations, and to get a rapid result that will build personal credibility, political capital, and momentum.

2. GO FOR SMALL EARLY WINS THAT CAN BE A SPEARHEAD FOR A LARGER BREAKTHROUGH.

Ask yourself: Why did I decide to run for office in the first place? What is the goal I care about? What are the things that really bother me? What could I translate into a "breakthrough project" that could potentially lead to a larger breakthrough in other related areas? When I go public with what I am up to, will people say, "That's ridiculous" or "This is what we have all been waiting for"?

3. BUILD A BIPARTISAN TEAM OF PROBLEM SOLVERS WHO WILL ACT AS CO-SPONSORS OF A BREAKTHROUGH PROJECT.

Get outside your office and talk to colleagues. Tell them you want to build a bipartisan team of problem solvers who will march toward common ground, while securing some early wins after the election. Talk about joining the team and becoming a co-sponsor of the breakthrough project you have in mind and discuss what would be involved.

4. Hold a one-day problem-solvers team off-site where you design a 100-day action plan.

The first item on the agenda is to appoint a co-chair from each side to help guide the "steering" team and drive the project to completion. The second is to build a 100-day action plan loaded with success factors. Focus on designing an early win:

- Identify the biggest sticking points and strategy for overcoming them
- Look for where there is a sense of urgency and where success is near and clear (think weeks, not months)
- Layout a set of coherent actions
- Get going right now, immediately, and get a result

5. Embrace the opportunity to build new skills and capabilities as you march toward common ground.

Leaders of teams often start with a push approach to changing attitudes and behaviors, thinking this will change results. My experience is that starting with a focus on rapid results creates a natural pull for changing attitudes and behavior. At the same time, it is important to practice "pause leadership" where you step back and reflect, to lead forward. Ask:

- How are we doing with building a shared sense of purpose, collaboration, and compromise?
- What's one thing we are doing that is working?
- What's one thing that could work better?
- What attitude or behavior change requests do we have of individual members?

6. HOLD WEEKLY TEAM MEETINGS ON AN INFORMAL BASIS AND ASK: WHAT'S HAPPENED? WHAT'S MISSING? WHAT'S NEXT?

Bring the group together regularly to stay aligned on the goal, clear hurdles, iron out conflicts, and act in a way that creates concrete measurable results and a rallying momentum. It is important to understand that "what's missing?" is different from "what's wrong." Think in terms of pondering what's missing that, if provided, would make a difference in the situation.

7. LEVERAGE THE SUCCESS OF YOUR FIRST BREAKTHROUGH PROJECT BY CREATING A WIDENING CIRCLE OF SUCCESSES.

There is indisputable proof that shared purpose, collaboration, and compromise can lead to breakthrough results going a long way toward changing behaviors. Showcase the breakthrough results that you have achieved, as well as the breakthroughs in skills and attitudes, and expand that to influence others in the institution.

Coda

Your First (Next) 100 Days in Politics was written with the idea of inspiring elected officials, political appointees, and public managers to find their greatness at a time when many are prisoners of pettiness. Perhaps the most important message of the book is represented by the cover image of our first president. It is there to remind you that *you are in the same business as George Washington*, whether you work at the national, state, or local level.

Your job, as it says in the Constitution, is to further the vision of America as the last, best hope on earth by upholding the ennobling values that are a container for that. Your job is also to be a unifier versus a divider, even in times of struggle and strife when people might seek to gain power by gravitating to one extreme side of the political fence or the other.

I write about the first 100 days because it's a time when you as a leader have a lot at stake in demonstrating to the people who put you in office that they made the right choice. I also write about the first 100 days because it is often the greatest opening you will have to bring about historic change and there is no time to be wasted. Just remember, whether you have a larger mandate or a smaller one, that the "clock is ticking from Day One" and you need to seize the window of opportunity before it closes.

This book is intended to inspire, empower, and enable you to do so.

About the Author

Robert Hargrove is a CEO, executive, and top team advisor, as well as a former co-director of the Harvard Leadership Research Project. Robert is the founder of Masterful Coaching and Venture Catalyst Partners. His clients have included the Chairman of the New York Stock Exchange, Fortune 500 CEO of the Year, European CEO Entrepreneur of the Year, and various presidential appointees.

Hargrove was awarded the Medal for Distinguished Public Service for his work at the US Department of Defense at the Pentagon.

Hargrove's early career involved conducting Leadership Weekends with over 30,000 people with the goal of developing the "Next Generation of Young Global Leaders." Over 70% of the participants surveyed said it was a "life-altering experience." During this time Robert had offices in Boston, New York, Atlanta, Tampa, Cleveland, London, Zurich, Montreal, and Seoul.

Hargrove works with leaders both in business and politics to prepare them for their first (next) 100 days. To see the master-classes, one-on-one coaching, and various tools Hargrove offers, visit us at www.MyFirst100Days.net.

Acknowledgements

I would like to acknowledge Susan Youngquist, my long-time partner and the editor of every one of my books. She often reminds me of the story told about Michael Angelo when asked about what image of David he had in his mind when carving the statue of David. His answer: *I don't have any image of in my mind, I am looking for the hidden David in the marble.* In this case, Susan was the sculptor who looked for the chapters, warm human stories, and practical how-to's that might otherwise be hidden in the pile of papers I sent her.

I would also like to acknowledge my long-time, committed, and loyal friend and secretary Hilary White, who did a brilliant and exacting job of copyediting the book. She is a person I can always count on in the 11th hour to help with what really needs to be done and I am very grateful to her for that.

Notes

INTRODUCTION: AN OPTIMIST'S PLAYBOOK

1　"Now, if … will be over," Abruzzese, Sarah. "Happening Upon a Look at an Optimistic Lincoln," *The New York Times,* June 8, 2007

2　"I assume … Great Depression." "The only … fear is fear itself." Roosevelt, Franklin D. "First Inaugural Address, March 4, 1933," https://www.billofrightsinstitute.org

3　"Their cause … shall overcome." Shogan, Dr. Colleen. "Lyndon Johnson and the 1965 Voting Rights Act," *The White House Historical Association,* https://www.whitehousehistory.org

4　"Listen buddy… not that nice." Stephen Colbert, "Stephen Colbert On Missing His Live Audience and Making Comedy a Family Business," interview by Terry Gross, *Fresh Air,* NPR, April 27, 2021, https://www.npr.org/2021/06/11/1005381024/stephen-colbert-on-missing-his-live-audience-and-making-comedy-a-family-business.

5　President Biden's approval ratings. "Biden continues to hold on to high approval ratings," *The Associated Press-NORC Center for Public Affairs Research,* May 10, 2021. https://apnorc.org/projects/biden-continues-to-hold-on-to-high-approval-ratings/

6　"A leader's job is to set the tone." MasterClass staff. "Doris Kearns Goodwin's 9 Tips for Bold Leadership, *MasterClass,* May 5, 2021, https://www.masterclass.com/articles/doris-kearns-goodwins-tips-for-bold-leadership

7　"I have never … than I am this very day." Ryan, Josiah. "Biden at the Lincoln Memorial," *CNN Politics,* January 20, 2021, https://www.cnn.com/politics/live-news/biden-harris-inauguration-day-2021/h_f29a6504102a20b4c7894b62c8ed2805

8　"There is no time … American families." (@POTUS, January 20, 2021) Twitter.com

9　"There is nothing … if we do it together." The White House – Get Involved, https://www.whitehouse.gov/get-involved/join-us/

10 "a house divided against itself cannot stand." Abraham Lincoln Online Speeches & Writings, "House divided Speech" Springfield, Illinois, June 16, 1858. http://www.abrahamlincolnonline.org/lincoln/speeches/house. htm

11 "That's not going to happen on my watch." Bade, Gavin. "Biden: U.S. locked in 'battle' with China for global influence," *Politico*, March 25, 2921. https://www.politico.com/news/2021/03/25/biden-china-press-conference-478052

12 "[I]t's one of our …thank you." Moran, Gwen. "Biden and Harris just gave a master class on motivating teams," *Fast Company*, February 5, 2021

13 "You are the center... the world." Ibid

14 "Everything you do... Americans." Ibid

15 "there is an awfully sick patient called the United States of American." Roosevelt, Franklin D., "Excerpts from the Press Conference, December 28, 1943," The American Presidency Project. https://www.presidency. ucsb.edu/documents/excerpts-from-the-press-conference-97

16 "I've never … I just see roads." Eagan, Lauren, "Biden Pitches Massive Infrastructure Plan in Louisiana," *NBC News*, May 6, 2021

17 Otani, Akane. "Record Share of Companies are Beating Earnings Estimates," *The Wall Street Journal,* May 3, 2021

18 "One-hundred … new administration," Smith, Allan. "McConnell says he's '100 percent' focused on 'stopping' Bidens administration," *NBC News*, May 5, 2021. https://www.nbcnews.com/politics/joe-biden/mcconnell-says-he-s-100-percent-focused-stopping-biden-s-n1266443

19 "The president … impeach." Sprunt, Barbara. "Cheney Will Vote To Impeach: 'There Has Never Been A Greater Betrayal By A President,'" *NPR*, January 12, 2021. https://www.npr.org/sections/trump-impeachment-effort-live-updates/2021/01/12/956192433/cheney-will-vote-to-impeach-there-has-never-been-a-greater-betrayal-by-a-preside

20 "We cannot … cannot be crossed." Gangel, Jamie and Warren, Michael. *CNN Politics*, May 3, 2021. https://www.cnn.com/2021/05/03/politics/ liz-cheney-doubles-down-trump-gop/index.html

21 "I will do … Oval Office." Hohman, Maura. "Would Liz Cheney run to keep Trump from the Oval Office? 'Whatever it takes,' she says," *Today*, May 12, 2021

22 "I intend… our party." Ibid

23 "The most … the private citizen." Brandeis University website, About Louis D. Brandeis. https://www.brandeis.edu/about/louis-brandeis.html

24 "Public sentiment … it nothing can succeed." Journal of the Abraham Lincoln Association, Vo. 41, No. 2 (Summer 2020), https://quod.lib. umich.edu/j/jala/

25   "just a 17-year-old high … right thing."Yancey-Bragg, N'dea. "Darnella Frazier, the teenager who recorded George Floy's death on video, says it changed her life." *USA Today*, March 30, 2020

26   "I suffered…things up." Yancey-Bragg. Ibid

27   "When you … in his neck." Yancey-Bragg. Ibid

28   "It changed my life…It has," Yancey-Bragg. Ibid

29   "Few will have the …this generation." Kennedy, Robert F. "Day of Affirmation Address, University of Capetown, Capetown, South Africa, June 6, 1966." Online at the John F. Kennedy Presidential Library and Museum. https://www.jfklibrary.org/learn/about-jfk/the-kennedy-family/robert-f-kennedy/robert-f-kennedy-speeches/day-of-affirmation-address-university-of-capetown-capetown-south-africa-june-6-1966

INTERLUDE: BEN FRANKLIN

24   "remember … if they could." Allen, Erin. "Remember the Ladies" *The Library of Congress Blogs,* March 31, 2016. https://blogs.loc.gov/loc/2016/03/remember-the-ladies/

24   Once he was … America." Isaacson, Walter. *Benjamin Franklin: an American Life.* (New York, Thorndike Press, 2003) 372

25   "an assembly of demigods" Williams, J. D. "The Summer of 1787: Getting a Constitution," *Brigham Young University Studies* 27, no. 3 (1987): 67-89. JSTOR Digital Library. http://www.jstor.org/stable/43041299.

26   "I smell … a monarchy." Ibid

27   "imploring … of Heaven" "and its blessings…deliberations," Eidenmuller, Michael E. *Great Speeches for Better Speaking,* (New York, McGaw-Hill, 2008)

28   "Gentleman… something." "Speak not…come here." "Listen first … think." "Gentleman, … conversation." Ed. "Benjamin Franklin's Famous Quotes" The Franklin Institute. Benjamin Franklin's Famous Quotes, https://www.fi.edu/benjamin-franklin/resources

28   "I firmly … is my country." O'Brien, Conor Cruise. "Thomas Jefferson: Radical and Racist." *The Atlantic,* July 3, 2019

30   "I doubt whether …they shall die." Ed. "Benjamin Franklin's Final Speech in the Constitutional Convention," *PBS.* https://www.pbs.org/benfranklin/pop_finalspeech.html

31   "The mutual … the physical world." Wood, Gordon S. "The Company of Giants," *The New Republic,* March 17, 2011

31   "it appears … of national government." "From George Washington

to Lafayette, 7 February 1788." National Archives: Founders. https://founders.archives.gov/documents/Washington/04-06-02-0079

31   "The happy ... the world." Swanson, Norma; Aud, Barbara. *A Constitution is Born: A Brief history of the Constitution of the United States of America, Tracing the Hand of God,* (United States, Aspect Books, 2016)

32   "A republic... can keep it." Swanson. *A Constitution,* 879

CHAPTER ONE: A HERO'S JOURNEY

36   "We are ... not be enemies." *President Lincoln's First Inaugural Address,* 1861, online at The Library of Congress, Wise Guide, March 2004. https://www.loc.gov/wiseguide/mar04/enemies.html

36   "American Needs ... Looks Like," Tom Friedman. "We Need Great Leadership Now, and Here's What It Looks Like," *The New York Times,* April 21, 2020

36   "Are great leaders born or made?" Doris Kearns Goodwin, *Leadership in Turbulent Times,* (New York, Simon & Schuster, September 2018)

40   "the Mayor of crazy town," "John Boehner on how the rise of ideologues harms America," *CBS Sunday Morning,* April 11, 2021 on YouTube. https://www.youtube.com/watch?v=fcLjUu6D5ck

40   "publicity seekers" "knuckleheads who are against everything." Ibid

42   According to historian ... Lincoln would not be known. "An Evening with Doris Kearns Goodwin," *The LBJ Library,* September 26, 2018 on YouTube. https://www.youtube.com/watch?v=8dEMuO5TSTQ

43   "Hurrah for the ... could hardly reply." Doris Kerns Goodwin, *Team of Rivals: The Political Genius of Abraham Lincoln,* (New York, Simon & Schuster, September 2006)

44   "We will try ... something." Debbie Aiken, "Remembering FDR's Commencement Speech at Oglethorpe," *Oglethorpe: The Source,* May 22, 2012

44   "Mr. President, before ... their advice." Meacham, Jon. "On the 50th anniversary of the Bay of Pigs, lessons in presidential humility," *PBS.* https://www.pbs.org/wnet/need-to-know/security/video-on-the-50th-anniversary-of-the-bay-of-pigs-lessons-in-presidential-humility/8490/

45   "Did you ... that all the time." "Jon Mecham & Doris Kearns Goodwin, A History of America's 'New' Presidents," *The Richmond Forum,* January 21, 2017 https://richmondforum.org/meacham-goodwin/

47   Where JFK said, "Let us begin," LBJ would say, "Let us continue." Caro, Robert. *The Passage of Power: The Years of Lyndon Johnson* (New York, Knopf Doubleday Publishing Group, 2013) 612

47   "Then what the hell is the Presidency for?" O'Donnell, Michael. "How LBJ Saved the Civil Rights Act," *The Atlantic,* April 2014

49   "the president's job is to care," O'Neil, Tyler. "The Latest Liberal Outraged Trump Held Up a Bible at a Church Is None Other Than Joe Biden," *PJ Media*, June 2, 2020. https://pjmedia.com/election/tyler-o-neil/2020/06/02/joe-biden-condemns-trumps-church-photo-op-fails-to-mention-the-church-had-been-on-fire-n483824

49   "Help is coming. Help is on the way." Associated Press staff. "Schumer: Help Is on the Way to NY After Relief Bill Passes," *U.S.News*, March 7, 2021

50   "gave me full authority ... direct about it," Bidgood, Jess. "John Kerry embarks on his latest mission: saving the world," *The Boston Globe,* March 19, 2021.

50   "obsessive zeal," "hyper prepared", and "ever optimistic." Ibid

50   "I just emphasize to everybody," he said, "this is exciting... the stakes couldn't be higher." Ibid

50   "We actually ... that we need." Remarks at the World Economic Forum, Davos January 27, 2021, Host Borge Brende interviews John Kerry. https://www.state.gov/remarks-at-world-economic-forum-davos-2021/

50   "We all have to ... with everybody." Ibid

51-52   "Literally overnight ... broke down crying." "It was just a ...overnight." Grim, Ryan and Gray, Briahna. "Podcast Special: Alexandria Ocasio-Cortez on Her First Weeks in Washington," *The Intercept*, January 28, 2019. https://theintercept.com/2019/01/28/alexandria-ocasio-cortez-podcast/

52   "I authored ... local governments." Ocasio-Cortez, Alexandria. "2 Years of Accomplishments in 2 Minutes," Facebook, December 11, 2020. https://www.facebook.com/OcasioCortez/videos/2-years-in-2ish-minutes/163713515497394/

55-56. "President Trump ... lot about him" Kim, Seung Min; DeBonis, Mike; Demirjian, Karoun; Hamburger, Tom. "Senate votes to pursue Trump impeachment trial after declaring the proceedings constitutional," *The Washington Post,* February 9, 2021

56   "On January 6, 2021... impeach the President." Raskin, Jamie. "Read Democrat Jamie Raskin's closing argument in impeachment trial of Donald Trump," *ABC News,* February 13, 2021. https://abcnews.go.com/Politics/read-democrat-jamie-raskins-closing-argument-impeachment-trial/story?id=75878802

56   "She was right... our people." Ibid

56   "Would you rather ... with one?" Intelligence Squared, "The Art of Political Power, with Robert Caro and William Hague," YouTube,

November 16, 2015. https://www.youtube.com/watch?v=rQHGZT-FpTEw

57   "I want to ... the center of action." Video seen at the John F. Kennedy, Presidential Library and Museum, Columbia Point, Boston, Massachusetts

57   "A president can ...in six years." Ibid

58   "My first reaction ... a feeling." Debenedetti, Gabriel. "Chuck Schumer Has Changed" *Intelligencer, New York Magazine.* April 16, 2021

58   "So that was ... trembled in awe." Ibid

59   "Big help is ... Help is here!" Video posted on Senator Chuck Schumer official Facebook page on March 10, 2021

62   "Great leaders are ... mechanics of influence." Meacham, Jon. *Thomas Jefferson: The Art of Power*, (New York, Random House, Inc., November 2012)

62   "Even if Schumer ... I call you back?'" Debenedetti. *Intelligencer, New York Magazine.*

63   "We can ... other's sentences." Debenedetti. *Intelligencer, New York Magazine.*

INTERLUDE: GEORGE WASHINGTON

69   "Do not ... you speak." Ed. "George Washington's Rules of Civility and Decent Behavior in Company and Conversation" Foundations Magazine, n.d. http://www.foundationsmag.com/civility.html

70   "King George... in the world." Achenback, Joel. "George Washington could have been a strongman, but kept giving power away," *The Washington Post,* July 28, 2016

71   "With a heart ... me by the hand." Price, Lynn. "With a heart full of love and gratitude I now take leave of you: George Washington' Farewell Toast" *Washington Papers,* January 19, 2018. https://washingtonpapers.org/heart-full-love-gratitude-now-take-leave-george-washingtons-farewell-toast/

72   "Long live ... Washington!" Ed. "President Washington's Inauguration in New York City" George Washington's Mount Vernon, n.d. https://www.mountvernon.org.

73   "No people ... United States." Ed. "Transcript of President George Washington's First Inaugural Speech (1789) https://www.ourdocuments.gov n.d.

73   "the preservation ... American people." Ibid

74   "party animosities...attachments" Ibid

74   "eternal … and right," Ibid

74   "sovereign … as he does." Chernow, Ron. "George Washington: The Reluctant President," *Smithsonian Magazine,* February 2011

76   "Few who are … drawn into precedent." Ed. "From George Washington to Catherine Sawbridge Macaulay Graham, 9 January 1790" *National Archives: Founders Online* n.d. https://founders.archives.gov/documents/Washington/05-04-02-0363

77   "If Washington … chose the right one." Chernow, R. *Washington: A Life* (New York, NY: Penguin Books, 2011)

78   "You have … tell me so we part." Ed. From Alexander Hamilton to Philip Schuyler, 18 February 1781" *National Archives: Founders Online* n.d. https://founders.archives.gov/documents/Hamilton/01-02-02-1089

79   "There is … greater friendship." Ed. "The Writings of George Washington, vol XIV (1789-1799)" Online at www.oll.libertyfund.org n.d. https://oll.libertyfund.org/titles/washington-the-writings-of-george-washington-vol-xiv-1798-1799?q=knox#Washington_1450-14_37

CHAPTER TWO: ONBOARD IS NOT ENOUGH

82   "Democrats … that way." Podcast: "Joe Rogan Experience #1295 with Tulsi Gabbard," YouTube, May 14, 2019.

84   "We will strive … but we must try." Dessem, Matthew. "Nancy Pelosi Responds to Republicans' Racist Fearmongering With a Paean to 'the Bipartisan Marketplace of Ideas'" *Slate,* November 7, 2018

90   "He was my tutor… important committees." Biden, Joe. "Joe Biden recalls Ted Kennedy as mentor who made a difference," *The Boston Globe*, March 30, 2015.

91   "Civil rights… have you here." Kaczynski, Andrew. McDermott, Nathan. "How Joe Biden worked with and praised a longtime opponent of civil rights," *CNN Politics*, May 28, 2019. https://www.cnn.com/2019/05/28/politics/kfile-joe-biden-stennis-latest/index.html

91   "it was like … unexpected quarter" Ibid

91   "Mr. Chairman … have to say." Ibid

92   "You see this … was for civil rights." Ibid

92   "He could see…my soul." Ibid

92   "they should … came from," Quilantan, Bianca. Cohen, David. "Trump tells Dem congresswomen: Go back where you come from," *Politico* July 14, 2019

92 "glass of water…would win" Chait, Jonathan. "What Joe Biden Is Teaching Democrats About Democrats," *Intelligencer, New York Magazine,* May 12, 2019

92 "The green …they call it." Ibid

93 "currency of the realm" Palmer, A., Sherman, J., & Lippman, D. "POLITICO Playbook: How to think about Pelosi's standoff with The Squad," *Politico,* July 11, 2019. https://www.politico.com/newsletters/playbook/2019/07/11/how-to-think-about-pelosis-standoff-with-the-squad-455632

93 "They are … votes they got" Hirschfeld Davis, J. "Tensions Between Pelosi and Progressive Democrats of 'the Squad' Burst Into Flame," *The New York Times,* July 9, 2019

92 "In a family… still family." Gay Stolberg, S. "'The Squad' Rankles, but Pelosi and Ocasio-Cortez Make Peace for Now," *The New York Times,* July 26, 2019

93 "I think … people like me," Edmondson, C. (2019, September 18). "How Alexandria Ocasio-Cortez Learned to Play by Washington's Rules," *The New York Time,* September 18, 2019.

93 "I realized …needed mad." Ibid

93 "They … walking committee." Ibid

94. "Day One … time you get there." Neff, Thomas; Citrin, James. *You're in Charge – Now What?* (Currency, New York, 2005)

97 "It's important … first place." "David Axelrod & Karl Rove: Teach Campaign Strategy and Messaging" *Masterclass,* Online. n.d.

102 "an institution … and dignity." Sorkin, Andrew Ross; Karaian, Jason; de la Merced, Michael; Hirsch, Lauren; Livni, Ephrat. "The Biden Spin on 'America First,'" *The New York Times,* December 2, 2020

105 'Good checklists … are above all practical." Gawande, Atul. *The Checklist Manifesto,* (London, Picador, December 2010)

INTERLUDE: ABRAHAM LINCOLN

108 "his breast … to commence." Donald, David Herbert, *We Are Lincoln Men* (New York, Simon Schuster, 2003) 273

108 "the good-looking ladies." Donald, David Herbert, *Lincoln* (New York, Simon & Schuster, 1995) 275

109 "Every man is … fellow men." *Abraham Lincoln's First Political Announcement.* Abraham Lincoln Online, Speeches & Writings. http://www.abrahamlincolnonline.org/lincoln/speeches/1832.htm

109   "A house ... cannot stand." House Divided Speech. Abraham Lincoln Online, Speeches & Writings. http://www.abrahamlincolnonline.org/lincoln/speeches/house.htm

109   "One day ... have stayed home." Interview of David Herbert Donald, Ph.D. "Extraordinary Teacher and Master Storyteller," October 19, 2007. American Academy of Achievement, https://achievement.org/achiever/david-herbert-donald-ph-d/#interview

110   "His ambition ... knew no rest." White House History, Abraham Lincoln, Sixteenth President 1861 -1865. www.clintonwhitehouse4.archives.gov

110   "Rarely was ... the event," Nicolay, John G. and Hay, John, *Abraham Lincoln, A History* (New York, The Century Co., 1890) 348

111   "see if you can't take better care of it." Whipple, Wayne, *The Story of Young Abraham Lincoln* (Germany, Outlook Verlag, 2018) p. 139

111   Those Cotton ... a hill of beans." Vidal, Gore, *Lincoln* (New York, Vintage, 1984) 99

113   "Any newly elected ... put their highest priorities in order." Nicolay, John G. and Hay, John, *Abraham Lincoln, A History* (New York, The Century Co., 1890) 318

113   "If I could ... would do that." Abraham Lincoln Online, Speeches & Writings. "Letter to Horace Greeley, August 22, 1862." AbrahamLincolnOnline.org http://www.abrahamlincolnonline.org/lincoln/speeches/greeley.htm

114   "I have been ... rube from Illinois." Noah Brooks, *Abraham Lincoln: The Nation's Leader in the Great Struggle Through Which was Maintained the Existence of the United States* (South Caroline, Nabu Press, 2010) 427-428

115   "Welcome to ... President-elect." Vidal, Gore, *Lincoln* (New York, Vintage, 1984) 7, 8

115   "Well to be ... gift to be shot." Ibid 19

117   Hay points ... course of conduct." Nicolay, John and Hay, John. *Abraham Lincoln: A History, V. 3* (Lex De Leon Publishing, May 2020)

117   "Honestly ... this one?" Robert Mankoff, "Lincoln's Smile," *The New Yorker,* Nov 28, 2012

118   "I swear I will ... have blankets." James G. Randall, *Lincoln the President,* 4 vols. (New York: Dodd, Mead, 1945–55), 3:21; Stoddard, "White House Sketches, No. IX"; First Auditor's Records

119   "matchless ... and beauty." Kearns Goodwin, Doris. "Doris Kearns Goodwin: 6 Essential Traits a President Needs," *A& E Television Networks*, History, January 31, 2019. https://www.history.com/topics/doris-kearns-goodwin-on-presidential-leadership

120 "In your hands… the aggressors." Ed. History.com. "Abraham Lincoln Inaugurated," *A& E Television Networks,* History, November 13, 2009. Online. https://www.history.com/this-day-in-history/lincoln-inaugurated

120 "as surely… of our nature." Ibid

123 "I must …first trick." Donald, *We Are Lincoln Men,* 149

124 "Mr. Seward …reach the sky." Ibid 150

124 "if it … must do it." Ibid 147

126 "You see …. own head." Vidal, Gore, *Lincoln* (New York, Vintage, 1984) 135

126 "Many things … than none at all." Ibid 136

127 "The … best of us." Michael Burlingame, *Abraham Lincoln: A Life, Vol. 2* (Maryland, John Hopkins University Press, 2013) Chapter 22 2407 https://www.knox.edu/documents/LincolnStudies/BurlingameVol-2Chap22.pdf

127 "better … than now." Learned, Henry Barret. "Some Aspects of the Cabinet Meeting" Records of the Columbia Historical Society, Washington, D.C. Vol 18 (1915)

127 "Now he … the ages." Kearns Goodwin, *Team of Rival,* 743

128 "We are all … here, here." Nicolay, John G. and Hay, John, *Abraham Lincoln, A History* (New York, The Century Co., 1890)

128 "with my … of slaveholders." "Cottage Conversation with Louis Masur, January 25, 2013" YouTube. https://www.youtube.com/watch?v=AXsdZMabB94

128 "The most … had ever met," Zeitz, Josh. "The Man Who Created the Lincoln We Know." *Politico Magazine,* April 14, 2015

129 "I am naturally … and feel." Interview of Eric Foner, "Lincoln's Evolving Thoughts on Slavery and Freedom," *Fresh Air,* NPR, October 11, 2010. https://www.npr.org/2010/10/11/130489804/lincolns-evolving-thoughts-on-slavery-and-freedom

129 "But will … question." "Lepore, Jill, "Abraham Lincoln's 100 Days," *The New Yorker,* April 29,2009

128 the inauguration…upon earth!" Ibid

130 "Fellow citizens … of earth." Ibid

130 "He would not … if he would." Pierce, Edward Lillie. *Memoir and Letters of Charles Sumner 1860-1074.* (Boston, Roberts Brothers, 1894) 113

130 "those emancipated…from tumult," Lepore. "Abraham Lincoln's 100 Days"

130   "I invoke the ... of almighty God." Ibid

130   "The cause ... inseparable." Ibid

130   "The Day of Days." Ibid

131   "At midnight... Jubilee has Come." Ibid

131   "I never, in ... signing this paper." "Do not let ... of freedom." Franklin, John Hope. "The Emancipation Proclamation, An Act of Justice," *Prologue Magazine,* Summer 1993, Vol. 25, No. 2, National Archives

CHAPTER THREE: THE LEADER SETS THE TONE

134   "We observe... as change." Kennedy, J. F. Transcript of President John F. Kennedy's Inaugural Address (1961). https://www.ourdocuments. gov/doc.php?flash=false&doc=91&page=transcript

134   "Let the... bitter peace." Ibid

135   "Let every... of liberty." Ibid

135   "and so my fellow ...country." Ibid

136   "I didn't...and carpet." Rott, N. "'Ask Not...': JFK's Words Still Inspire 50 Years Later," *WBUR News,* January 18, 2011. https://www.wbur. org/npr/133018777/jfks-inaugural-speech-still-inspires-50-years-later

136   "to help ...John Kennedy." Ibid

136   "I am paying...Green." Ed. "Ronald Reagan: 'I am paying for this microphone,'" *Real Clear Politics,* November 11, 2015. https://www. realclearpolitics.com/lists/debatemoments/reagan.html

137   "I won't...inexperience." Stephey, M.J. "Top 10 Memorable Debate Moments: Reagan's Age-Old Wisdom," *Time Magazine* (n.d.)

137   "The Great... two centuries." Bromund, T. R. "Reagan as Draftsman," *Commentary Magazine,* July 13, 2015. https://www.commentarymaga-zine.com/ted-r-bromund/reagan-as-draftsman/

138   "make it...of tragedy." Grier, Peter. "Challenger Explosion: How President Reagan Responded," *The Christian Science Monitor,* January 28, 2011. https://www.csmonitor.com/USA/Politics/The-Vote/2011/0128/Challenger-explosion-How-President-Reagan-re-sponded

138   "The president... patronizing anybody." Moyer, Justin Wm. "Exactly the Right Words, Exactly the Right Way: Reagan's Amazing Challenger Disaster Speech," *The Washington Post,* March 30, 2019

139.   "Ladies...the face of God.'" Reagan, Ronald W. "Explosion of the Space Shuttle Challenger Address to the Nation, January 28,1986." NASA. (n.d.) https://history.nasa.gov/reagan12886.html

139 "talk to… everyday words." Edwards, Lee. "What Made Reagan a Truly Great Communicator," *The Daily Signal,* February 5, 2018

145 "Before an…fought out." Ed. "Text of President's Address: President Calls for War Declaration, Stronger Navy, New Army of 500,00 Men, Full Co-Operation with Germany's Foes," *The New York Times,* April 2, 1917

145 "I hope …Republicans." Ed. "The Reagan Wit" CBS News, July 20. 2014. Online The Reagan wit - CBS News

145 "Mr. President…your pajamas." Ibid

145 "Mike Deaver …something else." Ibid

146 "Never… their hatred." Roosevelt, Franklin D. "October 31, 1936: Speech at Madison Square Garden." Miller Center, April 26, 2017. https://millercenter.org/the-presidency/presidential-speeches/october-31-1936-speech-madison-square-garden

147 "Will we…nobler story?" Democratic National Convention, Day 4. "User Clip: Jon Meacham DNC Speech." *C-Span,* August 21, 2020. https://www.c-span.org/video/?c4901180%2Fuser-clip-jon-meacham-dnc-speech

147 "We shall… never surrender…" Ed. "We Shall Fight on the Beaches," The International Churchill Society, April 13, 2017. https://winston-churchill.org/resources/speeches/1940-the-finest-hour/we-shall-fight-on-the-beaches/

INTERLUDE: FRANKLIN D. ROOSEVELT

149 "My little… the United States." Powell, J. M. (2015, October 04). "Grover Cleveland's Strange Wish." J. Mark Powell Author, Blog. http://www.jmarkpowell.com/grover-clevelands-strange-wish/

149 "He pulled … visiting scientist." Alter, Jonathan. *The Defining Moment, FDR's Hundred Days and the Triumph of Hope* (New York, Simon & Schuster 2006) 22

149 "first a seat …the presidency." MacGregor Burns, James. *Roosevelt: The Lion and the Fox* (New York, Open Road Media, 2012) 58

152 "Twelve thousand … speech had begun." Kearns Goodwin, Doris. *Leadership in Turbulent Times* (New York, Simon & Schuster, 2018) 170

152 "Mein Gawd… everything myself?" Alter, Jonathan. *The Defining Moment. FDR's Hundred Days and the Triumph of Hope (*New York, Simon & Schuster 2006) 117

152 "It's much … convention." Ibid

152   "Damn it ... candidate." Ibid

153   "Let it be ... foolish traditions..." "I pledge ... and courage..." "Give me your help...its own people." Ibid 119

154   "this means ... comfortable living." MacGregor Burns, James. *Roosevelt: The Lion and the Fox. New York* (Open Road Media, 2012) 253

154   "Hoover ... symbol of hope." "1932: FDR's First Presidential Campaign." See How They Ran! 1932. http://www.roosevelthouse.hunter.cuny.edu/seehowtheyran/portfolios/1932-fdrs-first-presidential-campaign/

156   "Absolutely not... seem easy." Kearns Goodwin, Doris. *Leadership in Turbulent Times* (New York, Simon & Schuster, 2018) 164

156   "as silent ... a grave." Cohen, Adam. "The Legacy of F.D.R." *Time Magazine,* June 24, 2009

156   "this great nation...action now." Ibid

157   "dominant note ... confidence." Ibid

157   "receive an extra day's pay." Ibid

157   "First rate ... rate intellect." President Clinton, Bill. "The Legacy of F.D.R. – Getting it Right," *Time Magazine,* June 24, 2009

159   "presidential barrage ... American history." Cohen, Adam. "The Legacy of F.D.R.," *Time Magazine,* June 24, 2009

159   "At the end ... own destiny." Schlesinger Jr., Arthur. "The 'Hundred Days' of F.D.R." The *New York Times,* April 10, 1983

159   "Who can ... social distress?" Ibid

160   "Get the note ... and starvation wages." FRANKLIN D. ROOSEVELT Public Papers and Addresses, Vol. V (New York, Random House, 1936), 624-25

CHAPTER FOUR: BUILD YOUR OWN TEAM OF RIVALS

164   "I feel ... fallen on me." Ed. "Harry S. Truman," https://www.whitehouse.gov/about-the-white-house/presidents/harry-s-truman/

166   "He quickly ... apparent to all." Eisenhower, Dwight D. "George Catlett Marshall," *The Atlantic,* August 1954

167   British Prime ... Marshall gave it victory." Runkle, Benjamin. *Generals in the Making: How Marshall, Eisenhower, Patton, and Their Peers Became the Commanders Who Won World War II* (Stackpole Books, Lanham, MD, 2019) v

167   "The cost of … another solution." Ed. "George C. Marshall Novel Lecture," December 11, 1953. https://www.nobelprize.org/prizes/peace/1953/marshall/lecture/

167   "Mr. President … president than you." ED. "Leadership, David Mc-Cullough," *Harvard Business Review,* January-February 2013

167   "He would … around me." Ibid

169   "I would by … ambition to excel." Ibid

169   "Getting fired … something else." (@MikeBloomberg, June 8, 2014) https://twitter.com/mikebloomberg/status/475667367725658113

170   "kinda goofy" Israel, Steve. "Why Mike Bloomberg has a shot," *The Hill,* February 26, 2011

170   "There is no … next mayor." Wolff, Michael. "The Ad Man" *New York Magazine,* November 19, 2001

170   "You're going to… Democrat." Flegenheimer, Matt and Haberman, Maggie. "How a String of Flukes Helped pave the Way for Mayor Michael Bloomberg," *The New York Times,* December 22, 2019

171   "Ever since .. so far?" Bloomberg, Mike. "You're in Charge: Build a Great Team." LinkedIn, January 31, 2020. https://www.linkedin.com/pulse/build-great-team-mike-bloomberg/

171   "I had … built a team." Ibid

172   "Great leaders … playing against you." Ibid

INTERLUDE: HARRY S. TRUMAN

178   "I have a … final words." Markel, Howard, Dr. "Franklin D. Roosevelt's painfully eloquent final words," *PBS New Hour,* PBS.org, April 12, 2018. https://www.pbs.org/newshour/health/the-quiet-final-hours-of-franklin-d-roosevelt

178   "Jesus Christ and General Jackson!" Glass, Andrew. "Truman sworn in as 33rd president, April 12, 1945," *Politico,* April 12, 2018. https://www.politico.com/story/2018/04/12/harry-truman-sworn-in-as-33rd-president-april-12-1945-511037

178   "Harry…is dead." Ed. "President Harry Truman Appoints Eleanor Roosevelt a Special U.S. Ambassador," RAAB Collection https://www.raabcollection.com/harry-truman-autograph/harry-truman-appoints-eleanor-roosevelt-special-US-ambassador

179   Is there …do for you?" No… in trouble now." Ibid

179   "Boys, last night … on my head." Ed. "Truman." *PBS,* Transcript of

American Experience Program with panel including Victor Reuther, David McCullough, Vernon Jarrett, Alonzo Hamby. http://www.shop-pbs.pbs.org/wgbh/amex/truman/filmmore/pt.html

179   "We have …nor will we." Neal, Steve. "Eleanor and Harry," *The New York Times,* August 25, 2002

180   "I hardly know Truman." Ed. "Harry S. Truman, 34th Vice President (1945)," United States Senate website. https://www.senate.gov/about/officers-staff/vice-president/VP_Harry_Truman.htm

180   "equivalent of dereliction of duty." Fleming, Thomas. *My Days with Harry Truman* (Boston, New Word City, 2011)

181   "Never had … a short period." Baime, A. J. *The Accidental President: Harry S. Truman and the Four Months That Changed the World* (New York, Mariner Books, 2017)

181   Bess Truman was … public no more." Ed. "Picturing History: February 10, 1945." Truman Library Institute, From the Archives, February 10, 2016. https://www.trumanlibraryinstitute.org/from-the-archives-2/

182   "Someday I hope … supporter below!" Ed. "Is the letter on display that Truman wrote in defense of his daughter's singing?" Harry S. Turman Library Museum, National Archives Records Administration. https://www.trumanlibrary.gov/education/trivia/letter-truman-defends-daughter-singing

182   "When you … the Presidency." Coutu, Diane, "Harry Turman's Reality-Based Leadership," *Harvard Business Review,* June 11, 2008

182   "this practice … own mind." DeGregorio, William A. *The Complete Book of U.S. Presidents. 7th ed.* (Fort Lee: Barricade Books, 2009)

183   Of Independence … will return." Ed. "Truman." *PBS*, Transcript of American Experience Program with panel including Victor Reuther, David McCullough, Vernon Jarrett, Alonzo Hamby. http://www.shop-pbs.pbs.org/wgbh/amex/truman/filmmore/pt.html

184   "His family …she could to help" Neal, Steve. "Eleanor and Harry," *The New York Times,* August 25, 2002. https://www.nytimes.com/2002/08/25/books/chapters/eleanor-and-harry.html

185   "I was appalled at how little he knew." Ibid

185   "He looks … great pressure." Neal. "Eleanor and Harry" Ibid

186   "share the … white supremacy." Evans, Farrell. "Why Harry Truman Ended Segregation in the US Military in 1948" History.com, November 5, 2020. https://www.history.com/news/harry-truman-executive-order-9981-desegregation-military-1948

NOTES 313

186 "a violently ... Lincoln haters." Leuchtenburg, William E. "The Conversion of Harry Truman," *American Heritage,* November 1991 Vol 42, Issue 7

186 'Everything's ... handle the n----s." Brown, DeNeen L. "How Harry S. Truman went from being a racist to desegregating the military," *The Washington Post,* July 26, 2018

187 "It took me ... work that way." Leuchtenburg, William E. "The Conversion of Harry Truman" *American Heritage*, November 1991 Vol 42, Issue 7

187 "Whatever my ...evils like this." Ibid

187 "Truman had a ... a different track." Frederickson, Kari. *The Dixiecrat Revolt and the End of the Solid South, 1932-1968* (Chapel Hill, The University of North Carolina Press, 2001)

187 "It is my deep ... our citizens." Evans, Farrell. "Why Harry Truman Ended Segregation in the US Military in 1948," History.com, November 5, 2020

188 "As Americans... all Americans." Brown, DeNeen L. "How Harry S. Truman went from being a racist to desegregating the military," *The Washington Post,* July 26, 2018

188 "Mamma won't ... implement it." Ibid

188 "I really ... the South," and a Baptist minister threatened, "If that... dogcatcher in 1948." Leuchtenburg, William E. "The Conversion of Harry Truman" *American Heritage,* November 1991 Vol 42, Issue 7

188 "A Georgian ... and humiliating." Ibid

189 "The military ... color of your skin." Evans, Farrell. "Why Harry Truman Ended Segregation in the US Military in 1948," History.com, November 5, 2020

189 Dr. Philleo Nash...was right." Ed. "Truman's Racial Ideas Changed, Letters Show," *The New York Times,* April 11, 1983

CHAPTER FIVE: YOUR FIRST (NEXT) 100 DAY PLAN

190 "Get ready... than you think." David Axelrod & Karl Rove Teach Campaign Strategy and Messaging, *MasterClass.* https://www.masterclass.com/

190 "The arc of... justice." Ed. "Dr. Martin Luther King Jr." Online at the Smithsonian Institution (n.d.) https://www.si.edu/spotlight/mlk?page=4

190-1   "The time … of happiness." Ed. "President Barack Obama's In-augural Address," National Archives and Records Administration. https://obamawhitehouse.archives.gov/blog/2009/01/21/president-barack-obamas-inaugural-address

191   "Abraham… political life." Caro, Robert A. *Master of the Senate: The Years of Lyndon Johnson III* (New York, Knopf 2002) xxiv

191   "There will… now lead." Kenneally, Meghan, and Rodriguez, Lissette. "First on ABD: George W. Bush's Inauguration Day Letter to Barack Obama," *ABC News Network*, January 19, 2017. https://abcnews.go.com/Politics/abc-george-bushs-inauguration-day-letter-barack-obama/story?id=44896610

193   "I begged… do it." Alter, Jonathan. *The Promise: President Obama* (London: Simon & Schuster, 2011) 395

193   "I'm feeling lucky." Ibid

193   "plans… everything." Ed. "Remembering World War II: Eisenhower Arrives in Europe." American Battle Monuments Commission, June 25, 2017. https://www.abmc.gov/news-events/news/remembering-world-war-ii-eisenhower-arrives-europe

193   "The planning… events unfold." Ibid

194   "The first thing… at least." Ibid

194   "to keep … help solve." Ibid

195   "I'm neither a dove… little bit of wisdom." Ed. "Owl-right start for ECB's Lagarde in first 100 days," *France 24 Live News*, August 2, 2020. https://www.france24.com/en/20200208-owl-right-start-for-ecb-s-lagarde-in-first-100-days

198   "The people … just to follow." "most elected … the first place." David Axelrod & Karl Rove Teach Campaign Strategy and Messaging, *MasterClass*. https://www.masterclass.com/

198   "The only… side of the complex." Ed. "A Quote by Oliver Wendell Holmes Jr." Goodreads. (n.d.) https://www.goodreads.com/quotes/8312003-the-only-simplicity-for-which-i-would-give-a-straw

200   "It takes six… iteration." Taylor, Gail. "Creating Work Products While Maintaining Post DesignShop KreW Integrity," MG Taylor Corporation, February 20, 1997. http://legacy.mgtaylor.com/mgtaylor/jotm/winter97/crworkpr.htm

203   "We as a … the world." Steinberg, Marty. "'Kinder, gentler' and other George HW Bush quotes" *CNBC* December 1, 2018

203   "We must … come from." Khalid, Asma. "Gov. Baker Calls on Leaders To Find 'Courage To Set Partisanship Aside' In Inaugural Speech, *WBUR News*, January 9, 2015. https://www.wbur.org/news/2015/01/09/charlie-baker-inaugural-speech-breakdown

205   "We've had … good laws" Keith, Tamara. "The First 100 Days: 'A Standard That Not Even Roosevelt Achieved,'" *NPR Maine Public*, April 29. 2017. https://www.npr.org/2017/04/29/525810758/the-first-100-days-a-standard-that-not-even-roosevelt-achieved

205   "If you say… not much." Ibid

205   "When you … account for it." Thanks to Mayor Laurie Maclean for conversations about her first 100-day plan

INTERLUDE: LYNDON B. JOHNSON

208   "I was three … as W.C. Linden." Beschloss, Michael. "Politics: Lyndon Johnson on the Record," *Texas Monthly*, December 2001

208   "helping… of circumstance." Holmes, Rick. "On the Road with Rick Homes: When poverty was a priority," *Mail Tribune*, March 29, 2018

209   "You know… United States." Germany, Kent. "Lyndon B. Johnson: Life Before the Presidency," University of Virginia Miller Center: US Presidents. https://millercenter.org/president/lbjohnson/life-be-fore-the-presidency

211   "When they came…belief in the future." Dallek, Robert. "Lyndon B. Johnson." *PBS News Hour*, Character Above All, An Exploration of Presidential Leadership: Essays. https://www.pbs.org/newshour/spc/character/essays/johnson.html

212   "He's a tall… jungle fighter." Bruck, Connie. "The Personal Touch," *The New Yorker*, August 13, 2001. https://www.newyorker.com/maga-zine/2001/08/13/the-personal-touch-3

214   "God, what…to take fishing!" "best of us… American people." Caro, Robert A. *Master of the Senate: The Years of Lyndon Johnson III* (New York, Knopf, 2002) p136 https://historynewsnetwork.org/article/685

214   "best of us… American people" Caro, Robert. "Books: LBJ Had a Bright Side and a Dark Side," *History New Network*, Columbian College of Arts & Science, The George Washington University. Online. n.d.

215   "don't try… talking about." "Sam Rayburn Quotations," QuoteTab, (n.d.) https://www.quotetab.com/quotes/by-sam-rayburn.

215   "just like a Daddy to me." Caro, Robert. *Master of the Senate: The Years of Lyndon Johnson* (New York, Vintage Books, 2003)158

215   "It was an… agreed to do it." Caro, *Master*, Ibid 476

215   "I like you … help you." Caro, Robert A. *The Path to Power: The Years of Lyndon Johnson I* (New York, Vintage Books, 1990) 616

216   "seemed… worries and desires." Caro. *Master* 136

217   "had visited … him to Congress." Caro. *The Path* 607

217   "I've just … anything you can.'" Caro, *The Path* 620

218   "him succeed… technically eligible." Burka, Paul. "A Monumental Man," *Texas Monthly.* January 1983

218   "the next time … kid the dam." Caro. *The Path* 637

219   "Oh, my … forget it" Schaub, Michael. "LBJ Shares the Spotlight—Finally—In Building the Great Society," *NPR Maine Public Radio,* January 31, 2018. ttps://www.npr.org/2018/01/31/579821758/lbj-shares-the-spotlight-finally-in-building-the-great-society

219   "knew … were buried." Inskeep, Steve, and Rudin, Ken. "A Brief History of Political Corruption," *NPR, Maine Public,* May 24, 2006. https://www.npr.org/templates/story/story.php?storyId=5427287

220   "We of the South…" Caro. *Master*

221   "as for … the desert." "Ask not … for him lately?" Caro, Robert. *The Passage of Power: The Years of Lyndon Johnson* (New York, Knopf Doubleday Publishing Group, 2013) 561

222   "Ask not … for him lately?" Ibid

222   "Come now … reason together…" Ed. "Let Us Reason Together," Constitutional Rights Foundation (Website). https://www.crf-usa.org/brown-v-board-50th-anniversary/let-us-reason-together.html

222   His colleagues … pull that one off." Caro. *Passage of Power* xxii

223   "Nigra bill … for 200 years." Caro. *Master* 954-955

224   "Rufus Cornpone… little porkchop." Tracey Gross interview with Robert Caro: "In 'Passage,' Caro Mines LBJ's Changing Political Roles". *WBUR News,* February 17, 2014 https://www.wbur.org/npr/276530368/in-passage-caro-mines-lbjs-changing-political-roles

225   "He was … didn't matter." Ed. "LBJ returns, under Robert Caro's scrutiny," *CBS News*, May 21, 2012

225   "a man without purpose… small corral." Caro, Robert. "The Transition." *The New Yorker Magazine,* March 26, 2012

223   "And right then… took charge." Caro. "The Transition"

223   "An assassin's … the Presidency." Larson, Sarah. "LBJ's War" Lets Us Eavesdrop on a President's Mighty Fall," *New Yorker Magazine,* September 6, 2017

223   "Mr. President" "He reacted immediately." Caro, Robert. "The Transition." *The New Yorker Magazine*, March 26, 2012

223   "almost a … carved in bronze." Ibid

226 "Do you want … keeping her?" "Now let's get airborne." Ibid

227 "I'm finished." Ibid

227 "It as if there … becomes President." Bruck, Connie. "The Personal Touch," *The New Yorker,* August 6, 2001. https://www.newyorker.com/magazine/2001/08/13/the-personal-touch-3

228 "I am going … died for." Dehgan, Bahman. *America in Quotations*, (Jefferson, N.C.: McFaland, 2003) 164

228 "He knew … summon people." Colman, John. "The Johnson Treatment: Pushing and Persuading Like LBJ," *Forbes Magazine,* July 30, 2018

228 "done more … hundred days." Greenberg, David. "The Hundred Days Myth," Miller Center UVVA (Website) October 24, 2016. https://millercenter.org/issues-policy/us-domestic-policy/the-hundred-days-myth

229 "I'm going … word." Kearns Goodwin, Doris. "The Divided Legacy of Lyndon B. Johnson," *The Atlantic,* September 7, 2018

229 "Well, what …Presidency for?" O'Donnell, Michael. "How LBJ Saved the Civil Rights Act," *The Atlantic*, April 2014

229 "We have … books of law." Ibid

229 "President … make men act." Reston, James. "Washington; The State of the President and Other Matters," *The New York Times,* January 8, 1964

229 "presidential … power to persuade." Neustadt, Richard. *Presidential Power: The Politics of Leadership* (New York, Signet Books, 1964) 11

230 "This man … ever known." Hardesty, Robert L. "The LBJ the Nation Seldom Saw," LBJ Presidential Library, (website). http://www.lbjlibrary.org/lyndon-baines-johnson/perspectives-and-essays/the-lbj-the-nation-seldom-saw

231 "Their cause … and prejudice." Ed. "President Johnson's Special Message to Congress: The American Promise." Speeches & Films: LBJ Presidential Library (website). http://www.lbjlibrary.org/lyndon-baines-johnson/speeches-films/president-johnsons-special-message-to-the-congress-the-american-promise

231 "When a man … revealing begins." Caro. *Passage of Power*

232 "Dick… stand in my way." Ed. "Destiny of Democracy." The 1964 Civil Rights Act – LBJ Presidential Library (website). http://www.lbjlibrary.org/assets/uploads/general/DestinyOfDemocracy_1964CivilRightsAct.pdf

232 "The best … owner." Reston, James. "The State of the President and Other Matters," *The New York Times,* January 8, 1964

233   "Johnson loved … in that context." Coleman, John. "The Johnson Treatment: Pushing and Persuading Like LBJ," *Forbes*, July 30, 2018

233   "an incredible… advantages." Ibid

234   "Public … can succeed." Zarefsky, David. "Public Sentiment is everything: Lincoln's View of Political Persuasion." Journal of the Abraham Lincoln Association. Vol 15, Issue 2. Summer 1994

235   "a St. Bernard …scratch marks." Coleman, John. "The Johnson Treatment: Pushing and Persuading Like LBJ," *Forbes,* July 30, 2018

236   "Shame, Shame, Shame." Moyers, Bill D. "What a Real President Was Like," *Washington Post,* November 13, 1988

236   "I'm calling … is ringing" Dallek, Robert. "Lyndon B. Johnson." PBS News Hour, Character Above All Essays. (n.d.) https://www.pbs.org/newshour/spc/character/essays/johnson.html

237   "What is… to know." Caro. *Passage of Power* 697

237   "You and I … listen to Dirksen!" O'Donnell, Michael. "How LBJ Saved the Civil Rights Act," *The Atlantic*, April 2014

238   "deliver Republican … seal the deal." Ed. "On Civil Rights: June 10, 1964." The Dirksen Congressional Center (website). https://www.everettdirksen.name/print_basics_histmats_civilrights64_cloturespeech.htm

239   "Mr. President … improved it." McMillian, Brad. "Effective Bipartisan Leadership," *Peoria Magazine*, November 2011

239   "It was a scene … the 19th century." Ed. "The Civil Rights Act of 1964," The United States Senate, Art & History (website). https://www.senate.gov/artandhistory/history/civil_rights/cloture_finalpassage.htm

239   "America grows… It is here!" Ibid

CHAPTER SIX: SHARED PURPOSE, COLLABORATION, AND COMPROMISE

242-3   "The presidency… leadership." Leuchtenburg, William Edward. *The FDR Years: On Roosevelt and His Legacy* (New York: Columbia University Press, 1997)

244   "The First… Achieved" Keith, Tamara. "The First 100 Days: 'A Standard That Not Even Roosevelt Achieved'," *National Public Radio*, April 29, 2017. https://www.npr.org/2017/04/29/525810758/the-first-100-days-a-standard-that-not-even-roosevelt-achieved.

247   "the very … American ideals." Glass, Andrew. "Former Sen. George Norris dies at 83, Sept. 2, 1944" *Politico,* September 2, 2015

250 "The single most important... president." Kessler, Glenn. "When Did Mitch McConnell Say He Wanted to Make Obama a One-Term President?" *The Washington Post,* January 11, 2017

250 "It was the... stimulus." Carroll, James R. "The Obama-McConnell Cold War," *U.S. News & World Report,* June 22, 2016

250 "Professor ...one in the room." Ibid

250 "I never put... of baseball." Ibid

254 "There are... answer." Ed. "Congress's Problem Solver: DSA Interview with Rep. Josh Gottheimer," *Direct Selling Association* (Press Release) April 2, 2019. https://www.dsa.org/events/news/individual-press-release/congress-s-problem-solver-dsa-interview-with-rep.-josh-gottheimer-(d-nj.

254 "I was ...the sake of it." Ibid

INTERLUDE: PROFILE IN COURAGE?

261 "Sadly... of impeachment." Speaker Pelosi makes a statement on status of house impeachment inquiry – *CNBC* YouTube, Streamed live on Dec 5, 2019, https://www.youtube.com/watch?v=8UC9vLWUH0g

261 "I get it... where will it?" Milbank, Dana. "No wonder Jonathan Turley's dog is mad," *The Washington Post,* December 4, 2019

265 "the Senate...impeach official" Ed, About Impeachment, United States Senate website, https://www.senate.gov/about/powers-procedures/impeachment.htm

265 "do impartial justice....and laws." Ed., Analysis and Interpretation of the U.S. Constitution, Constitution Annotated website, https://constitution.congress.gov/browse/essay/artI-S3-C6-1-3-2/ALDE_00000709/

266 "kook," "crazy," "unfit for office" Leibovich, Mark. "How Lindsey Graham Went From Trump Skeptic to Trump Sidekick," *The New York Times,* February 25, 2019

266 "race baiting... public office." Gay Stolberg, Sheryl. "What Happened to Lindsey Graham? He's Become a Conservative 'Rock Star'," *The New York Times,* November 2, 2018

266 "We have ... golf with him," Leibovich. "Trump Sidekick"

266 "I try to ... compliment." Gay Stolberg. "Conservative 'Rock Star'"

266 "being in ... good for him." Ibid

267 "There's a funny ... great again." Ibid

267 "I have ... conservatives," Leibovich. "Trump Sidekick"

267 "What happened to me ... damn thing." Ibid

268 "What is ... name?" Ibid

268 "What's the ... family owned?" Ibid

268 "To every ... behind you." Ibid

269 "The House ... road," Snell, Kelsey. "McConnell: 'I'm Not Impartial' About Impeachment," *NPR,* December 17, 2019. https://www.npr. org/2019/12/17/788924966/mcconnell-i-m-not-impartial-about-impeachment

269 "It is their duty to investigate...national election." Ibid

270 "Dad, my sitting here ... life for our family." Gambino, Lauren. "'Here, right matters': Vindman stands ground amid Republican onslaught" *The Guardian,* November 19, 2019

271 "Do not worry...telling the truth." Ibid

271 "this is the country ... right matters." Ibid

271 "he considered ... for the United States." Demirjian, Karoun; DeBonis, Mike; Zapotosky, Matt. "Trump said his Ukraine call was 'perfect.' Impeachment witnesses testified otherwise." *The Washington Post*, November 19, 2019

273 "troubling ... extreme." Edelman, Adam; Allen, Jonathan. "Here's the price Mitt Romney is paying for standing against Trump," *NBC News Now,* Jan 6, 2020. https://www.nbcnews.com/politics/trump-impeachment-inquiry/here-s-price-mitt-romney-paying-standing-against-trump-n1072111

273 "loser," "fool," and "pompous ass." "slippery ...secret asset" Ibid

274 "I am here ... partisan level." Firozi, Paulina. "How Romney's vote to convict Trump paid homage to his rabble-rousing Republican father," *The Washington Post,* February 6, 2020

274 "I don't believe... he understood it." "'Appalling': Bolton reacts to Flynn's pitch for martial law," *CNN Politics*, Interview of John Bolton with Wolf Blitzer, December 19, 2020. https://www.cnn.com/videos/politics/2020/12/20/trump-oval-office-meeting-martial-law-bolton-tsr-sot-vpx.cnn

274-6 "The Constitution ... grievously wrong." Ed. "Romney Delivers Remarks on Impeachment Vote" February 5, 2020. Online at Romney Senate Government Website, www.romney.senate.gov

276 "Every single vote... who you are." Gregorian, Dareh. "Schiff's powerful closing speech: 'Is there one among you who will say, Enough'!"

NBC News Now, February 3, 2020. https://www.nbcnews.com/politics/trump-impeachment-inquiry/closing-argument-democrats-say-not-removing-trump-would-render-him-n1128766

277 "I have to say … very effective." Gay Stolberg, Sheryl. "Emotional Schiff Speech Goes Viral, Delighting the Left and Enraging the Right," *The New York Times,* January 24, 2020

277 "If you… movement." Keilar, Brianna. "GOP ignored their own warnings about Trump" *CNN News* on YouTube, January 11, 2021 https://www.youtube.com/watch?v=6FXuXqzUO9E

277 "I'm thinking…president?" Ibid

277 "We need … disavow the KKK." Ibid

278 "You sir are the distraction … democracy." Ibid

278 "We're on the verge … out of his mouth." Ibid

278 "There is only …that's called demagoguery." Ibid

278 "Mark my words… going to end." Ibid

279 "a bullet … on Live TV" Fuchs, Hailey. "A man charged with threatening Pelosi also mused about shooting the Washington mayor, prosecutors say," *The New York Times,* January 13, 2021.

280 "To be … human morality." Ed. "The John F. Kennedy Profile in Courage Award," John F. Kennedy, Presidential Library and Museum. https://www.jfklibrary.org/events-and-awards/profile-in-courage-award/about-the-book

CHAPTER SEVEN: SECURE EARLY WINS

283 "What is particularly … to recover." Ed. "America's Dying Cities," *Newsweek,* January 21, 2011.

281 "I think the fact … old habits." Finley, Allysia. "South Bend's 'Beta' Test for Mayor Pete," *Wall Street Journal,* February 14, 2020

283 "hey, we're …in charge of." Gabriel, Trip. "What Being a Mayor Taught Pete Buttigieg," *The New York Times,* February 14, 2020

283 "If there's … and deal with it." Ibid

284 "It's not like… before you were." Gomez, Henry J. "What Happened When Pete Buttigieg Tore Down House in Black and Latino South Bend," *BuzzFeed News,* April 9, 2019. https://www.buzzfeednews.com/article/henrygomez/mayor-pete-buttigieg-south-bend-gentrification

285 "took a second … play a strong role." Gabriel. "What Being"

286   "He brought … entire thing." Ibid

286   "There was … perfectly fine." Ibid

286   "It led to … office." Ibid

287   "I will encode …with U." Jardin, Xeni. "Chicago mayor Lori Lightfoot has 2 words for Donald Trump," Chicago, Boing Boing, May 29, 2020. https://boingboing.net/2020/05/29/chicago-mayor-lori-lightfoot-h.html

287   "keep … lying mouth." Marshall, Glenn. "Lightfoot responds to Trump's debate comments: 'Keep Chicago out of your lying mouth'," *WGN9*, September 30, 2020. https://wgntv.com/news/chicago-news/lightfoot-responds-to-trumps-debate-comments-keep-chicago-out-of-your-lying-mouth/

288   "We are … her in April," Wall, Craig. "Critics give Lightfoot D grade as she nears 100 days in office," *ABC News*, August 26, 2019. https://abc7chicago.com/politics/lightfoot-nears-100-days-in-office-with-d-grade-from-critics/5494411/

288   "My job is … constituency." Ibid

289   "Get going … circle of successes." Schaffer, Robert H. *The Breakthrough Strategy* (New York, Harper Business, February 1990)

290   "Each small … larger breakthrough." Ibid

www.ingramcontent.com/pod-product-compliance
Lightning Source LLC
Chambersburg PA
CBHW062157270326
41930CB00009B/1569